THE AUTHOR

Nicholas Fogg has enjoyed a varied career in education, journalism and the arts, and has written for a number of national broadsheet papers. Other books by him include *Brunel's Flagship*, *Portrait of a Town: Victorian Photographs in the Collection of Shakespeare's Birthplace Trust* and *Merrymaking and Frolic*.

THE VOYAGES OF THE GREAT BRITAIN

Life at Sea in the World's First Liner

NICHOLAS FOGG

CHATHAM PUBLISHING
LONDON

STACKPOLE BOOKS
PENNSYLVANIA

Dedication

To the beloved memory of Jacob, who linked England and Australia

This edition first published in Great Britain in 2004 by
Chatham Publishing,
Lionel Leventhal Ltd,
Park House, 1 Russell Gardens, London NW11 9NN

And in North America by
Stackpole Books,
5067 Ritter Road,
Mechanicsburg,
PA 17055-6921

British Library Cataloguing in Publication Data
A catalogue record for this book is available from the British Library

ISBN 1 86176 235 6

Typeset by Dorwyn Ltd, Rowlands Castle, Hants
Printed and bound in Great Britain by The Cromwell Press, Trowbridge, Wilts

Contents

List of Illustrations

PREFACE

'A Line to New York'

The SS *Great Britain* is the most significant surviving artefact of a transport revolution that occurred with bewildering speed in the first half of the nineteenth century. Until then, methods of transport were the same as those in the Ancient World, powered by the natural energies of man and nature – human and animal muscles and the force of wind and water.

It was the application of newly-discovered industrial processes to communications that fired this revolution. The results were astonishing. The fastest sailing ship might make the passage from Liverpool to New York in 30 days. With the advent of the *Great Western* steamship in 1838, the time was halved. Before the coming of the Great Western Railway, a fast coach might cover the 115 miles between Bristol and London in 14 hours. The earliest train service took only four hours. As early as 1839, telegraph wires which could transmit a message and receive a reply within minutes were snaking their way beside the railway tracks. This revolution affected not only the time taken to travel from one place to another. One simple example will serve to demonstrate that it changed man's perception of himself. Before the coming of the railways, each locality had its own time, determined by its geographical relationship to the movement of the sun. The hands of a clock, erected in Bristol in 1838, show both Greenwich Mean Time and 'Bristol Time', which was 6 minutes earlier. But the arrival of the railways meant that time had to be standardised.

The Brunels

This huge revolution was centred on Great Britain, the only country which possessed the technology to develop it. Great engineers drove it forward: Richard Trevithick, George and Robert Stephenson, Thomas Telford and many others. The most celebrated of all was Isambard Kingdom Brunel, the son of a French engineer and inventor of great intuition and energy. His father, Marc Isambard Brunel, had to flee the Terror in France because of his royalist sympathies. He became City Engineer to New York and won a competition to design the Capitol in Washington, although it was never built on grounds of cost.

Marc Brunel had invented a means of manufacturing block-pulleys for ships and in 1799 the British Government commissioned him to install it at Portsmouth Dockyard. He married a local lass, Sophia Kingdom, and their only son was born at Portsea on 9 April 1806. The boy was educated privately and his early years were spent within the tranquil affluence of his family, but in 1814 disaster struck when Marc Brunel's business investments progressively collapsed. The prospect of penury stimulated his inventive powers. He had observed the action of the shipworm, whose shell plates permitted it to bore through timber and push debris out behind, and in 1818 he patented his tunnelling shield, a machine with a giant iron casing that could be pushed forwards to bore through soft ground in a similar fashion. But this remarkable invention, which formed the blueprint for the device in use today, did not save his finances. In 1821, he was imprisoned for debt, but he was released after the Duke of Wellington secured him a government grant. This enabled him to send his son to France to complete his education.

In 1825, Marc Brunel embarked on a project to utilise his invention to bore the world's first tunnel under a navigable river between Rotherhithe and Wapping on the Thames. As Resident Engineer, he appointed his 19 year-old son. The project was fraught with difficulty. Five times water broke through and work was suspended because of lack of capital after two years. It was resumed in 1835, but it was not completed until 1842, when Marc Brunel was knighted.

Isambard Kingdom Brunel was not part of this second phase. During one flooding of the tunnel, he had rescued a trapped man. He was awarded the Silver Medal of the Royal Humane Society, but as a result of his brave action, he was severely injured. He was confined to bed for several weeks and then went to Bristol to convalesce. It was a decision that changed his career. On his recovery, Brunel was appointed Consulting Engineer to the Bristol Dock Company (BDC). He developed a firm friendship with the Quay Warden, Captain Christopher Claxton, and they began an innovative and creative partnership. Brunel entered a competition to design a bridge over the Clifton Gorge in Bristol. His proposal was eventually accepted, but his famous suspension bridge, 'my first child, my darling', as he called it, was not built until after his death.

As a result of his growing reputation, Brunel was appointed to survey the line of the proposed Great Western Railway (GWR) between London and Bristol. 'I am the Engineer of the finest work in Britain', he wrote. Indeed it was. It incorporated two great works, the flattest brick arch in the world on the bridge spanning the Thames at Maidenhead and the world's longest tunnel at Box, which was lined with 30 million bricks.

The Great Western

At a board meeting of the GWR in 1836, one of the directors expressed misgivings about the length of the proposed line. 'Why not make it longer and have a steamship go from Bristol to New York and call it the *Great Western*?' Brunel is said to have retorted. Another director of the GWR, Thomas Guppy, proposed the formation of the Great Western Steamship Company (GWSC) to establish such a regular service between Bristol and New York. Capital was subscribed and Brunel appointed to design the ship (he gave his services for nothing). At 1320 tons she would be the largest ship ever built. A Bristol shipbuilder, William Patterson, 'a man open to conviction and not prejudiced in favour of quaint or old-fashioned notions in ship building' was appointed to build her.

Brunel had been interested in the design of large steamships since 1829. By the start of Victoria's reign, the paddle steamer had proved its viability in coastal waters, but the lucrative transatlantic route was dominated by fast Yankee sailing packets. A school of thought existed that no steamship could carry enough coal for a transatlantic crossing under continuous steam power, but Brunel supported the then-controversial view that water resistance does not increase proportionately to the ship's size, enabling the relative size of the engines to decrease.

A half-pay naval officer, Lieutenant James Hosken, was appointed to command the *Great Western* which was launched on 19 July 1837 before a crowd of 50,000 people. The GWSC's rivals started to take heed. Determined to steal Brunel's thunder, the British and American Steamship Company chartered a smaller steamship, the *Sirius*, and fitted her out for a transatlantic voyage. She sailed from London on 28 March 1838. The *Great Western* followed from the same port three days later, with Brunel on board, her owners confident in the knowledge that the *Sirius* would have to coal in Cork.

Two hours after the *Great Western* set sail, fire broke out in her funnel which spread to the deck. Hosken immediately ran her onto a mud-bank. As Brunel was helping fight the flames, the charred rung of a ladder collapsed from under him and he fell 18 feet into the boiler room. Knocked unconscious, he nearly drowned in the water that had gathered there. In great pain, he was rowed ashore to the care of a cottager on Canvey Island. On his insisting that he had recovered, the ship set sail again 12 hours later.

While the indefatigable Brunel supervised repairs at Bristol, the *Sirius* left Cork on 4 April. Four days later, the *Great Western* set off again. When the *Sirius* docked in New York on the morning of 23 April, she became the first passenger steamship to cross the Atlantic, but her bunkers were empty and she only reached her destination by burning barrels of resin from her cargo. The *Great Britain* arrived later that morning. Her voyage had taken a record-breaking 15 days 5 hours and her bunkers still contained 200 tons of coal. It had been demonstrated conclusively that a steamship could cross the Atlantic without running out of fuel.

'On the broad, blue water', wrote the *New York Herald,* 'appeared this thing of life ...'

> She looked ... rakish, cool, reckless, fierce and forbidding ... As she neared the *Sirius,* she slackened her movements and took a sweep round ... At this moment the whole Battery sent forth a tumultuous shout of delight at the revelation of her magnificent proportions. After making another turn towards Staten Island, she made another sweep and shot towards the East River with an extraordinary speed. The vast multitude rent the air with their shouts again, waving handkerchiefs, hats, hurrahing!

The speed, reliability and comfort of the *Great Western* soon eclipsed the Packets. She made 64 crossings of the Atlantic between 1838 and 1843, becoming the first holder of the Blue Riband of the Atlantic.

The Great Western Railway was inaugurated on 30 June 1841, but Brunel's grand dream of a through passage to New York was frustrated by the inertia of the BDC. The launch of the *Great Western* revealed the port's limitations. She could only get up the Avon on high tides, so passengers had to be ferried to her anchorage at Kingroad in the Bristol Channel and cargo was handled by lighters. Despite its failure to provide adequate facilities, the BDC still charged a levy of £212 per voyage. When the GWSC requested that the dock entrance be widened, the Company replied that it was 'manifestly unjust' that it should be baulked of its profits by 'the building of ships too big to enter the harbour'. The realisation that the transatlantic trade could be lost led the Bristol Corporation to establish a committee of interested parties, but its ambitious proposals were rejected by the BDC. The inevitable happened. In 1842, it was decided to base the *Great Western* in Liverpool, which charged lower port dues and possessed the incalculable advantage of possessing facilities for ships to moor at the quayside. The ship would only return to Bristol for repairs and maintenance.

Despite her success, the *Great Western* had serious weaknesses. Her sails had to be used in concert with her engines and paddlewheels were inefficient under ocean conditions. It was costly to build wooden ships strong enough to withstand the stress from the engines and the proportion of the available space occupied by the engines meant that the ship was, in the words of Thomas Guppy, 'disadvantageous from a pecuniary point of view'.

She soon faced fierce competition. The celebrated Liverpool ship-owner, Samuel Cunard, had founded the British & North American Royal Mail Steam Packet Company (later the Cunard Line) after the Admiralty advertised for tenders to carry the Royal Mail to North America. The GWSC, which had its ship built, appeared certain to win the contract, but Cunard had three ships on the stocks and a far better chance of maintaining a service, and his tender was accepted.

PART ONE: 'THIS WONDERFUL VESSEL'

ONE

'She is Truly Beautiful'

To counter the competition from Cunard, Brunel proposed building another ship, *The City of New York*, and a large quantity of African oak was bought for her construction. He knew that the *Great Western* represented the limit of what was possible with wooden construction, but the size and efficacy of iron ships was restricted by obvious problems with the use of magnetic compasses on board. However, the Astronomer Royal, Professor Airey, devised a system which seemed to solve the problem. It was installed on board the *Rainbow*, a small iron paddle steamer which visited Bristol in 1838. Brunel inspected her and decided to build his new ship of iron.

Another important factor was that iron plate was, for the first time, readily available at competitive prices. The plates were shipped down the Severn from the Coalbrookdale Foundry at Ironbridge to the Great Western Dock in the Floating Harbour, which may have been intended as a repair facility for the *Great Western*. Now huge warehouses and workshops were erected there and construction machinery installed. Brunel's team did not simply transfer traditional ship building techniques to iron construction. Because of her unprecedented length of 322 feet, the ship had to have a rigid structure, so the hull was built with five watertight bulkheads – a recent innovation. Thomas Guppy stressed the vital implications of this development. 'When an injury is sustained in one compartment only, it may absolutely preserve a vessel from sinking.' The ship's paddlewheels would be the largest ever built. No known forging method could create an engine shaft of the dimensions required to drive them, but the Scottish engineer, James Nasmyth, solved the problem by designing, fabricating and patenting a powerful steam hammer which was to become an important tool of the Industrial Revolution.

The ship's keel was laid on 19 July 1839. She was to be built with her bottom at working height supported by scaffolding above the dock floor. Ten months later, another experimental ship arrived at Bristol, fitted with a screw propeller instead of paddlewheels. In

1835, Francis Pettit Smith, had patented a design which placed the screw between the sternpost and the rudder. This overcame the technical problems of many early designs, which were caused by the screw being placed abaft the rudder. The appropriately-named *Archimedes* was launched as a prototype ship to test it. Thomas Guppy reported favourably on the new design and the Board of the GWSC decided to suspend work on the paddle-drives for three months while Brunel investigated the issue. His report was so favourable that 'undaunted by the novelty and vastness of the experiment, the Directors resolved to adopt this mode of propulsion'. The decision to use a screw aroused criticism. Many eminent nautical men contended that, with the propelling force in the stern, the vessel would run very wild in a head wind. Although this view was wrong, it undermined confidence in the new ship and this took some time to overcome.

The engine planned for the new ship was redundant. No large engine existed that was designed to drive a screw, so Brunel adapted the 'Triangle' paddle engine patented by his father. The ship's name was changed to the *Great Britain.* At 3675 tons displacement, she would be by far the largest ship ever built: the world's first fully-powered, screw-propelled steamship. Two hundred gas burners were installed at the Great Western Dock so that work could proceed day and night. Since she would be too large to pass through the gates of the Cumberland Basin, it would be necessary to widen them and the BDC agreed that this should be done

The *Great Britain* was designed as a steamer with auxiliary sail to save coal in favourable winds. The six-bladed propeller was the first large one built. Its huge shaft was regarded with wonder by all who saw it. She was also the first ship to be fitted with a balanced rudder and bolted rudder post, linked by chains to the ship's wheel. Because its line of pivoting ran near the centre, it was easier to turn than conventional rudders. The steering was so light, she was said to handle like a yacht. As one observer put it: 'This wonderful vessel will combine a greater number of varieties and untried principles than ever before united in one enterprise.' All modern ships may be considered to be descended from her.

Building

The hull of the *Great Britain* bulges on each side, a skilful design feature that maximised internal space, and is 'clinker-built', constructed of iron plates that were shaped and riveted on the spot by the strength and skill of Bristol workmen. The hull has always been remarkably watertight. She has bows like a clipper's for fast sailing.

The figurehead was the royal coat-of-arms, with motifs on each side symbolic of art and industry. Her stern was designed in the style of an old man o' war, with elaborately decorated windows and the gilded arms of the City of Bristol.

The *Great Britain* may be described as the first ocean liner. Passenger comfort was greater than on any previous ship, with steam heating in the cabins and function rooms. The beautiful Dining Saloon, which was used by First Class passengers for meals and recreation, aroused the admiration of all who saw it. Twelve gold and white columns ran down the centre and twelve on each side. Mirrors were skilfully installed to give an impression of great spaciousness. A superb Brussels carpet was specially designed for the room.

In rough weather, Saloon (First Class) passengers could stroll on the long, covered Promenade Deck. The doors off it led to the cabins, two Ladies' Boudoirs and the Captain's Quarters. The weather deck was laid with pine planks. Fascinated passengers could watch the engine working through the huge skylight over the great drive wheel which protruded above the deck. The extensive wooden bridge was open to the elements, although canvas screening gave some protection. A bulge round the base of the funnel housed a tank into which seawater was pumped to provide preheated water to the boiler below. The resultant brine had to be pumped out regularly.

The *Great Britain* was the first ship to be registered as a six-masted schooner. As there were no technical names for her masts, they were known by the days of the week, starting on Monday and excluding Sunday. In full sail, they could carry 1700 yards of canvas, which was only nine-tenths the capacity of a frigate less than a fifth of the size. The rigging was made from iron rather than the traditional hemp. It stayed taut in all weathers and held the masts at any angle required. The mainmast was the only metal one and was stepped to the keel and square-rigged. The other masts carried fore-and-aft sails and were hinged to the deck, which allowed them to be moved when the rigging was adjusted. *The Times* compared the ship to a laundress's yard, 'with the props and wires for hanging out the clothes'. The idea was to save labour, with ten men on a watch rather than the twenty-five needed on a square-rigger with the same area of canvas. The officers' quarters were in the forecastle, with 'other ranks' directly below. The galleys were on the plated upper 'tween deck. Below were the engines, boilers and coal bunkers.

The Launch

The launch of the *Great Britain*, or rather, the flooding of her dry dock, was on 19 July 1843, in the presence of Prince Albert, who came down by train from London and was escorted to the ship by the Mayor, Aldermen and Dean and Chapter, in a procession headed by a troop of cavalry. 'Triumphal arches abounded and inscriptions hung across the streets'. Bristol was *en fete* as thousands watched from the surrounding hills. 'All the shops are shut', reported the *Bristol Mirror*, 'and business entirely suspended. Every church has displayed its flags, the ships have been dressed out in a variety of colours, peals have been rung, and cannon fired; indeed every demonstration has been made that loyalty and rejoicing could inspire.'

To commemorate the occasion, a local printer published a humorous poem in the Somerset dialect, entitled *Jarge's Trip to Bristol, And How He Related the Wonders of the Day to His Uncle Ben*

> Nunck, did I ever tell thee o'my Bristol trip
> Da zee Prince Albert en gurt iron ship,
> How Mary went wi' I – (thee's know Mary, my wife)
> En how I got frightened maust out o'my life.

The 'fright' was the railway journey from Somerset.

Thomas Guppy escorted the Prince over 'the noble ship' and answered his 'many and minute' questions. The engines had not been installed, but for the sake of appearances, a temporary funnel and masts had been erected. The Prince returned with 'much courtesy and condescension the marks of respect with which he was everywhere greeted', while a 'splendid' regimental band enlivened the scene.

While water was let into the dock to float the ship, Prince Albert attended a banquet for 520 people in the Patternmakers' Shop. In the centre of the royal table was a clockwork model of the *Great Britain* in full sail. A diner was gratified to note that the demolition of the delicacies proceeded 'quietly and ... the West Country air appeared in no wise to have disagreed with the Royal appetite.' A magnificent sight greeted the guests as they left. The water in the dock had risen to the level of the Floating Harbour and the *Great Britain* had been lifted high. There had been a heavy shower and the spectators across the water had hoisted their umbrellas so that Brandon Hill looked like a large ants' nest.

The official party passed along a raised gallery to a pavilion which had been erected near the dock gates. Mrs John Miles, the wife of a Director of the GWSC, performed the ceremony. She had launched the *Great Western* on the same day 6 years before. At the moment she swung the champagne bottle towards the bows, the ship moved forward. The steam packet *Avon* had begun to tow before the shore warps were released. The towrope snapped and the bottle fell into the water. Prince Albert soon procured another and hurled it against the hull. It well and truly smashed, showering broken glass over the workers shoving against the ship's sides to prevent her scraping the wall.

Soon after her launch, the *Great Britain* was hauled back into her dock for fitting out and for the installation of her engines. In the following April she was ready to be towed over the harbour to Mardyke Wharf, but she stuck on the sill of the dock. A diver was sent down and found that a piece of wood was wedged beneath her. All was well when this removed, but it must have caused concern about the ship's ability to pass through the much more formidable obstacle of the Cumberland Basin. The BDC had failed to widen the lock gates after learning that they would be liable for any damage caused in the attempt. 'A nice laugh against the Bristol people', wrote local Vicar's son, William Prideaux, 'for building a vessel they could not get out of Dock.'

Early Voyages

James Hosken, the commander of the *Great Western*, was appointed as the first captain of the *Great Britain*. Despite impressive credentials, subsequent events were to show that he may not have been the wisest choice. In the meantime, he suffered the frustration of seeing his new command apparently permanently moored at Mardyke Wharf. While she was there, William Fox-Talbot took the earliest photograph of her. A number of notables paid a visit, including the King of Saxony, the French Pretender 'Henri V' and Prince Wilhelm of Prussia, who was to become the first Kaiser. The King of Saxony and his party were impressed by the ship, but expressed the fear that if she were raised at 'once under the bow and stern by two waves, the weight of her machinery might break her in two'. It would take some time to overcome such scruples.

In July, a plan proposed by Brunel to widen the lower locks was accepted by the BDC provided the GWSC met the costs. To get the ship through this first stage, a massive wooden cradle was built and sunk beneath her. This provided enough buoyancy to enable her passage into the Basin on 26 October 1844. It was decided to attempt to get the ship through the outer locks on the December high tides. Everything possible was removed to lighten her: stores and equipment, coal, top-masts and yards. The first attempt was made on the morning of 11 December, but it soon became clear that the ship was in danger of becoming jammed as the waters fell, so she was hauled back.

The evening tide was due to be slightly higher at 33 feet. Gangs of masons under Brunel's 'practiced eye' tore up the coping stones and removed the road bridge over the locks. Despite a severe frost and a cutting easterly wind, an enormous crowd assembled to watch the *Great Britain*'s rapid passage into the river, hauled by the tug *Sampson*. The correspondent of the *Illustrated London News* was struck by her 'splendid appearance' as she entered the dock. On each side, barrels of blazing tar lit up 'the giant ship, the water and the faces of the multitude'. The difficulty in getting the ship out of the Floating Harbour confirmed a decision to base her in Liverpool. It was to be 25 years before port facilities were built at Avonmouth. By then the focus of maritime trade had shifted elsewhere. Next morning, the *Great Britain* was towed to Kingroad. On her way down river, she got up steam. On being released from her tow, she made a satisfactory trial trip round the Holms during which she was completely under the command of the helm.

Two days later, a large party dined in the saloon. Numerous toasts were raised. 'Overwhelming cheers' greeted the one to Captain Claxton. He was, declared the *Bristol Mirror*, 'the life and soul of undertaking and most sincerely do we rejoice with him on the magnificent result of his unwearied exertions.' Curiously, no glass seems to have been raised to Isambard Kingdom Brunel. In more sober moments, the Directors must have reflected on the huge cost of building the ship, which to date was precisely £117,295:6:7d. In addition the works at Great Western Dock had cost £53,081:12:9d and the work on the locks, £1330:4:9d.

Official interest in the ship's potential was intense. Captain Hosken was asked to send reports on her performance to the Admiralty. Already the ship's revolutionary design was gripping the popular imagination. 'It is considered', wrote William Prideaux to his brother, 'that paddle wheels ere long will be entirely laid aside as the Archimedean Screw seems so much better in point of speed and appearance.'

On 14 January, the *Great Britain* was officially registered and given the number – 25967 – that she retained throughout her career. A medal was struck to commemorate her maiden voyage which began on 23 January when she embarked for London and her final fitting out. She was short-handed and the crew was composed 'chiefly of that indifferent class usually shipped for short runs, to whom of course, the rig of the ship was perfectly new.' Off Lundy, the ship hit a gale, but came through well, although some rigging was lost and buckling occurred on the forecastle deck. Despite the heavy seas, the engines continued 'as steadily as if they had been on land', but, with virtually no ballast, she rolled considerably. Many of the crew were laid up with seasickness. When the ship arrived in the Thames, amazement was expressed at her ability to manoeuvre in the crowded river. She was moored off Blackwall for five months and visited by an average of 1500 people a day. The *United Service Gazette* expressed the popular mood of wonder. 'The *Great Britain* is the largest vessel that has been constructed since the days of Noah.'

On the afternoon of 15 April, Queen Victoria and Prince Albert were given a tour of the ship by Captain Hosken. The Queen expressed amazement at her enormous length, a third longer than any battleship. As she was going down to the Engine Room, where Brunel was waiting to explain the machinery with a scale model, she seemed a little nervous and asked Captain Hosken if she was near the bottom of the steps. He told her that there was only one more and offered her his hand, 'without a thought of court etiquette and the Queen received it quite simply'. This bluff naval courtesy upset some courtiers, who remarked that he should have offered the Queen his arm. She was not perturbed and asked for him to be presented at her Drawing Room reception next day.

On 12 June some eighty passengers embarked on a leisurely cruise around the coast to the ship's home port of Liverpool. After embarking and disembarking more passengers at Cowes, she proceeded to Plymouth, where she was greeted by the ringing of church bells and thousands of people who rushed to the shores of the Sound. 'The western Hoe, even to the edges of its precipitous limestone quarries, was deeply fringed with persons of both sexes and all ages, who heartily cheered the iron wonder.' Further sea trials included a day-trip round the Eddystone Light with 600 passengers, who were amazed that the ship could sail backwards by reversing her engines. On the passage to her next port-of-call, Dublin, where she received another enthusiastic reception, one of her cylinders gave out and the ship proceeded on one engine. On her arrival in Liverpool, she underwent an inspection in the Queen's Graving Dock and was then opened to the public, averaging 2500 visitors a day.

On 26 July, the *Great Britain* sailed for New York with just fifty passengers – she still had to overcome fears about her safety – and 600 tons of cargo. The crossing went without incident, taking 14 days 21 hours at an average speed of 9.4 knots. The engines ran continuously until she sounded off the Canadian coast. Her tendency to roll was undiminished and there were complaints of excessive vibration. At noon on 10 August, her imminent arrival in New York was telegraphed and thousands rushed to greet her. The press reception was equally enthusiastic. The *Scientific American* regarded her as 'the greatest maritime curiosity ever seen in our Harbour.' 'She is truly beautiful ... The monster of the deep, a sort of Mastodon of this Age', enthused the *New York Herald*. 'The great problem whether or not a steamer of the magnitude and construction of the *Great Britain*, and her incorporating her principles of propulsion, could make a successful trip across the ocean, is now satisfactorily and happily solved.' More than 12,000 people paid to go aboard during the ship's stay in New York. At a dinner in honour of Captain Hosken, the first toast was to 'The Merchants of Bristol – the first to risk their wealth in Transatlantic steam navigation. The thanks of both nations are justly their due.'

The return voyage began on 30 August, with fifty-five passengers and a cargo composed largely of cotton. The best day's run was 287 miles. The ship lost her topmast in a storm and a sailor had his arm smashed while attempting to move the debris. An amputation was performed on the spot by the surgeon and £25 was collected by the passengers for the injured man. Despite this setback and difficulties in keeping up steam, the passage was accomplished in 15½ days at an average speed of 9 knots. On her return to Liverpool, the ship was dry-docked. Her plates, contrary to expectation, were found to be free from fouling.

To demonstrate the ship's capacity for a rapid turnaround, the second voyage began 12 days later, with 102 passengers aboard. She ran into bad weather from the start and averaged less than 7 knots for the first 2700 miles. Her foremast was carried away. Amidst strong winds and coastal currents, Captain Hosken failed to keep her clear of the Nantucket shoals. She probably touched ground and her propeller was severely damaged. On 13 October she took shelter for 10½ hours at Holmes Hole. On arrival in New York two days later, she was dry-docked. Two arms and a blade of the propeller were missing and nearly all the rivets were loose. These were tightened and a blade removed to preserve the ship's balance.

The *Great Britain* sailed for home on 28 October under reduced power, with only twenty-three passengers. Five days later, an arm of the propeller began to strike the stern post very hard. Captain Hosken ordered the engines to be put astern. After two or three good thumps, the arm broke off. Fortunately, the massive stern casting stood up to this punishment. The ship went forward on low steam, but soon after another arm broke, so the voyage continued under sail alone, the engines turning just enough to reduce drag. Progress was slow in a virtual calm. On 6 November the winds picked up, but, later that day, the last blade of the propeller broke off. Two days later, it was decided to stop the shaft with the remaining half arm fixed in a vertical position. This boosted the ship's sailing qualities and on 17 November she anchored in Liverpool Bay after a voyage of 20 days: a commendable time under the circumstances. The passengers presented the Captain with an address of congratulation.

After these mishaps, the *Great Britain* underwent a thorough refit. She was fitted with two bilge keels in an attempt to reduce her propensity to roll. A new propeller with four blades weighing 7 tons was built at the Bristol Works and shipped aboard the *Great Western* as she returned from her winter refit. It was decided that any advantages accruing from the unique wire rigging and hinged masts were more than offset by 'attendant evils', so they were replaced with fixed ones. The sails on the mast directly behind the funnel had a propensity to catch fire and so it was removed. 'Thursday', the main mast, was refitted with square rigging.

Enthusiasm had waned and only twenty-eight passengers embarked on the third voyage to New York in the following May. Although the propeller was more efficient, a fractured air pump led to a shutdown of the engines for 6 days. But the new rigging came into its own and the ship made good progress under sail. When the engines were restarted, she steamed at half speed and the passage took 20 days. She was again dry-docked for repairs. On the return run, she seemed to get over her difficulties, crossing in 13 days, averaging in one 24-hour period a speed of 13 knots. A target of 13 days out and 11 home seemed achievable.

These successes led the GWSC to tender again for the mail contracts, which were due for renewal, but it appeared that Samuel Cunard would again be successful. The Duke of Beaufort was persuaded to put down a question in the House of Lords, asking why 'the company which opened steam communications with America' had not had the opportunity to gain the contract. 'I know nothing of it', wrote Lord Ellenborough, the First Lord of the Admiralty, to Henry Goulborn, the Chancellor of the Exchequer. 'Will you let me know something about it?' Goulborn's reply sheds light on the failure of the GWSC to gain the contracts. He conceded that the company had a grievance, but it was well known to be in a parlous financial state. 'Between ourselves ... they are nearly, if not quite, bankrupt ...'

The fourth transatlantic voyage began on 8 July, with a respectable 108 passengers aboard. Despite touching bottom again as a result of faulty navigation in thick fog off the Newfoundland Banks and a broken driving chain on the return trip, each crossing took around 13 days. The outward mishap rebounded to the company's advantage, for it was popularly construed that a wooden ship would never have survived such a misfortune, but the *Great Britain* was about to face an even sterner test.

TWO

'The Most Egregious Blundering'

It was a measure of the growing confidence in the *Great Britain* that, on her next voyage out on 22 September 1846, she carried a considerable cargo and 180 passengers, the highest number to have embarked on a transatlantic crossing at that time. The total was boosted by the presence of forty-eight little girls aged between six and twelve from Madame Weiss's *Danseuses Viennoises*, a celebrated German dancing troupe.

The night was dark and wet. After a concert in the saloon, the passengers prepared for bed. In the words of a clergyman who was on board, 'all was bright, joyous and happy'. At around 10pm, a light to starboard puzzled the watch. Captain Hosken assumed that it was Chicken Rock Light on the Calf of Man, but in fact it was St John's Light on the Irish coast. In what the *Nautical Magazine* described as 'the most egregious blundering', the ship ran ashore in Dundrum Bay in County Down. Captain Hosken put the engines astern, but it was to no avail. She was stuck fast. The passengers were startled to hear cries of 'Stop her!' 'Aground! Aground!' 'The breakers! The breakers!' 'We are wrecked! Oh we are wrecked!' 'To add to that moment of woe', lamented *The New York Tribune*, 'the lightning glared, the thunder bellowed portentously from a thick curtain of overhanging cloud, and the rain began to fall in torrents.'

An officer on deck told Mr Tucker, a clergyman from Bermuda, that there was something wrong with the compass and compared its bearings with the one in the fore part of the ship. The opinion prevailed that it was the cause of the disaster, but Captain Hosken averred that there was nothing wrong with it. During the remainder of the night, blue lights were lit and guns fired amidst distressing scenes. Although no-one was injured, many people were very ill; the *enfantes Viennoise* were crying hysterically around Madame Weiss. Several passengers, 'who ought to have shown firmness, betrayed lamentable weakness'. Captain Hosken remained cool and composed, frequently consulting his charts. 'Oh, I cannot tell you the anguish of that night', wrote a young lady passenger. 'The sea broke over the ship, the waves struck her like thunderclaps; the gravel grated below. There was the throwing overboard of the coals; there were the cries of children, the groans of women, the blue lights, the signal guns, even the tears of men; and amidst all rose the voice of prayer.'

The prayers were the initiative of a group of clergy led by the Reverend S H Cox of New York. Few can have doubted his view that their survival was 'wonderful demonstration of the providence of God', when daylight revealed that the ship had passed through two dangerous reefs, the Cow and Calf Rocks, to run onto the only beach on the coast. One passenger slept through the whole business. Although leaking, with 10 feet of water in her hold, the ship was so well-built that she was not badly damaged, but there was no immediate hope of refloating her.

The local populace must have been astounded by the sight of the world's largest ship aground in their bay. At 4am, boats came alongside and some people were taken ashore. As the tide receded, the other passengers were lowered over the sides. Some were carried on the backs of local men while others enjoyed the comparative luxury of a seaweed manure cart. The little girls of the *Danseuses Viennoise* amused themselves by gathering seashells. 'There was an effective coastguard', continued the young lady passenger, 'but at one time, the Irish assembled in such numbers that we feared a riot. We walked through an Irish bog and lay down on the floor of an Irish cabin, where we found plenty of bread, some bacon and divided an egg into three. With much fatigue we came on to Belfast and Liverpool. To my astonishment, all the luggage was saved.'

When news of the disaster reached Bristol, Captain Claxton left for Ireland. On arrival, he generously, but somewhat surprisingly, exonerated Captain Hosken from all blame. Hosken claimed that he had been 'betrayed' by the omission of St John's Light from the latest Admiralty chart and that he did not know of its existence, but the Admiralty was to deny this oft-repeated assertion. The two lights were very different. St John's Point Lighthouse was 195 feet above sea level and showed one bright light for 45 seconds each minute. The Chicken Rock Lighthouse was 396 feet above sea level and had two lights which revolved alternately every two minutes. Not all were to agree with Claxton's assessment, although the compasses may have been at fault. At least Hosken could reflect on who were 'true and who were false friends'.

On 31 October, as a gale was blowing up, Claxton set sail and drove the ship 130 yards up the beach, above the high water mark, to protect her from the waves. The leading salvage experts, Alexander Bremner and his son James, built a breakwater from pieces of bulk timber, but it was hardly completed when a fierce gale 'laid this labour of man's hands prostrate, smashing the bones like so many reeds'. Claxton submitted a design for a new breakwater to Brunel, but it was difficult to obtain materials in such a remote place. He experimented with various timbers and found young beech wood the most effective. On 7 November, a survey of the ship was completed by Mr W Billington, who reported that the bulging of the plates on the starboard side had caused the rivets to spring open, admitting the ebb and flow of the tide. Several holes were drilled through the ship's bottom to prevent her from rising and falling. During spring tides there was up to 17 feet of water in the hold and at low water she was left dry, except for a small quantity of water in the 'dock' she had formed in the sand. At high tide she swung to and fro and appeared 'much sprung and strained'. She had lost her rudder, although her propeller was only slightly damaged. Despite his gloomy prognosis, Mr Billington considered that the difficult task of refloating the ship could be accomplished. Mr Mackintosh, a military accoutrement-maker, shared this view and came up with a 'novel' scheme to install a semi-circle of explosives around the bows of the ship, with a line of smaller charges along a channel to the sea. Tugs would start pulling and when the explosives were fired, the water at her stern would be lifted with enough force to loosen the sand and set her afloat. The firing of smaller charges would ensure that the wave continued to drive the ship towards the sea. 'The grand point', he concluded, conceding the obvious, 'must be to ensure such a precise arrangement of the explosive materials as to prevent any untoward injury to the ship.'

Brunel arrived at Dundrum Bay in December and was grieved to see his ship,

> lying unprotected, deserted and abandoned by those who ought to know her value and ought to have protected her, instead of being humbugged by schemers and under-writers ... The result is that the finest ship in the world, in excellent condition, such that £4000 or £5000 would repair all the damage done, has been left and is lying like a useless saucepan kicking about on the most exposed shore that you can imagine, with no more effort to protect the property than the said saucepan would have received on the beach at Brighton ...
>
> The ship is perfect, except that at one part the bottom is much bruised and knocked in holes in several places. But even within three feet of the damaged part there is no strain or injury whatsoever ...

The slight damage to the stern demonstrated the need to take precautions 'if' she were to be saved.

> I say 'if', for really when I saw a vessel, still in perfect condition, left to the tender mercies of an awfully exposed shore for weeks,

> while a party of quacks are amusing you with schemes for getting her off, she is in the meantime being left to go to pieces. I could hardly help feeling as if her own parents and guardians meant her to die there ... What are we wasting precious time about? The steed is being quietly stolen while we are discussing the relative merits of a Bramah or a Chubb's lock to be put on at a future time. It is really shocking ...

Brunel wrote a scathing letter to Claxton which gives an insight into his work ethic.

> You have failed, I think from that which causes most of the failures in the world, from not doing quite enough. I would impress on you one principle of action which I have always found very successful, which is to stick obstinately to one plan (until I believe it to be wrong) ... and push that to the utmost limits before I allow myself to wander into others; in fact, to use a simile, to stick to the point of the attack, however defended, and if the force first brought up is not sufficient, to bring ten times as much but never to try back upon another in the hope of finding it easier. So with the fagots – if a six-bundle fagot won't reach out of the water, try a twenty-bundle one, if hundredweights won't keep it down, try tons.

Brunel increased the number of fagots to 5000, held in place by any available weights, including chains and parts of the ship's engines. The breakwater swayed with 'the mighty waves ... like the trees of the forest in a gale', but proved highly effective in protecting the ship through the winter storms. During violent gales in February, around a hundred fagots were washed away and the sea constantly swept over the funnel, but the breakwater held. Its very success caused a further problem. Its base became a solid mass, so that its eventual removal was exceedingly difficult. The disaster placed severe strain on the already-straightened GWSC. The *Great Britain*, it transpired, was grossly under-insured. To keep the company afloat, the *Great Western* was sold to the West India Royal Mail Steam Packet Company for £24,750.

In the spring of 1847, Claxton ordered that the *Great Britain*'s upper deck and her coal bunkers be tightened. On a high tide, the ship rose 4 feet. She was kept at this height by pulling her to one side and filling the resultant gap with stones, but she would rise no further. To solve the problem, the Bremners ordered the construction of twenty huge crates. Each was filled with 50 tons of sand and attached to chains which went over pulleys fixed on large vertical baulks of timber and then passed through pulleys attached to the side of the ship. This effectively doubled the weight of the sand. Screws capable of lifting 160 tons were placed near the hawsepipes on a stout timber frame supported by an immense wooden structure. The levers on the landward side were ballasted by one of the large iron lifeboats filled with sand. Any available weights were piled at the ends of the timbers – chains, anchors and engine parts. Thus very little of the ship's surface was exposed to the action of the sea.

On 19 July, when preparations were nearly complete, it was felt advisable, in view of the imminent spring tide, to make an attempt to lift her. Claxton thought she would be more difficult to 'move than a granite rock', but, to the amazement of all, she rose so rapidly that the pumps had to be opened to prevent her rising any higher. Unfortunately, the pumps proved inadequate to hold the ship at the required height, so that when the tide came in, a number of boxes and baulks were damaged. To prevent a recurrence, the pumps were improved and thousands of small piles were driven through the sand to the bedrock. On these were laid the foundations for vertical supports. An 'ingenious contrivance' was created to ensure that, as the ship rose, the shoring repositioned itself. Huge wedges were hauled under the fore keel and bilges and stones were projected under the vessel through long chutes running down her sides. The 'gratifying result' was that on 29 July the ship was raised enough to enable boilermakers from Portsmouth Dockyard to patch her bottom plates. The largest of a considerable number of holes was 6½ feet square. At low water, a deep trench was cut through the sand from the stern of the ship towards the sea. In August, she was moved a short distance to a level ridge of rocks and a few days later she was pulled clear by HMS *Birkenhead* and *Scourge.* Such was the renown engendered by the Bremners' bold rescue that a scale model of their lifting device was a feature of the Great Exhibition of 1851.

The ship was still leaking considerably, so she was towed to Belfast for further patching-up. Next day, the *Birkenhead* towed her across the Irish Sea, as 300 perspiring naval ratings manned the pumps. As she approached the Mersey Bar, the wind rose to a half gale. The towropes snapped and the inflow of sea through the leaks increased. It seemed as if the Herculean efforts of the previous 11 months might be in vain, but the ropes were reattached and she was towed into Prince's Dock.

A survey undertaken by Fawcett, Preston and Company extolled the materials used in the construction of the *Great Britain.* 'We do not conceive that it would have been possible under similar circumstances to stop holes of the size mentioned, in the bottom of a wooden vessel; and we may further remark that the iron of which the frame and plates are made must have been of the most excellent quality.' The report was not good reading for the GWSC. It was estimated that it would cost £15,886 to repair the ship's structure and a further £5808 for her engines and boilers. At an acrimonious General Meeting, the directors were berated by angry shareholders for refunding the stranded passengers their fares. The *Great Britain* was put up for sale and the GWSC was wound up. On 14 April 1848, the ship's effects were auctioned in Liverpool. Wonder was expressed at the scale of the shipboard establishment. Amongst the goods on sale were 228 hair mattresses, 406 feather pillows, 580 blankets, 970 linen sheets, 1556 towels and 781 pillow cases. Efforts to find a buyer failed. The ship was put up for auction on 11 September, but failed to reach the reserve price of £40,000. She was finally sold in December, 1850 for £18,000, less than a sixth of her original cost, having amassed a considerable backlog of dock dues.

The buyers were Gibbs, Bright and Company, the Liverpool branch of an old shipping concern. They had decided to convert her for a service to Melbourne. The recent discovery of gold at Ballarat had transformed Australia from a land of exile to a place of opportunity.

A New Ship

The 12,000-mile voyage to Australia was beyond the range of contemporary steam power, unless the expensive, lengthy and erratic process of coaling en route was undertaken, so William Patterson was commissioned to change the vessel from a sail-assisted steamship to a steam-assisted sailing ship. At the Queen's Graving Dock in Liverpool, 350 men were hired to carry out the work. The number of masts was reduced to four, although the sail area was increased to 300 square yards, with broad-rigging on the second and third masts. The main mast was now abaft newly-installed twin funnels which were unusual in being side-by-side. Each served three new boilers which doubled the steam pressure.

New engines were installed by John Penn and Sons of Greenwich. Although at 500 horse-power they possessed only half the nominal power of their predecessors, they proved to be more efficacious. They were very similar to those designed to drive paddlewheels and consisted of a pair of oscillating cylinders 82½ inches in diameter. Motion was transmitted to the screw shaft by cogwheels, with direct gearing to a cast iron triple-bladed propeller, which could be detached from its shaft to turn freely when the ship was under sail alone, thereby reducing drag. Above the boilers was a blacksmith's shop. Nearly all the parts of another engine were stored nearby in case of breakdown. To make the ship more stable, the iron keel, which was about 2 inches deep, was replaced by a 17-inch one made of oak cased with zinc plating.

Passenger numbers were increased to 730 by adding an upper deck. As a result, the ship floated several feet lower in the water, a testimony to the strength of her design. As this brought the hawse-pipes, through which the anchor cables ran, nearer the surface, they were sealed and new ones installed higher up. For the first time, the ship offered 'steerage' accommodation. A passage to Australia cost £16 – more than half a year's wages for a farmhand – and Intermediate (Third Class), £18. Passengers brought their own bedding, linen, soap, cutlery and a 3-gallon water keg and cup. A dark narrow gangway led down to the cabins, where they were packed 'as close as bees in a hive' next to the engines, with a shared washstand and four undivided berths on each side of a confined and narrow passage.

Passengers in the Fore Saloon (Second Class) were berthed in part of the new deckhouse. The accommodation was 'very comfortable and well lighted' with a steward in attendance. Cutlery was provided, but passengers had to bring their own bedding, linen and soap. The After Saloon (First Class) cabins were on the Promenade Deck. Although still luxurious by previous standards, they were cramped, measuring 9 feet by 6 feet. They contained two bunks, a sofa and a shelf. Unlike the other classes, passengers were provided with 'every requisite', which was hardy surprising, since the passage cost twice that of Second Class.

A new dining saloon was located in the deckhouse, with a partition separating Fore and After Saloon passengers. This elicited the same admiration as its predecessor. It is probable that many fixtures, like the 'innumerable mirrors' were simply transferred there. The seats were covered with crimson velvet and the room contained 'everything that luxury could invent to make the meal agreeable'. It was much remarked upon that the flooring and passages were now covered with rope matting and carpeting, which eradicated 'the clatter and noise so disagreeable, and injurious to invalids and delicate persons, in ordinary passenger ships'. The Ladies' Drawing Room was now in the stern, with its large windows, and 'the comfort of the fair passengers was much enhanced by the presence of a "darling" little piano'.

Further forward were the officers' and seamens' sleeping-quarters and mess rooms, the doctor's surgery, barber's shop, steward's pantry, bar, bakehouse, three galleys and carpenters' and joiners' workshops. The resplendent dining saloon was converted to steerage accommodation and as an extended cargo hold. This, together with the compactness of the new engines and boilers, meant that cargo capacity increased to nearly 1000 tons. In order to boost shipboard rations, live animals were carried. There was a cow house and accommodation for 160 sheep and 40 pigs, with a large hen coop on deck.

Barnard Robert Matthews, who succeeded James Hosken to the command of the *Great Western*, was appointed as the new captain of the *Great Britain*. He was an experienced sailor, having commanded sailing ships on many transatlantic voyages, following the emigration boom after the Great Famine in Ireland. Although he possessed social graces, he could be 'crusty and disagreeable'.

On 1 May 1852, the ship embarked on a trial voyage to New York, which took 13 days and 7 hours. She encountered severe gales, but shipped very little water onto her decks. Her new stabilisers were proven in the most practical way. It was claimed that none of the 350 passengers she carried out and home was seasick, but this hardly accorded with subsequent experience. After her return from New York, Captain Martin, the company's Marine Superintendent, asked John Gray, a 17-stone Shetlander, to join the ship's complement as Second Officer. Born on Unst in 1819, he came from a nautical family, his father being a fisherman and the Sheriff Officer of the island, and a great-uncle, Arthur Anderson, M.P, a founder of the P&O Line. Gray had pursued a successful career in the merchant marine, rising to command the *Loodiano*, a Liverpool clipper, when he was barely thirty. Mrs Gray disliked the idea of her husband stepping down in rank to join the *Great Britain*, but he was a far-sighted man and accepted the offer.

THREE

'The Celebrated'

The capacity of the *Great Britain* to make regularly-timed trips transformed the route to Australia and opened up the new land. Until she began her service to Melbourne, many travellers chose to take the lengthy and expensive route via an overland crossing of the Suez isthmus, rather than embark on the arduous voyage around the Cape of Good Hope.

Something of the ascendancy that the *Great Britain* established on the Australia run was caught by a *Times* correspondent in 1965. The ship had long been marooned as a wreck in the Falklands when he was taken to see her by an old boatman who referred to her as 'The Celebrated'.

> The bare old hulk in the quiet cove on your right as you sail up Port William was the great iron masterpiece conceived by Brunel, the biggest ship of her day, the first screw-driven to cross the Atlantic.
>
> 'But it wasn't that', said the old man, 'which made her the Celebrated. It was her success on the British-Australia run. Liked better than any other in all the 25 years she made the trip. Even when the bigger and better ones came along people still preferred her. Australians used to get on at Melbourne and Sidney and travel up to Brisbane just to say they'd been on her.'

It was not only in terms of passenger traffic that the contribution of the *Great Britain* was vital in building the new land. She built a virtual monopoly in the gold trade, and in 1853, she carried the first bales of wool exported from Australia. Cotton was another major cargo.

Tearful Adieus

The *Great Britain* sailed for Australia on 21 August 1852, carrying 630 passengers (the most she would carry on the route), a crew of 138 and a full cargo which included gold and silver specie valued at £1 million. With such riches aboard, she was equipped to resist attack. Six 8-pounder guns were mounted on deck and she carried arms and ammunition for 100 men including muskets and pikes to repel boarders.

The owners predicted that the voyage would take 56 days. This time, they had secured the valuable Royal Mail contracts. In their eagerness to obtain them, they had guaranteed delivery in Melbourne within 60 days. The ship bunkered with 1400 tons of coal, which was considered sufficient for the entire passage, but it was decided, wisely as it turned out, to take on fresh supplies at Cape Town and colliers were sent ahead.

Allan Gilmour was 17 when he embarked with his father, a widower, and younger brother, Matthew, aged 14. His father's business in Glasgow had suffered in the great reverses in the cotton trade during the economic crisis of 1848. When the depression continued, his partners decided to send him to Melbourne to open a commission house. The rest of his family was to stay in Pollockshields until he could send for them.

Mr Gilmour cannot have looked forward to going to Australia. He had heard that, because of the huge influx of immigrants brought about by the gold rush, houses could not be got in Melbourne for 'love or money', so he had provided himself with a 'Model Tent', which was large and square with a substantial frame. On a longer term basis, he shipped out separately, to arrive after him, a prefabricated house and store built of galvanised iron. The 'tearful adieu' after family worship on the Sunday mirrored many such sad partings. At the gate, Allan's Aunt Jane masked her distress with curt Presbyterian dourness. 'Be off with you!' From Glasgow they took a steamer to Liverpool.

No such sadness was felt by Edward Towle, a young man of 22 from Draycott in Derbyshire. He embarked with his elder brother, Ben, who was 24, in a spirit of adventure with new worlds to explore. When they arrived at the dockside, much encumbered with luggage, crowds of people were scrambling to get aboard the steamer that was to take them to the ship. With characteristic resource and aplomb, they boarded a vessel berthed alongside, pitched their luggage 'safely over the chasm' and leapt after it. They soon reached the 'Leviathan of steamers and after much struggling to ascend its stupendous sides', reached the deck on which hundreds of people were massed. The overcrowding was exacerbated by the bags of coal stacked against the rails. Their cabin in the Fore Saloon had six bunks and a single washbasin. It was well-ventilated, but very cramped. Only with difficulty could two people get dressed at the same time. The situation was not helped by the presence of a large box, which they assumed belonged to a surgeon, 'a serious and rather soft-looking chap', who was occupying one of the berths.

Like many other voyagers, the Towles were hoping to make their fortunes in the gold fields. 'We are a rough looking lot', wrote Stephen Perry, a young man in Steerage. 'There is a dash of every nation here ... Nearly all the passengers are going to the diggings and I only hope there is gold enough for all.'

The Prodigious Steamer

Thomas Murray Park, although he was only 5 years old when he embarked with his family in the After Saloon, recalled half a century later the excitement when the *Great Britain* slipped her cable and got under way at half past two.

> We had many friends to see us off, and get our luggage put into the cabin. The ringing of the first bell hurried those with their preparations to get onto the tugboat that lay alongside. Then the bell was rung a second time giving its warning note that time was rapidly passing away and that people must get ready for the shore. Then came the final warning by the ringing of the bell for the third time, and the Officer at once set about clearing the ship of visitors ... The Tug-boats kept as near as they could with safety to themselves, also the bands kept up a lively set of tunes to cheer us on our way.

It was a hot day and the crew was dressed in their white summer uniforms. John McFall, the Boatswain, completed the ceremony of piping up the gangplank at one o'clock and then climbed the mast. He had been ill, so despite the heat, he felt chilly. As the ship passed his home at Everton, he looked across the water with a 'full heart' and thought of his 'heart's treasure', his wife, Catherine. Another who gazed ashore with a heavy heart was Simeon Cohen, a 20 year-old Jew from Liverpool. He was being sent to Melbourne by his family to set up in business, but he was leaving his 16 year-old sweetheart, the beautiful and accomplished Cecilia Wolfe. He must have wondered if he would ever see her again.

The American Consul in Liverpool, the writer Nathaniel Hawthorne, was invited by Mr Bright to join the 'prodigious steamer' on her passage out to sea.

> There is an immense enthusiasm amongst the English people about this ship, on account of her being the largest in the world. The shores were lined with people to see her sail; and there were innumerable small steamers, crowded with people, all the way out into the ocean.

The ship fired her guns at regular intervals and HMS *Arctic*, which was moored in the Harbour, and the cannons at Parry's Pleasure

Gardens responded. The smaller craft saluted with pistol or musket shot. 'On every side resounded the most enthusiastic huzzars to which the passengers responded: some with cheers, some with tears ... the steamers dropped off one by one, each saluting us with a hearty cheer before departure until ... we were left alone on the mighty deep.'

As the ship passed Holyhead Light that evening, Edward Towle felt a mood of reflective melancholy, which was however soon dispelled.

> For the first time in my life I felt myself alone in the world and a stranger. One half of my life in all probability is gone, a new and, I trust, brighter era is about to dawn.

He retired at ten o'clock, still not having met all his cabin mates, and slept soundly, despite his 'novel bed'. He decided always to get up first to enjoy 'a clear cabin and a clean basin'.

When the rest woke up, they examined each other curiously. The Hodgetts brothers, Joe and William, seemed 'civil and obliging'. They were equipped for the diggings, 'with every requisite but one ... the habit of bodily labour'. William was medically qualified. His wife, whom Edward regarded as rather beneath his social station, was in the women's quarters. The dormitory accommodation on board meant that only those in the After Saloon could share with their spouses. The berth opposite was occupied by George Mansell, 'a wild looking Irishman ... a genial looking fellow, but always in fun. He appears to be like all his compatriots, all impulse and as unstable as the water upon which we float.'

It was the Sabbath. At eleven the ship's bell tolled for an idiosyncratic service in the Saloon conducted by the Captain. He read prayers and then announced he had no time to preach as he wanted 'to take a sight of the sun', but he promised a sermon at the evening service. The 200 worshippers were attentive and seemed very devout, but the Captain forgot to preach.

The excessive number of passengers in the Fore Saloon caused chaos at mealtimes, But this was eased by forming two sittings. 'We now get comfortably served', wrote Edward Towle, 'and very fair provisions for shipboard'.

As the ship hit the full force of the Atlantic, she rolled in the heavy swell. Seasickness was rife and sufferers climbed over the sacks of coal to 'make their contributions to Neptune'. A wag described it as being 'hauled over the coals'. Ben Towle felt queasy, but could not go below because it made him feel dizzy. The Hodgetts brothers were very ill. They were grateful when Edward fetched them tea and began to be more communicative. On the train from Manchester he had met Mr E H Foulks, a young man 'possessed of the most exuberant spirits and a taste for fun that nothing can abate. He is very sick, but in spite of it all, laughs at everybody in the same predicament and more particularly if they do not fire straight.' The berthmates turned in early that evening and all slept well, except the surgeon, who rose early and fouled the basin, so depriving Edward of his morning wash. It was decided that he was a 'nasty beast' who was 'evidently selfish and must be dealt with accordingly'.

In the family cabin, Tom Park's father was very busy.

> First he got my mother to bed, then Sissy and myself were stowed away. My poor Mother was very ill. She was, at the best of times, a poor sailor: here, with ... masts creaking, blocks and chains rattling, sailors tramping on deck making all as secure as they could, and every now and then, the ship would give an extra roll, as if she would never recover herself and roll over. My poor mother suffered very much during that long night; many and many a time she wished herself on shore, back in dear old Liverpool. To make matters worse, some of the crockery fell from the racks.

One day when his mother was halfway up a companionway, the ship lurched and she slipped, cutting and fracturing her leg. She had to spend a long time in bed. She had some practical medical knowledge and suggested to the ship's doctor that he apply bread poultices to the wound, but he insisted on linseed ones, which caused her 'untold suffering'. It was only when she persuaded him to try her remedy that she improved.

Three days out, the Towle brothers decided to gain revenge on the surgeon by getting rid of the huge trunk that was still blocking up the cabin. Singing the shanty '*Cheerily boys, Cheerily boys eh oh*', they heaved the 'ponderous receptacle' into the passage. They made a lot of noise and nearly knocked the cabin door off. To their surprise, the trunk turned out not to belong to the surgeon at all, but to George Mansell, but he took the incident in good part.

Tom Park became a great favourite with the sailors and often went into the forecastle to see them. One started to make him a model of a brig and the boy watched him day by day, cutting out masts and yards and then the rigging. At last it was finished and he became its proud owner. One fine day he thought that it would like to see his ship sail, so he went to the cabin and got a cotton reel. Captain Matthews had been solicitous of the comfort of his After Saloon passengers, arranging for a platform to be built in the bulwarks where gentlemen could lounge or play games, freeing the deck for the ladies and children. Tom scrambled onto it. Everyone was intent on their games, so no-one noticed him as he lowered his boat into the water.

> Just as I had got it into sailing trim, the cotton broke and the end went over the side. I reached out for it ... The ship was heeling over and this caused me to slide to the edge of the platform.

Tom's father heard the cry of 'Save the boy' and raced to the rail. He grabbed his leg as he disappeared overboard and hauled him back on deck. Tom was not pleased. 'All I wanted was my ship that was being left astern at the rate of 12 miles per hour, so you can imagine what chance I had of being saved if I got in the water.'

The ship was making steady progress in a northerly trade wind. 'Though it does not blow hard enough', the Captain told Edward Towle, 'it still helps us a little.' Edward noticed that the stacks of coal were diminishing rapidly. 'As the coals are consumed we get lighter and lighter.' The voyage seemed to be going well. An exhibition of personal curios was organised by the passengers and Captain Matthews established a 'police force' to guard it drawn from volunteers amongst the passengers.

The Manchester Table

Edward Towle had become a member of a 'sort of club' of seventeen young men who took meals together. Since most of them came from that area, it became known as the 'Manchester Table'. 'By this combination we have obtained many advantages in our eating and drinking and attendance.' The latter was important as there were insufficient stewards to provide a proper service at table, but the friends had one allocated to them exclusively and an 'increased gratuity' encouraged him to procure them 'valuable luxuries'.

Captain Matthews, who may have felt vulnerable to the criticisms that some passengers were starting to voice, found some respite on this affable table, joining the chums for dinner one evening and buying champagne. 'He retired after being most heartily cheered and said we were the noisiest set of people he ever met with in his life ... We eat more, sleep more and laugh more than any other party on board the ship.'

In this spirit of ribaldry, they devised a set of rules 'for the better regulation of our meals and manners'. Transgressors were fined 2/11d, the price of a bottle of wine. This was enjoyed so much that it was decided to extend the range of infringements. The provocative and frivolous regulation was added that any 'gentleman' who felt 'insulted or aggrieved by another' should deposit his money with the Chairman and level his charge against the 'aggressor', who was also obliged to hand over 2/11d until he could clear himself. No sooner was this rule passed than Mr G D Holt handed over 2/11d and accused Mr H Hartley of putting a pin on his seat that had penetrated a 'certain part of his person'. His neighbours at table were 'greatly incommoded' by his resultant inability to sit still. Hartley replied that the charge was a fabrication to get a bottle of wine out of him and challenged Holt to submit his wound to examination. When he refused, it was decided that he should pay up. Hartley laughed and jabbed his thumb at him insultingly. Holt promptly bit it, so Hartley immediately preferred another charge. Since everyone had witnessed 'this unwarrantable seizure', Holt was condemned to pay for another bottle. He was very annoyed and made rude remarks to his neighbours who brought further charges so he had to pay for even more bottles. Naturally, he got indignant about the 'prejudiced' way in which matters were being conducted and 'half angry and half in joke', grabbed Mr Foulks, who was sitting opposite, by the hair.

> Mr Foulks returned the compliment. They pulled and tugged at each others heads until Mr Holt's hair gave way and a handful was left in Mr Foulks' hands. Mr Holt then got into a furious rage. He wished to destroy everybody at the table, but Mr Cox, the First Officer, appeared at this critical juncture, calmly reprimanded the ungentlemanly conduct of the whole proceedings, inspected the lock of hair which had been torn from the brow of Mr Holt, and declared his intention of keeping it as a memorial of Mr Holt's spartan like endurance of so foul an insult.

A few days later, the tabular tribunal sat in judgement on its Chairman. Charles Worral had got drunk one night and insulted a lady. It was decided unanimously to expel him from the chair and elect another in his place.

Every evening Edward and his companions sat on what they dubbed their 'country seat': the long curving sofa which ran under the stern windows.

> We talk of our homes and those we have left behind us, our future hopes and prospects and our anticipated return, if not rich, at least with something to keep us comfortable. We can look upon the waves and admire their crested tops tinged by the silvery light of the moon. Joe then gives us a song, Ben a stave on the cornet and my flute has to contribute to our mutual amusement though almost drowned by the noise of the breaking waves. At 11, we go the rounds of the ship, visit the engine room, the forecastle, the fore saloon, the upper and lower deck just to see (by way of a

joke) that all is right before we turn in, and sleep too soundly even to dream of home.

In the morning, they were woken by the crowing of the cocks and the quacking of the ducks of the shipboard poultry farm. 'There is one cock which has a particular crow that amuses us very much. Every day we expect to hear his last crow and every day our expectations are disappointed.'

'Like a Fiddler's Elbow'

A moment of high drama occurred as the ship approached the Canaries. There was a good breeze blowing in the early hours, so it was decided to test the mechanism for detaching the screw. This was duly done and the studding sails were set. When the wind dropped, it was decided to attach it again, so the free revolving of the propeller was stopped. As a result, it acted 'like an oar in the water to a moving boat'. The ship shuddered almost to a standstill. She no longer obeyed the helm and was at the mercy of the winds. She was rolling tremendously. The sacks of coal piled round the bulwarks spilt their contents to block the gangways and lots of crockery was smashed. Above the wind, the voice of John Gray was heard, commanding that all the sails should be struck. 'In an instant he seemed to possess the gift of ubiquity and his energy seemed to rouse the crew to their utmost exertions.'

Before the order could be obeyed, the fore studding sail boom, a spar two feet in circumference, snapped in two and fell to the deck. Before the debris could be cleared away, the top mast studding sail boom crashed down. The passengers who were on deck were asked to help strike the sails and set to 'work in right earnest'. Miraculously, no-one was injured and the broken booms were rapidly replaced. John Gray was not averse to a leg-pull and told the passengers that he had seen the yard arm dip into the water. Some believed him, but most dismissed it as a sailor's yarn.

That evening there was a sudden squall. John McFall saw the new lower studding sail boom 'knuckle like a fiddler's elbow'. Without instant action, all the sails would be lost. The passengers on deck were again enlisted. The scene was chaotic. 'Ropes were swinging about in all directions', wrote Edward Towle, 'and giving us such whacks on the head.' The confusion increased as darkness fell. John McFall forgot that the passengers did not understand nautical terms and shouted to them to pull the weather brace, brail up the spanker and haul down the gaff. For about an hour, they hung on like leeches to any rope that happened to be dangling about and swung backwards and forwards like 'so many pendulums' as the vessel rolled from side to side. 'Sometimes coming athwart one another and extracting an involuntary but painful grunt.' The Captain was on deck in his dressing gown and nightcap. Edward's trousers were tied up with a handkerchief under a nightshirt besmirched with tar and dirt. Mr Foulks found it impossible to treat the matter seriously. When a Frenchman appeared on deck, enquiring 'Vat is the matter?', he seized him by the collar. 'Don't you see? The ship is sinking, while you stand there like a lazy lubber. Down below with you and fetch your lifebelt quick as lightning and then come here and bear a hand and mind you salute me, sir, for I am Second Officer of the ship.' The bewildered Frenchman went below, returned with his lifebelt and saluted Mr Foulks, who remained incognito in the darkness. In the resulting panic George Mansell rushed below, grabbed his lifebelt and inflated it with 'a vigour and resolution which nothing but the idea ... that his life was in danger could have inspired'. He was to get a lot of ribbing about it.

Rising Tensions

Much of the difficulty with sailing the ship was caused by the crew's unfamiliarity with her. They were also short-handed. Many of the sailors declared that they had never been worked so hard. The mishaps had made the ship extremely dirty, with coal dust everywhere. This did much to fuel rising discontent amongst the passengers, which was exacerbated by overcrowding and the steadily increasing heat. Gambling, drinking and quarrelling were on the increase.

The routine of shipboard life was disturbed by a number of incidents. An Irishman, 'a poor old man over 50, who had married a young girl of 17 who meekly follows him around', claimed that £40 had been stolen from him and got the Captain to organise a search of the crew's quarters. The money was eventually found in his own luggage. The sailors marked him down for revenge. Edward Towle also had his differences. When he asked Mr Cohan, the Captain's clerk, a question, this disagreeable young man shook his finger at him insultingly and told him to mind his own business.

On another occasion, one of the cooks accidentally mashed the tea with salt water. The angry passengers threw it overboard and a deputation went to complain to the Captain. He explained the mistake and the matter appeared to be settled, but that evening, a passenger called James Horsefall made 'several severe and unwarrantable' remarks to him. The Captain took it stoically, but when Horsefall continued to rail, he told him that he would not be insulted on his own quarter deck. If he had anything to say, he should say it on shore at the Cape. Unless he left immediately, he would be placed under arrest. As he left, a sudden lurch of the ship laid him prostrate on the deck, much to the amusement of those who had witnessed the altercation and its 'unfortunate but ridiculous termination'.

Complaints about the food led to a protest meeting in the Fore Saloon attended by some 200 people. Edward Towle was surprised by the eloquence of the speeches. Mr Cox, the First Officer, responded with some convincing explanations which appeased the discontented. Some benefits ensued, and excellent jam and other little luxuries appeared. Edward Towle found most of the food to be of the 'best quality' and thought that no-one with any justice could complain, but even he drew the line at the salt beef. 'It is really so hard, tough and salt that I can never take it at all.'

There were more volatile sources of tension. 'We have a gentleman here by the name of Scott who has a very pretty wife', wrote Stephan Perry, 'and I believe she thinks she will leave him and take another lord even before we arrive at our destination. There has been what the ladies call miffs and he won't leave a moment ... Then there are some young men who go below at midnight drunk and come out in the passages with a little bowie knife exercise. Then others that get chained up for being drunk and disorderly.' Two such gentlemen fell out during a 'Bacchanalian revel' and arranged to fight a duel when the ship reached the Cape.

Further tensions surfaced in the cramped and congested sleeping quarters. Mr Foulks' neighbour in the upper bunk was 'an exceedingly quiet and silent young' man by day, but once asleep, he would begin his 'usual nocturnal song'. In exasperation, he administered an 'eloquent' punch from below. The head of his 'attic friend' slowly projected over the side and looked at him as if silently enquiring what was the matter and then it slowly withdrew. The snoring soon recommenced, so Mr Foulks administered another admonitory punch. The head again slowly projected and whispered 'elho' [*sic*].

> Upon receiving no answer the head, with a ludicrous expression of silent wonder again withdrew. Five minutes more elapsed when the snoring recommenced louder than before. Mr F gave him such a smart rap that the head protruded this time rather more quickly and gazed right down into Mr F's berth as if seeking an explanation of this unceremonious attack. At last it quietly ejaculated:
>
> 'Is anything the matter?'
>
> 'Ah, to be sure', said Mr F. 'You are snoring like a seahorse and blowing like a grampus. Can't you be still and let folks sleep quietly.'

Before the head was withdrawn, the countenance presented a mingled expression of regret and despair which haunted Mr Foulks for the rest of the night.

As the heat intensified, the new staves supporting the upper bunks contracted. A fat man weighing 17 stone crashed down on his neighbour and, not surprisingly, 'very much damaged him'. In another cabin, a Welshman in the bottom bunk raised his legs at right angles during a nightmare and thrust the Scotsman above him up to the roof and held him there fast. He bellowed and struggled. The cabin was in an uproar. Nobody in the darkness could ascertain the cause of the disturbance. The Welshman woke up and immediately pulled his legs away. The bunk and the Scotsman came crashing down. A great deal of kicking, struggling and cuffing ensued before things were explained and the matter ended in hearty laughter.

The temperature soared as the ship sailed southwards. 'If you move to see our reeking temples and our steaming faces, you would indeed pity us', wrote Edward Towle in his lengthening letter home. 'There is no remedy for it and no means of cooling ourselves or of obtaining anything that is cool.' Many people spent the night on deck, but Edward considered that the damp atmosphere and 'being rather too near Sierra Leone' made this dangerous. This was the era of Livingstone's explorations and the perils of the Dark Continent, even from well out at sea, had fired the popular imagination.

Crossing the Line

As the ship approached the Equator, the crew prepared for a 'Crossing the Line' ceremony. Passengers were sworn in to solicit contributions towards the merriment from their fellows. The names of those who refused to cough up were carefully noted. On the great morning, a rocket ascended, both ends of the main yard were lit up with blue fire and a trumpet sounded to greet the arrival of John Gray, disguised as King Neptune's Lieutenant. He was accompanied by an assistant. Large goggle eyes were painted on his face and he was wearing a fur cap, a long beard, a stout flannel overcoat and knee boots under a coloured apron. He hailed the Captain and gave him a dispatch from his Lord and Master. Passengers who rushed to the bows to get a better view were deluged when the ship's hoses were set on them.

The Captain welcomed the emissaries and read out the letter before tacking it to the mainmast.

> His Sultanic Majesty Neptune begs to inform the Captain of the *Great Britain* that he is fast approaching his territories and by the indicator he finds he has upwards of 800 children on board some

> of whom are cultivating mustaches, a privilege I alone claim on the Equator and all who dare to infringe render themselves liable to have the wrong side of the razor used on their faces. I beg you to acquaint them of this fact. I will however forego harsh measures with them on your account, having been so kindly treated by you on board the Catherine in 1847. I fear that my duties to the Westward will prevent my making a long visit to your ship this evening at which time I will see that the line is opened for your passage through unmolested. Hoping to give you a hail at about 9pm ...

The Deputies pretended to board their boat, which was made from half a tar barrel, which was lit and dropped astern.

The afternoon was spent in preparing for Neptune's arrival. The sailors got dressed up in the capstan square. Intruders received a bucket of water or flour over their heads. The hose continued to play on unwary passengers. Edward Towle was sure it would 'be a wet business' and donned his tarpaulins and sou'wester.

When preparations were complete, four sailors stood on the fore-yard and on deck, each holding two patent lights to welcome the sea god aboard with 'a perfect blaze'. The yards were illuminated with blue lights, On the dot of nine, a voice hailed the ship through a speaking trumpet from over the bow 'in the most unearthly tones'. Two rockets were fired as Neptune stepped over the side. He accompanied by his wife, 'a modest, unassuming looking lady'; twelve myrmidons; his secretary with a huge book under his arm; a barber with a two-foot razor and a bear who carried a bucket of 'lather' made from tar and other abominations and a 20-inch lather brush. A huge tub of water was placed near Neptune, who sat under a canopy formed by a sail, his ambrosial locks hanging down to his waist and his trident in his hand. His first order was any passengers remaining on the forecastle would be shaved.

As they fled, one tripped headlong into the tub. Neptune joined in the laughter. He then blew his trumpet and demanded of the Captain the name of the ship, the port where he was bound, the number of passengers and whether any births or deaths had occurred on the voyage. Unrestricted license followed. The hose was again turned on the unwary spectators. Those perched in the rigging were pinned down in the torrent. The secretary opened his 'awful book' and read out the names of the stewards. The myrmidons were dispatched to find them. One was produced, struggling and fighting, but to no avail. The bear began to lather and the barber to shave him. When Neptune asked him where he came from, he fell for it. He opened his mouth to reply and the lather brush was shoved into it. He was then pitched headfirst into the tub. All the stewards suffered the same fate except Hughes, the waiter on the 'Manchester Table', who locked himself in the Fore Saloon pantry, lit his pipe and regaled himself with grog. The four 'middys' were next. The Captain, who had taken up position in the fore rigging, pleaded for the youngest through his megaphone, but Neptune was inexorable and he was duly soused.

Attention now turned to those who had made themselves unpopular. First in line was Cohan, the Captain's arrogant young clerk, who Edward was not alone in finding obnoxious. After a long search, he was found to have locked himself in a cupboard. Three sailors offered to let him off if he would stand them a bottle of brandy. He agreed, but when he opened the door, he was grabbed by a fourth and dragged on deck. Again the Captain tried to intervene, but Neptune told him that he was not in command and should not interfere. As Cohan bewailed his nemesis, the Captain sent a man to rescue him, but he was laid prostrate by a whack on the eye. Uproar ensued. The yells of excitement 'could have been heard for miles'. Cohan was ducked, shaved and ducked again.

The fellow who had caused the furore about the money thought that the ship had been taken over by mutineers who intended to throw him overboard because he was Irish. He locked his stateroom door and retired to bed. This availed naught and he was dragged out in his nightshirt. His berth was filled with empty bottles, pieces of meat and other debris. As he was brought on deck, he begged then to spare his life, his grey hair floating in the wind, the 'very picture of despair'. The Towle brothers felt sorry for him and their cry of 'Shame' was taken up by other spectators. This produced a reaction in his favour, so he got off relatively lightly. He was tumbled head first into a tub of water and 'by aid of hose and pump, sent trotting back to his room', minus much of his scanty clothing.

Shaving was now deemed 'superfluous from excess of subjects', so the victims were confined to a ducking. First in line was James Horsefell, the busybody who had wrangled with the Captain about the tea. The selection knew no favours. Reginald Bright, son of one of the ship's owners, slipped on deck and John McFall played the hose within 6 inches of his face. Everybody was soaked. 'Sure such a watering was never seen before'.

After a couple of hours of such romps, the cry went up that Neptune was about to depart. As he climbed over the side, blue lights on the masthead signalled his return 'to his own domain'. Soon after, his chariot, another blazing tar barrel, was seen astern. The Captain, by altering his course to the east, made it appear that the barrel was moving westwards, an astonishing effect which 'puzzled even a few of the knowing'. The Sea King forgot his Consort. 'Mrs Neptune disgraced herself and her royal spouse, for she was found beastly drunk under the hatchway.'

To the Diggings

As the *Great Britain* made good progress down the African coast, conversation was dominated by her anticipated arrival in Cape Town. It was hoped to meet a homeward-bound mail steamer, so people were writing letters home. Numerous parties were being formed for the diggings. The Towle brothers decided to join the Hodgetts, who were equipped with tents, mining tools and medicines. Somewhat condescendingly, Edward though that William Hodgett's lowly marriage might prove an advantage in the outback. 'The young woman will not be afraid to rough it ... and she will prove invaluable in cooking our meals.'

The fifth member of the party was Thomas Attrill, a 'quiet, strong and active young fellow', who owned a cart and harness. Edward regretted that he had not brought a cart, but found that his neighbour at table was bringing out a dozen. He offered to sell him one for a cheaper price than he could have shipped it. Edward was worried about 'rogues' in Australia and suggested that the various groups went to the diggings together for mutual protection and assistance. 'If a cart sticks fast 30 persons can extricate it much sooner than six.'

FOUR

'This Tremendous Rock'

When the *Great Britain* was 850 miles out of Table Bay, she ran into more heavy gales. The fore stay sail blew away and the fore try halyards broke, bringing the huge sail down onto the deck. The ship rolled so much that a man fell out of his berth and broke his nose. At breakfast, crockery smashed and the tablecloths were covered in mustard, vinegar and tea.

With the currents against her, the ship could only make headway under full steam. A crisis loomed when the engineer reported that coal stocks were considerably lower than the logs indicated. There was just three days supply if the winds continued to blow – and they were four days steaming from Cape Town. Captain Matthews called an emergency meeting of the officers. The decision was unanimous; to run back before the wind and currents the 1086 miles to St. Helena. The Captain was hopeful of getting help from the warships harboured there, as the Royal Navy was obliged to render assistance to ships carrying the Royal Mail.

To appease the passengers, the ship's position was falsified to make her appear further from the Cape than she really was. This was an ill-judged deception, for a number of passengers did their own daily calculations. Incredulity was expressed when the Captain acknowledged the 'error'. 'As all the officers and midshipmen calculate the position of the ship, it was singular they should all have made the same mistake.' In response to such criticisms, Captain Matthews ceased to post the daily position and a wag pinned a note to the mainmast offering £5 reward to anyone who could reveal where they were.

At a meeting of passengers, the Captain explained that lack of power could have caused the ship to drift towards the coast. Many expressed indignation with the owners. The ship's journal alleged that, to maximise profits, part of the hold had been loaded with merchandise rather than coal. The Captain felt obliged to issue a statement, setting out the facts and leaving the passengers to decide who was to blame. Although this was an honourable move, it was a mistake. It would have been better to have allowed discontent to focus on people thousands of miles away. Many of the passengers were desperate to get to Australia where they hoped to make their fortunes.

Any delay might cause them to lose the opportunity, so the Captain was the target of much vituperation.

The owners' optimism about the passage time, born of their eagerness to win the Royal Mail contracts, was to prove costly for the company which incurred penalties totalling £3000. Yet if the schedule was over-optimistic, there is no doubt that Captain Matthews burnt up vital coal in pursuing it. Until the *Great Britain* was compelled to turn back, she was on schedule to reach Melbourne in 50 days, which would have been four days faster than the best time she ever achieved. The weather conditions were exceptionally bad. On 19 July the *Glaucus*, a sailing vessel bound from Liverpool to Valparaiso, met the *Taurine*, one of the *Great Britain*'s colliers, beating against heavy winds. Her captain signalled his anxiety that he might arrive after the ship he was to coal.

As soon as the turn-around was decided upon, the passengers and crew set to work to rehoist the sails. Such was the enormous weight of canvas that it took six hours of solid work. Steam was reduced to a level which was just enough to prevent drag and, running before the wind that had previously obstructed her, the *Great Britain* achieved the good speed of 11 knots. Morale was still low. Edward Towle felt that the Captain's 'disagreeable and arbitrary manner' had turned the passengers against him. He considered Mr Cox, the First Officer 'a much superior man' and Mr Gray, the Second Officer, 'as good a sailor ... I am pretty sure', he added, 'what opinion they entertain about matters on board and the navigation of the ship'. The debris on deck had not been cleared and John McFall reckoned she would be one of the dirtiest vessels ever to put into St Helena. He had no doubts where the blame lay. 'With a competent commander we should be well on between the Cape and Australia. This one, I am sure he is not fit to be here.' The unrest was becoming potentially serious. His letter to his wife reveals that the crew were arming themselves with pistols and dirks at nights, 'so if there is a row who knows what to expect ... I shall keep to myself if I can.'

The antipathy between passengers and Captain was mutual. 'I believe some of them have irritated him to a very great extent', Edward Towle wrote, 'and have acted with a freedom and independence rather annoying to the despotic sway assumed by the Captain of a ship.' 'The passengers have scandalised this ship shameful', wrote John McFall. 'I would hardly believe they would have been so mean.' Drunkenness and fractiousness increased. On one occasion some passengers who had taken too much grog were making a great din. The Captain happened along and hazarded that a passenger named Vivian was responsible 'as usual'. In fact he was not there, but when he heard of it, he threatened to give the Captain 'a sound drubbing' if he badmouthed him again. 'The consequence is', wrote Edward Towle, 'that the Captain is irritated against everyone and treats us with a great deal of hauteur.'

St Helena

The *Great Britain* arrived at St Helena at midnight on 22 September. The harbour was very deep and the 3-ton anchor was released in 20 fathoms. The noise of its enormous chain running through the hawsepipes sounded like thunder.

> Large sparks of fire flew up and caused a brilliant light from the friction caused by the rapid descent of this ponderous machine. The moment it touched the bottom all the people set up a tremendous shout. They really seem very crazy sometimes and totally unable to control their feelings.

Edward Towle was moved to behold 'the dim and dark outline of this tremendous Rock, the last abode of the most extraordinary man the world ever produced, and it was long before I could make up my mind to turn in and try to bury in sleep the emotions which the close proximity to the last sad scene of his fallen glory awakened within me.'

Next morning, Allan Gilmour admired the 'grand sight' of the high bare cliffs looming above them. The picturesque little port of Jamestown nestled in a valley. A long flight of steps known as 'Jacob's Ladder' ascended to the principal battery, to which a road zigzagged circuitously. Captain Matthews gazed out more gloomily. Instead of the anticipated warships in the harbour, there was only the steam frigate, HMS *Penelope*, which had lost several men during the capture of Lagos. John McFall wondered how the *Great Britain* would be able to leave. Her coal stocks were reduced to around 80 tons. There was less than 100 tons available on the island at the exorbitant price of £5:17:0d a ton, and the *Penelope* could supply some 150 tons. All possible hands were recruited to shift the coal: sailors from the two ships, soldiers from the garrison and any passengers willing to earn some money. The island's 'darkies' were recruited to cut several hundred tons of wood at £3 a ton to make up the shortfall. Soldiers were employed to saw and store it. It would be a lengthy process.

The local newspaper recorded the passengers' criticisms of the Captain's seamanship and many people sent letters back to England. Edward Towle was typically cheerful, declaring that he was 'not very particular about where Gibbs, Bright & Co. choose to forward us next. The novelty of seeing a strange country is full compensation for the loss of time we have to submit to.'

The passengers waited eagerly for permission to go ashore, which was granted after breakfast. Swarms of boats lay alongside to take people for a penny each. A dozen of Edward Towle's messmates engaged one. When they got ashore, they astonished the locals by leapfrogging all the way to Jamestown. Prices had soared because of the ship's visit. 'There was never more business caused in a town by a ship before', wrote Stephen Perry. At the only hotel, breakfast cost 7/- and dinner 10/-. 'The working classes are principally negroes and half caste', Edward Towle noted. 'The latter are an extremely well made race. Apollos in shape though not in feature with a remarkably appealing intonation of voice and free from provincialism.'

The group decided to go straight to Napoleon's tomb. Two people were sent ahead to find a place for lunch. The steep climb of five miles was very tiring. It was the start of the southern Spring and they were struck by the luxuriant greenery of the valleys with coconut trees, dates and huge cacti growing in profusion. Aloes were planted at the roadside and a 'peculiar' tree called a Jackson's Willow was in full bloom. When they reached a height of about 2000 feet they were drenched in the clouds and felt extremely cold.

Longwood

Longwood, the place of Napoleon's exile, was one of the most famous and at the same time, for obvious reasons, least visited houses in the British Empire. The Victorians took a different view of the man their parents had regarded as a tyrant and an impostor, regarding him as a romantic and tragic figure, languishing far from his homeland, his destiny unfulfilled. Prints of his grave, with its neighbouring willows, were a familiar sight.

For most people on the *Great Britain*, the one bonus of their unexpected sojourn was the chance to view this famous sight. John McFall obtained a mere three hours shore leave during the stay, but made a visit to Longwood his priority. 'I held out my hand to you', he wrote to his wife, 'to come with me and see Napoleon's grave. You won't come? Very well. I'm going.' Thomas Park and his family were deeply moved by the place. 'We could easily imagine the long, weary watches of Napoleon as he looked out over the vast Atlantic, in the vain hope of a rescue from this island home by some passing French ship.' Such sentiments sound somewhat inflated for a 5 year-old. Perhaps his family told him about it in later years.

Edward Towle found it 'impossible to behold the last resting place of this great man without feelings of deep and intense emotion'. The pals recognised the famous willow as they descended from the chilly heights, but it did not appear as graceful or as luxurious as it did in the prints. Over the valley, tall cypresses gave the place a mournful look. Napoleon's body had been removed some years before and the tomb was in a very bad state of repair, but Edward was not ashamed that his 'eyes felt unusually full of moisture while meditating on the lofty spirit that had once lain entombed there. I thought of his misfortunes and not of his faults, and the instability of all human greatness.'[1]

Such lofty sentiments were lost on his companions, who were trying to reach the branches of the willow. The reason it appeared stunted was that it had been stripped by souvenir hunters. Edward climbed up and managed to break off a twig. They walked on to Napoleon's house, which had been turned into a mill and looked small and uninviting. Edward was sad that the fallen Emperor had been given such a humble residence, but was gratified to see the magnificent 56-room mansion 200 yards farther on, which his death had prevented him from inhabiting. It remained 'a monument of England's generosity to a fallen enemy. I only regret it was not done sooner'. The house had never been occupied and was let at £60 a year. It was surrounded by excellent farming land, capable of producing several crops a year, but the farmers were 'ignorant and lazy'.

The two sent on ahead had found a little pub kept by a mulatto couple a mile away. The way there was bordered by peach trees in blossom and guavas with ripe fruit of which the pals partook plentifully. The pub was agreeably situated below the brow of a hill, which sheltered it from the unvarying south-easterly trade wind. Tall camellia japonicas flowered profusely in front. The mists descended as they arrived and later a gale blew up. A return to the ship was out of the question so they decided to stay the night. After demolishing a meal of fresh meat and poultry, they felt in 'comical humour' and promised an old negress some grog if she would sing for them. After clearing her throat, she exhorted a promise that they would not laugh. 'We innocently agreed, not anticipating the self control we should be obliged to exercise during the performance.'

'She commenced in a droll nasal twang much to our amusement which nearly made Ben burst – "Twas down in Cummin's garden a bery long time ago." Here the old lady stopped and said it was necessary that we should join in the chorus but the real fact was she knew no more of the song and was only dodging about to gain time in the hopes of obtaining the grog which was now handed to

1 The Emperor Napoleon had died on 5 May 1821. He was buried beside a stream in which two willows were reflected. In 1840, his remains were collected on a French warship and taken to Paris where they were reinterred at Les Invalides.

her. She tried again: "Twas down in Cummin's garden a bery long time ago." The friends tried to join in, but could not catch the time, so they reprised: "Twas down in Cummin's garden a bery long time ago." '

At bedtime, an argument ensued about the sleeping arrangements. There were only two beds. Frederick Phillips, who weighed 14 stone, got one. Bedding was spread on the floor in two rooms for the others. Four of them rushed into one room and a pillow fight ensued to decide who would sleep where. Edward and two companions bolted the other door and slept soundly until four o'clock when the household was woken by a great crash. Phillips had fallen out of bed. The fragile wooden building shook and the landlady was greatly alarmed. The friends got back to the ship at six next evening. After a hearty tea, they tumbled into their beds and slept as soundly 'if not sounder than in our own beds at home'.

John McFall was in an 'awful hole'. He had been given the unenviable task of working the boats which were shipping the timber on board. The heavy surf at the landing knocked the workers off their feet.

> Whack! She would go on the rocks, down we would fall on our faces and over would come the water and thirty soldiers working with us. You may think how I like it when I tell you I was quite sea-sick.

On the day after their return to the ship, the Towles went fishing with Joe Hodgetts. They caught some eels and Ben hauled in a 'comical looking fish called a Jack'. They were keen to go for a swim, but were afraid of sharks. They saw some mulattos bathing so Edward ventured in. Joe went in up to his knees, but Ben 'declined hazarding the experiment'. While Edward was in the water, he asked the 'little scamps' whether there were any sharks about. '"Oh, yes, plenty shark, but they never touch black man, can't see him." You may depend on it after this intimation of the sharks' good taste, I made my way out again and regarded my limbs with the utmost complacency and affection.'

Sandy Bay

Next day, Edward and Ben left their laundry with a local washerwoman and set off to hike the 15 miles across the island to Sandy Bay with two young men named Williams and Webber. Joe Hodgetts was playing cricket for the *Great Britain* in a match against the officers of the garrison. The defeat of the ship's team was largely due to his modesty. His bowling skills were 'not discovered until too late to retrieve the game'.

The companions first climbed the 630 steps up the virtually-perpendicular 'Jacob's Ladder'. Then they went up a barren road where countless cacti flourished. They were intrigued by the little ice plants, whose leaves concealed globules of water, which dissolved in the hand. After climbing silently for two miles, they came to Plantation House, the Governor's residence. The lodge keeper suggested that they should make a detour to climb Diana Peak, at nearly 2700 feet the highest point on the island. He warned them not to do it without a guide, but when they could not find one, they decided to make the attempt anyway.

They trudged on for miles up a very rough track. Their shoes were smothered in mud and dirt and the clouds came over and drenched them. They came on a narrow rock ledge with a precipice on each side, but so overgrown with trees 'that had we fallen we should probably have lodged in the branches'. They held on by the long grass and made their way with considerable difficulty. They reached the peak, only to discover there was another, higher, one beyond. Despite feeling weary, they persevered to the top, where a splendid view of the entire island repaid their efforts. A beautiful valley lay at their feet, full of orange and lemon groves with romantic little villas scattered over the slopes.

Somewhat recklessly, they decided to climb down the other side, which was quite precipitous. They tied themselves together with handkerchiefs, hoping that, if one fell, the others would save him. Progress was slow and the descent more and more difficult. After struggling a short distance, they decided to retrace their steps. It was getting dark, they had had nothing to eat and they had no idea where they would stay the night, but they 'trudged away merrily'. The prospect 'was anything but inviting, nothing but barren rocks piled upon each other in the most fantastical shapes met our view'.

They passed some 'negro' huts and discovered that the Sergeant in charge of the battery lived with his family in the only house in Sandy Bay. Edward had seen 'few men with such a benevolent countenance and his wife seemed to share in all his kind wishes to make us comfortable.' Some negroes had just brought some fish to the door, so 'this amicable couple' sent off a messenger for 'other necessities' and them set to work to prepare tea 'and did more than the laws of hospitality could possibly require'. The Sergeant told them that he intended to quit the army as soon as he qualified for his small pension and that he hoped to meet them in Australia within ten months.

Beds were prepared. Completely exhausted, they retired early. After an hour, they began to scratch themselves in a 'fearful manner'. They lay awake until four when they managed to get a little sleep. Ben thought the itching was caused by bedbugs, but the others reckoned the place too clean for that and that their assailants were mosquitoes. Edward and Ben were relieved to take a dip in the sea before breakfast. When they returned, a negro was waiting to tell them that the *Great Britain* was sailing that afternoon and that passengers had to embark by one o'clock.

Their generous host refused payment, but, when pressed, let them reimburse his expenses. After saying their farewells, they set off at a cracking pace, which soon brought Williams and Webber to a standstill. Despite the brothers' exhortations, they insisted on a 5-minute rest before embarking on the slow 5-mile climb. They were again enveloped in cloud and thoroughly drenched. Things looked bleak when they took what they thought was a shortcut and lost their way. They were due on the ship in less than two hours and the going was rough. The drear prospect of being marooned on the remote island bore down upon them.

At half past eleven, they reached the summit and began the slow descent into Jamestown. There was a dilemma when the road forked. If they went the wrong way, they would literally and metaphorically miss the boat. Fortunately, three officers from the *Penelope* rode up and gave them directions. Since the route was clear, the Towle brothers, anxious to pick up their laundry, accelerated away from the other two. They arrived at 12.15pm. The Blue Peter was flying at the *Great Britain*'s masthead.

They could not find the washerwoman, so they gave up their laundry as lost and went aboard. 'We never stepped the deck with so much pleasure as we did at that moment. We examined our snug little berths with the greatest satisfaction and went about the old ship as if we had regained our best friend. Joe was ready to welcome us and was greatly alarmed by our absence. We shook each other till our arms were almost dislocated and vowed no expedition of this sort should ever separate us again.' They were delighted to find that the washerwoman had brought their clean linen aboard and that the much-maligned surgeon had paid for it. Williams and Webber arrived just before the anchor was weighed. On her way out of the harbour, the ship passed close to the *Penelope*, which fired a salute as her sailors cheered.

The visit to the island had a beneficial effect on service in the saloon. Ten St Helenians had been recruited to meet the chronic shortage of stewards.

'Another Dust'

At first progress was good in fine weather and the passengers got back into their daily routines, which, for some, included getting drunk and there were frequent quarrels, so the Captain banned the sale of spirits for a few days and cracked down on individual drunks.

Drink may have been behind a bizarre theft. A sheep had been slaughtered in the abattoir, and that night a large joint of it was stolen. A £5 reward was offered by the Captain for the discovery of the thief. After the meat was found hidden in the Fore Saloon, a cabin boy alleged that 'a rather respectable' man was the criminal. He was put on trial with the Captain presiding as Chief Magistrate and William Hodgetts acting for the defence. The verdict of the jury of fellow passengers was that there was no positive proof against him, but the Captain had been right to order the enquiry. It was generally considered that the man took the mutton as a joke 'while in a state of beer ... but without felonious intention'.

Mr Battersea, a young Irishman, was another whom drink got into trouble. He was amicable enough when sober, but always in scrapes when drunk. He was summarily ejected by his cabin-mates with the Captain's approval. The stewards took pity on him. Each night they tracked him down in his drunken state and put him into a bed they made up for him in the corridor. One evening, Battersea came into the Towles' cabin to beg a pipe of tobacco and bemoan his outcast state. Mischievously, Edward suggested that, since Mansell never retired before Lights Out, he have a snooze in his bunk. 'Without hesitation and full of Irish fun and Irish whiskey', he duly turned in. In five minutes, he was 'in a happy state of oblivion'.

When Mansell got back, he undressed in the dark and groped his way into bed. When he perceived that 'something unusual impeded his further progress, he started back in great alarm and rushed into the passage, shouting 'Stewart, Stewart', (meaning Steward).' The steward rushed into the cabin and held his light into the bunk. 'Why, it is that confounded Battersea. He gives us more trouble than any-one on board the ship. Come, bundle out Mr Battersea and let Mr Mansell get into his berth.' The response was a negative grunt, so the stewards tried to pull him out. Battersea, indignant at being disturbed, kicked and struggled violently. The berthmates shouted encouragement, but he was eventually ejected from the cabin.

Other passengers had been awoken by the noise and gathered in the corridor in various states of undress. They goaded Battersea into making an assault on the cabin. On his hands and knees, he darted between Mansell's legs, who was laid prostrate by the sudden lunge.

> The merriment this created was unbounded. We now had Battersea's head and Mansell's legs in our cabin. We held on to Battersea's head while the Steward and his party ... hauled away at his legs, and Mansell kicking and calling out underneath that

> he was 'going to be killed entirely'. The fun increased while roars resounded from one end of the corridor to the other. 'Now Battersea, now Mansell, two to one on the Connaught boy' until I really felt great alarm for Battersea's neck which was stretched to an unusual manner. The whole fore saloon was now in an uproar and the people from the midship berths pressing into the corridor to know what was the matter, caused a fearful crush.

Battersea's temporary bed was thrown about. The Officer of the Watch heard the din and came down and got some 'tremendous whacks' from the numerous projectiles that were flying about. After he had quelled the disturbance, it turned out he had a sense of humour, for he agreed not to report it to the Captain.

Battersea did well out of the fracas. The stewards found him another berth which he would never otherwise have got. Next day, the incident was the talk of the ship. Some of the Irish passengers considered that Mansell had been insulted and insisted that William Hodgetts, who they considered to have taken the 'most conspicuous part against him', should apologise. Edward Towle insisted that he was the instigator, but no-one believed him.

> We were none of us particularly alarmed at Mr Mansell's pugnacious propensities. Mr M. looked very pale all day, evidently much alarmed at the course his friends deemed it right for him to pursue to defend the honour of 'Ould Ireland'. Hodgetts informed them that the only apology he could make was to say that it was not done with any malicious feeling towards Mr Mansell, but only for the sake of a joke. Irish honour was easily appeased when a joke was mentioned and the glow of health once more bloomed upon the cheeks of Mr Mansell.

Soon after there was 'another dust' with the Captain about misbehaviour by a member of the 'Manchester Table'. Captain Matthews sent for the Chairman, Moses Critchley, and demanded the identity of the 'sinner'. When he refused to give the name, the Captain said that he would be obliged to enforce the rules regarding 'emigrants' on board ship. He replied that they were not emigrants but 'merchants and passengers' and 'if he attempted to impose any such laws upon us we should take the law into our own hands'. Edward perceived that the Captain's problem was his failure to recognise that this 'most fearless and independent set of men ... ripe for the diggings' who were 'extremely well disposed towards each other' were 'a different set ... from the half starved emigrants he has so often landed on the shores of America.'

Cape Town

Three days into the run to Cape Town, the winds turned hostile. There was only enough coal for five days steaming. John Gray told Edward Towle that an easterly gale would drive them 'just where the winds please to take us'. Fortunately, the wind turned next day. Every available stitch of canvas was set and the ship bowled along. A cheerful smile animated Mr Gray's weatherbeaten visage.

As the ship approached Cape Town, Captain Matthews embarked on an exercise in public relations. The biscuit served at table improved distinctly. The boats and the guns were painted, the decks holystoned, the masts scraped and the ship's sides washed and painted. 'Rather an artful dodge', thought Edward Towle, 'considering the complaints the passengers will make on arriving there and the publication of the *Great Britain Times* which is to be done at the Cape.' The armoury was also refurbished. The ship carried a valuable cargo and the possibility of lawless colonials attempting to board her while she lay in Table Bay was not discounted. The long-awaited land was sighted at 8am on 10 October and the ship dropped anchor in Table Bay at 12.30pm. Despite the adverse weather, her colliers had all arrived. Coaling would take a week, which must have delighted the Towle brothers, but more impatient travellers would not have been pleased. The agents had been active at getting the coal into lighters, so, despite the fact that the ship anchored on a Sunday, a good quantity of coal was brought aboard. Next morning. Allan Gilmour was fascinated to watch the 'coolies' unloading it, 'most deliberately, there always being a lot of them to each rope used for hoisting the coal bags from the lighters. Whilst thus leisurely pulling one end, one or more generally danced some steps, as all hauled together to the words of "I put my money in the Savings Bank, Ahonda, honda hey." ' He had learnt from the sailors what it meant when 'the table cloth was spread' over Table Mountain. Later that day, the wind began to blow in violent squalls, loading stopped and a number of ships put to sea for safety.

Captain Matthew's effort to win friends impressed the correspondent of the *Cape Monitor.*

> It is a proud station for anyone to fill, to command and manage this epitome of a kingdom which the *Great Britain* presents. And the testimony of his passengers, officers, &c., show that the command has fallen into the most worthy hands. Capt. Matthews is a kind, considerate and attentive man, unceasing in his zeal to secure comfort to every one on board, and in the interest of his employers.

The passengers that the reporter met must have been selected by Captain Matthews with some care. Nor did he refer to the unfortunate delays. For him the ship quite simply epitomised Victorian progress.

> A visit to the *Great Britain* will afford a demonstrative lesson of instruction in art, science and economy such as has never been witnessed before in this colony. To young people particularly, such a lesson would be invaluable as showing how much can be accomplished by science, art, and systematic order in every arrangement, whether of human action, or the power of machinery and adaptation of ingenuity.

A new era in global communications was envisaged, with the possibility of a 26-day passage to The Cape becoming a reality.

> Two years ago if any one held forth such an expectation as within probability, he would have been considered marvellously sanguine, if not a visionary, but now all doubts are removed, and a trip to England or Australia in this travelling city, instead of being a penance for the time, as voyaging used to be in former days, is but a sojourn for a short period, surrounded with every comfort and luxury that reasonable man could expect or desire.

While the ship was coaling, the passengers went ashore. Cape Town at that time was not a large place. Some passengers even referred to it as a village. There was a flourishing saddlery trade there and Allan Gilmour bought bridles as 'a spec', having had heard that they were fetching twice the price in Melbourne. Later he went on a hike with some other passengers around Table Mountain. Their lateness in returning caused some alarm since a huge 'tiger' [*sic*] had been seen to cross a path they had taken. They had not made his acquaintance, but it was too late to get back on board, so the officers of the garrison kindly offered them beds for the night.

The bunkering was completed by the end of the week. Once again, sacks of coal blocked the deck. As the ship sailed, a small boat pulled out from the landing place. In her stern were 'three natives of the Celestial Empire', who came aboard with their luggage, The inherent racialism in Victorian society asserted itself. 'Loud were the protests about having these Chinamen forced upon us.' The saloon passengers refused to admit them and it appeared that they would have to return ashore. Captain Matthews had probably agreed to take the Chinamen as Fore Saloon passengers to offset some of the soaring costs of the voyage. Realising that it would prove contentious with his extremely difficult passengers, he brought them aboard at the last moment. The ploy failed and he was obliged to hold a meeting at which a compromise was reached. The Chinamen were allowed to travel in the saloon, but partitions were erected so that they were not in contact with the other passengers.

Captain Matthews' troubles were not over. The ship hit a very heavy swell on leaving harbour and began to roll alarmingly. It was realised that it was caused by the deck load, so many of the sacks of coal that had been so laboriously loaded were thrown overboard. Then, some days out of Cape Town, ominous reports circulated that one of the Chinamen was seriously ill. Panic ensued. Every possible disease was mentioned, but in fact the poor fellow had suffered a severe asthmatic attack and died a week before the ship reached Melbourne. Some of the stewards were Chinese and they organised the funeral. 'Believing that the journey after death was a long one', they placed provisions and a small bottle of wine beside him and put some small coins in his hand to pay the toll on entering the gates of Paradise. Iron weights were placed at his feet and the canvas was sewn up in the Union Jack. The sailors bore the plank with the remains shoulder high to an opening on the upper deck where the Captain read the burial service from the Book of Common Prayer. One end of the plank was raised and the body slid gently off.

Many passengers watched the rite from the stern. 'You can picture yourselves the horror and surprise of all', recalled Tom Park, 'to see the body rise out of the water about breast high, just under the stern of the vessel. There it stood upright for a few seconds, then it gradually sank lower and lower into the water, and finally disappeared under the waves ... This distressing incident was caused by the sailors forgetting to make air holes in the canvas for the air to escape.'

FIVE

'Gold is like Dirt'

Hobson's Bay in the Melbourne outer harbour was reached on 11 November 1852, after a voyage of 82 days, amidst predictable excitement from passengers and crew. There were over 200 ships in port. Gold-rush fever had caused most of their crews to abscond to seek their fortunes at the diggings, leaving just the captain and mate behind. Many ships had been put up for sale to pay the harbour dues. The only hope of obtaining a crew for the voyage home was to pay the men's money in advance. On the *Rip Van Winkle*, the captain had mistreated the crew on the trip out, so on their arrival in Melbourne they locked him in his cabin and 'every soul went bag and baggage'. He was obliged to offer £100, cash down, per man, to find a crew to sail her back to Liverpool. Another ship faced even greater problems. Typhus had broken out and half her complement of 400 people lay dead on board while she remained in quarantine. On the *Great Britain,* the Third Officer exacted a solemn pledge from each crew member that he would stay with the ship. 'Rest assured', John McFall wrote to his wife, 'I have pledged my word to Mr Samson and I will not break it, though it is very tempting as we have only to say the word and there is plenty who would get us safe away and give us an ounce of gold per day to go with them to the diggings.' Others were not as scrupulous. Within four days of their arrival, three sailors and a baker had escaped ashore.

In anticipation of going ashore, many passengers hauled their luggage on deck. Boxes were piled up in great confusion. It proved impossible to disembark such numbers with any speed. Massive inflation had hit the fees charged by the local boatmen, who disdained offers of as much as £1 to row passengers the mile to the shore. Captain Matthews offered the crew of one boat £5 to wait while he fetched a parcel for them to deliver, but they disdained the offer and went off. Many passengers were marooned on board for as long as five days before they could get on a steamer to take them up the River Yarra to Melbourne. They had to load their own luggage aboard, struggling and shouting in the terrific heat. As Mr Gilmour was climbing down the ladder into the tug, he caught hold of a slack rope and fell into the water, which had the reputation of being shark-infested. His son Allan had to be forcibly restrained from leaping after him. Mr Christie, the Duty Officer, shouted to him to swim to the side of the steamer. In a prodigious feat, he then went down a rope hand over hand, put his feet under the stranded man's armpits and, by sheer strength, lifted him clear of the water and held him there until one of the ship's boats rescued him.

To alleviate a desperate situation, Captain Matthews agreed that the ship's boats be used to row people ashore for a small fee. Oarsmen were recruited from amongst the passengers, including Edward Towle who thought it time to start 'his labours at money making'. Each boat held about 70 people. They were extremely heavy and difficult to row. Several of the recruits were unclear how to handle an oar. A strong breeze was blowing and the boat was lowered with some difficulty. Immediately it was blown a long way to leeward. After great exertions, they succeeded in landing their passengers safely. Waiting on the quay were around 60 people who had gone ashore and wanted to return to the ship. The crew offered to take them for 5/- each, but they declined to pay, probably because most of them did not have any money. Typically, Edward Towle did not want to leave them exposed to the danger of being robbed and suggested that they take them for nothing. The crew was divided about this, but eventually agreed and the crowd rushed aboard. As soon as the overloaded boat set out, a fierce squall drove it towards the shore. The waves came over the gunwales and the rain fell in torrents. The passengers screamed that they were going to be drowned, until the confusion was so great that the rowers refused to pull another stroke.

Edward proposed that the only way to save the boat was for Thomas Attrill to take sole command, but he was unable to get a hearing, although he pointed his pistol at one obstreperous fellow. The passengers had had enough of the hair-raising adventure and wanted to get back on shore, but return was impossible as long as the squall lasted. Edward, who had stuck to his oar until his hands were raw, berated them as cowards. His generosity in offering the free trip was forgotten and they threatened to pitch him overboard. When the wind abated, they took to the oars again and through great exertions got back to the quay. The passengers were delighted to have 'escaped a watery grave'.

Although it was getting dark and the boatmen on the wharf said they would never make it, Edward proposed making another start. This time they pulled well to windward to give them scope to be driven off course if the squall blew up again, which it did with renewed fury. All they could do was to keep head on to the wind. To make matters worse, darkness fell and they could no longer see the ship.

They were drifting to leeward and were too exhausted to do much about it. Edward proposed pulling towards a steamer which was astern of them and sheltering in its lee until the squall passed. They came alongside her boat, but another squall blew it out of reach as they were about to grab it. As they were drifting away, a man came on deck and threw them a rope. They made a last 'expiring' effort to reach it, but it fell short. It was thrown again and this time it was caught and made fast. The man hauled them on deck one by one, 'more dead than alive'. The ship was called the *Launceston* and the man was the skipper. Only he and the mate were on board. The crew had succumbed to gold rush fever and run off to the diggings.

The skipper said that they would never reach the *Great Britain* in such a wind. He advised them to wait until the squall dropped and invited them to his cabin for grog and biscuits. They soon forgot their toils and began to enjoy themselves. After two hours, they heard a familiar song across the water and knew at once it was a search party from the *Great Britain*. They hailed them as they passed and Mr Cox, who was in charge, ordered that their boat be taken in tow. Edward realised that he intended to maroon them, so he swarmed down the rope and held on until the others joined him. Mr Cox ordered a rowing party aboard and demanded that each of the pals should pay 5/- for their trouble. A little sailor called Peters was put in charge and hugely enjoyed the sight of them coughing up. He told them that they had made three forays to look for them and had just given them up for lost. Somewhat tactlessly, he said they were not bothered about their fate, but they did not want to lose the boat.

Next day, Edward Towle went ashore with Thomas Attrill to reconnoitre a campsite. On the steam tug which was being used as a ferry, he got into conversation with her engineer, a 'dirty looking fellow', and was astonished to learn that he was earning two guineas a day. Reports of enormously high prices in Melbourne were not exaggerated. The standard wage was £10 a week and a common labourer could pull in at least £5 (a farm labourer in England earned around 10/-).

'This place beats all I ever see', wrote John McFall. 'Gold is like dirt amongst them that go to the diggings ... A carpenter will not lift tools under £3 a day ... Sailors is in demand here, from £16 to £25 or sometimes £30 per month to go in the coasters.' He ran into a man he knew who had been a gatekeeper at the Albert Dock in Liverpool. He had just returned from the diggings and sent home £400. He was going back and was expecting to go home 'independent' in three months. A construction boom meant that building workers were in great demand, but 'clerks, gentlemen and fine ladies' would starve. There was, however, one opportunity for men of education. The huge influx of immigrants meant that extra police were being recruited and positions were 'gladly accepted by people formerly in good circumstance, not a few of the *Great Britain*'s passengers availing themselves of this opportunity'. Perhaps some cited their experience in the shipboard police force.

Those who had brought goods to sell capitalised on the high prices. Allan Gilmour sold his bridles for twice what he had paid for them. 'The first money I ever made.' The report that housing was unobtainable in Melbourne was correct, so Mr Gilmour secured a plot in 'Canvas City', south of the Yarra. Around 1000 tents were aligned to form streets along which wagons delivered groceries, meat and water. They slept on mattresses laid on their trunks. Another trunk served as a table. Allan did the cooking and washed their clothes in the river, laying them out to dry on the bank. He tried ironing them, but found this collected dust. The summer heat was often oppressive. The north wind blew up clouds of dust and the temperature could soar to 120° in the shade.

'Fleas, Bugs, &c'

After a grand official reception, the ship sailed on to Sydney, arriving two days later. Those passengers who remained in the Fore Saloon were upgraded to the After Saloon to avoid the 'rough customers' who had come aboard. After undergoing repairs, she returned to Melbourne on 18 December. Ten days later, a magnificent ball in the Dining Saloon was attended by some 300 colonial notables. 'I do not think we will leave the country till New Year', wrote John McFall, 'to be home in the middle of March and see my heart's best pleasure.'

The *Great Britain* sailed for home on 4 January 1853. Many passengers were hardened men returning from the gold fields, and the level of drinking was high, even by the standards of the outward voyage. Some had made – and some would lose – fortunes from prospecting. One midshipman saw a lump of gold weighing 1lb gambled in a card school. Young Simeon Cohen had done well in business in Melbourne, but could not live without his beloved Cecilia and, 'much to the detriment of his commercial affairs', was returning home. The ship had to beat her way home against adverse trade winds and bunkered at Cape Town, St Helena and Vigo. The wood that was taken on board at St Helena was swarming with fleas and other biting bugs and these infested the Saloons for several voyages, despite the berths being fumigated.

Back in Liverpool, the *Great Britain* underwent an extensive refit to prevent a recurrence of the coal shortage. The boilers were altered and the number of masts was reduced to three, all square-rigged. It was decided that on future return voyages from Australia, the ship would follow the trade winds around Cape Horn and circumnavigate the globe.

Mr Cox retired as the ship's First Officer. He was replaced by John Gray and Mr Chapman became Second Officer. Gray persuaded his cousin, a 25 year-old Shetlander named Ramsey, to join the crew. He was engaged for two other voyages, but John Gray thought highly of him and persuaded him to withdraw. Since he was the sole support of his aged father and his sister, Gray must have provided for them during the three months that the *Great Britain* was in dry dock.

The Second Australian Voyage

The *Great Britain*'s second Australian voyage began on 11 August 1853. The harbour was again crowded with boats. Hundreds of people afloat and on shore cheered her departure. On board were the newly-wedded Mr and Mrs Simeon Cohen, who were accompanied by the bride's twin brother and seen off by her father. Also in the Fore Saloon were Mr and Mrs Angus Cameron and their five children, aged between eight and ten months. He held an important position in the colonial administration.

Although the Gold Rush still exerted its obsessive attraction, it had passed its peak, so the number of travellers was less than half that of the previous voyage. Nevertheless, the 319 passengers included many young men who were hoping to reap the riches. One such was Felix Spiers, who may have already grasped that not all the fortunes made in gold rushes were made by the diggers. Another was Robert Saddington, who was pleased to find that he had only four berthmates, all Germans, in his Fore Saloon cabin. 'Excepting their dirty habits', they were 'allowedly the most respectable foreigners on board.' He grew to admire Dr Sickler, 'a most intelligent and humane man', who he rated above the ship's doctor. He was to treat many of the passengers and crew on the voyage without charge.

After a 'wretched' tea of 'bad sugar and "patent" concentrated milk with excellent bread and butter', Robert took a stroll on deck and turned in early. He was kept awake by the loud and choice language from the next cabin of an Australian called Charley and a young Englishman, whose parents were 'wealthy if not respectable'. This was a nightly problem and Captain Matthews posted a notice prohibiting swearing on pain of a fine, but the respite was only temporary. Robert woke at five and found that he was the only person in his part of the ship not to have been bitten by 'the most disgusting

Fleas, Bugs, &c' – the residue of the visit to St Helena. He killed nine while dressing and the slaughter continued all day.

The ship ran into hostile winds from the time she dropped the pilot and steamed all the way to Madeira, where she hit calms. The bad weather had an adverse effect on little Isabella Cameron, aged eight and the newlywed, Cecilia Cohen, who both became violently ill. The weather must have led Captain Matthews to recall the mishaps of the previous voyage. 'The calms have had anything but a soothing effect on our esteemed Captain', wrote Robert Saddington. 'He has been very cross.' Many passengers regarded him as a 'crabbed old fellow'. Resentment was felt when he changed the rules to restrict the Fore Salooners to the deck area before the mainmast, whereas they had previously been allowed some way aft.

The Fore Salooners considered the provision of baths to be part of their terms of travel, but none were available in their accommodation, so many people used the ones in the After Saloon. An Irishman was taking a bath there when the Captain, Purser and Supply Officer (or 'Supercargo') banged on the door and told him to open up. When he emerged, he was told never to enter the wrong part of the ship again. This caused further outrage amongst the Fore Salooners. Feelings were further exacerbated that evening. Some Fore Salooners persuaded the Cook to play his fiddle for a dance on deck. A good time was being had by all when a message came from the Captain ordering the man to go and play in the After Saloon section. This annoyed the dancers so much that numerous 'Riff Raff' and 'Blackguards' repaired to the Aft Deck and behaved very insultingly.

> The Captain rose up in great wrath and commanded the Fore Saloons to go forward immediately and never dare to come beyond the Main Mast on pain of being lashed to it. A long colloquy ensued between the Captain and some passengers and all retired to rest very angry with each other and resolving to rise early for the purpose of testing the Bath Question.

At 4am, the baths were in full play, with water flying about by the bucketful. The protest had its effect. A compromise was reached on the baths and the Fore Salooners were allowed some way aft of the mainmast again.

Sao Vincente

The prolonged adverse weather meant that coal stocks were running low, so it was decided to bunker in the Cape Verde Islands. Little Isabella Cameron had continued to ail. Now her baby sister was suffering from water on the brain. 'I am sorry to say we have a death on board', wrote one of the stewards, John Lewis to his wife on 23 August. 'It occurred this afternoon. It was a sweet little girl about seven years old from bronchitis in the throat. I saw it breath its last in its mother's arms. It will be some time before the scene will be erased from my memory.' Robert Saddington noted that, with a landing in prospect, many passengers did not give this 'solemn occurrence' much thought.

At 7.15 next morning, what many passengers took to be a cloud appeared on the horizon, but the sailors declared that it to be the island of Sao Antao, whose majestic peak soared to 7000 feet. Its sister island of Sao Vincente ('St Vincent') was reached at seven bells (11.30am). Beyond the nondescript little deep-water port of Mindelo the hills rose steeply. Monte Verde, the highest peak at nearly 2,500 feet, was enveloped in cloud for most of the day. Robert Saddington wrote home, to impart 'some little idea of the place ... to those who are never likely to visit it (and it will assuredly be no great loss to them)'.

Mr Miller, the British consul, came aboard. After a few minutes consultation, the passengers were allowed ashore. The Captain and many of the After Saloon passengers attended Isabella Cameron's funeral. The ship's flags hung at half mast as her coffin was rowed over to the Seamen's Cemetery.

After this sad departure, Robert Saddington went ashore with eight friends. One of them, Fred Smith, had visited the island before and had a friend living there who he hoped would recommend a good place to eat. He was pleased to be able to take his dog ashore. He had paid £5 for its passage, but it had suffered grievously with seasickness and had been thought unlikely to live. The group had been long enough at sea to feel 'very strange sensations' when they stood on land. They were in a merry mood and had a 'thorough good laugh' at a native boy they met.

> He was of a darkish copper colour with black curly hair, but he had a gait which I think must be peculiar to the Islanders for we observed it in all men. The stomach protruded in a frightful manner and the back seemed hollowed out at least 1½ inches. He was in a state of nudity as indeed are all the male children.

Most of the men on the island dressed in 'European style' in shirts and calico trousers. The women went barefoot and wore headscarves and a simple chemise tucked in around their waists.

Behind the taller buildings on the quay were irregular rows of single-storey houses built of mud and stones. Most were thatched but some had tiled roofs. Nearly all of them were shops and all sold wine. The streets were unpaved and devoid of pavements. Fred found his old friend in a wine shop and dinner was arranged in a house owned by the Customs Officer. The first price quoted was a dollar a head (5/-), but the friend's local knowledge got it down to 1/8d. The dinner was excellent: stewed chicken, kid, fish, rice, eggs, biscuits and potatoes washed down with brackish water and Madeira wine at 1/6d a bottle. Conversation was conducted in 'broken English, execrable French and one or two stock words of Portuguese, but it formed capital amusement for all of us'. Robert thought that Rosa, their waitress, was the only pretty girl he saw on the island. Glasses were raised to 'Queen Victoria', 'Captain Matthews' and 'The Ship's Officers'. There would have been even more toasts, but the host managed to convey that another party from the ship was waiting to dine.

That afternoon they explored the town. They were disappointed to find that there was no fresh fruit available, but Robert was pleased to note all the British goods on sale: Allsopp & Son's Ale, willow pattern plates, earthenware bearing the insignia, 'Evans, Swansea & Glasgow' and cases of cotton goods marked 'Hoyle y Cia'. Later, he walked with a friend to the Seamen's Cemetery, where little Isabel Cameron had been buried. People had carved their names on the white railings, so they added their own and then climbed up to the Battery, where they found five Portuguese soldiers with six small cannons and a pile of rusty cannonballs. The bay was alive with boats passing to and fro from the *Great Britain.* They then went for a swim on the beach. The loose sand reminded Robert of Broadstairs, but he acknowledged that the intense heat was not a feature of the Kent resort.

Back at the ship they found terrible chaos. A shark had taken bait from a hooked line. A sailor thrust a boathook at it, which it had snapped in two. It was harpooned several times from a boat and, after a great struggle, hauled onto the aft deck and its eyes and liver cut out. John Gray suddenly realised that this great commotion was taking place directly above the cabin of the poor bereaved Mrs Cameron and her sick baby and ordered the fish thrown overboard.

This did not bring an end to the confusion. 'Our poor ship', Robert recorded,

> was taken possession of by the Blacks who were continuously singing out 'Hi Hi – Hi Hi – Hold on! High 'nough – Lo go.' The coals were brought alongside in Iron Barges. The 'Niggers' nearly all of whom come from Sierra Leone have 1 dollar per day for their hire and 'precious slow' they are. One Rascal whistles all day; another blows an instrument somewhat resembling a flute

> making an almost unearthly noise, and about 8 or 10 more will pull up a Bag of Coals stamping frantically with their naked feet shouting 'Orga Orga Orga Le go'. Every place and every thing is covered with dust.

That evening, John Lewis wrote to his wife again. 'I mentioned the death of the sweet child and now I have to say that its sister, Elizabeth, is just gone into the world of spirits. It was unwell when its sister died but not dangerous. The poor mother is almost heart-broken. I think if she does not get better soon, she will be the next.' The baby was buried beside her sister.

Many passengers were fishing from the bows of the ship, but 'more lines were lost than fish caught'. Robert Saddington went ashore again with Fred Smith, who lost his dog. They inspected the new cathedral which was unfinished. 'Nor does it look likely to be. It looks more like a barn having just the bare walls and roof with a stand in front holding three bells.' They went for a swim, but there were warnings of sharks. On the other side of the bay they found a splendid place completely enclosed by rocks. the bottom was sandy and the water reached head height.

Back at the ship, the 'Blacks' were still noisily and languidly loading coal. Many passengers had returned from shore in 'a state of disgusting intoxication' and were 'babbling aloud an account of their proceedings'. One man was so drunk that he had to be hauled aboard on a sling. Another was lying in a hotel in such a state of inebriation that it was thought unwise to move him. A number had formed liaisons with the local women. 'Suffice it to say', Robert wrote home, 'the whole Island is a sink of iniquity where every kind of abomination is practiced.'

Next morning the friends went ashore to swim in their favourite spot. A small ship had brought grapes, fowls and pigs from San Antao. Mr Lane, the Supercargo, bought the lot for the After Saloon, except for one basket of grapes. The pals followed it into town and bought five bunches. The ship's arrival had the same effect as in St Helena. Prices soared. Robert was charged 2/6d for a pint bottle of lemonade, but wine was much cheaper than on board, so the friends laid in a few bottles, which were very cooling when added to filtered water.

The *Great Western, en route* from the West Indies, was expected at any time, so passengers wrote letters home. Captain Martin, the Marine Superintendent, decided to return to England on her. A widow in the Lower Cabin had turned washerwoman and taken passengers' laundry ashore. That evening, she returned drunk, swearing and crying that she had lost her child and all the clothes. Most people thought that she had sold the clothes and abandoned the child. Nevertheless she returned to shore to look for them. Next morning, the pals went for their last swim in their 'Natural Bath' and when they returned, the widow was back on board, having found her child and some of the laundry. Even the man who was drunk in the hotel had returned. Large numbers of flies had also come aboard to join the St Helenan bugs.

Coal was stacked on the foredeck almost to the top of the bulwarks. It would remain there for two days until the engines had burnt enough to make space in the bunkers. The Upper Deck was crammed with water casks and hen coops, the products of Mr Lane's forays. After many people went down with diarrhoea, the ship's doctor pronounced the water unfit to drink.

Soon the Blue Peter was flying. At two o'clock, a cannon warned any passengers still ashore of the ship's imminent departure. Captain Martin started to row himself ashore to await the *Great Western*. In half an hour another cannon announced that the *Great Britain* was under way in a splendid north-easterly. Two sailors fell overboard and might have perished unseen, but fortunately Captain Martin was still rowing round the ship and raised the alarm.

As he gazed his last at Mindelo, Robert Saddington was pleased he had been there, but he was 'heartily glad to leave'.

> When in England I might perhaps have expressed astonishment that the Representative of our Nation had a very large salary for such a little place, but nothing would induce me to live there. Society there is none besides the British and American consuls and one other Englishman to whom all the wine shops belong.

Next day, at the Methodist service, the preacher condemned the 'disgraceful proceedings ashore'. He called on all to remember that there 'is forgiveness and plenty of redemption through Jesus Christ to all who seek it'. Others felt a different kind of remorse as 'regretfully many' suffered the effects of over-indulgence. Dr Sickler refused to treat these cases for nothing as he considered them self-inflicted. That Sunday morning, a stowaway presented himself. He was from Madeira and would have done better to have remained there. Later in the voyage, he fell down a hatchway and was seriously injured.

The 'Crossing of the Line' ceremony soon followed. It was intimated to Robert Saddington that he might have been selected as a victim, so he emptied his pockets and wore his lightest clothing, but the threat came to nothing. Perhaps mindful of the excesses of the previous voyage, the shaving of passengers was forbidden. The main target was one of the cooks, a 'most quarrelsome fellow', who had made himself very unpopular by deliberately ruining the sailors' food. He turned very violent at the prospect of a ducking and the Captain ordered him to be put in irons.

As the ship entered colder climes, Robert unpacked a parcel of warmer clothing. To his great disgust, it was infested with 'three families and about 25 other bugs. I instantly took my knife and slaughtered some, but finding that some would undoubtedly escape, I took the parcel on deck and threw the paper overboard, consigning the intruders to a watery grave.'

A high seas romance occurred when Frederick Hutchinson from the Fore Saloon, who was hoping to obtain a governmental position in Sydney, found happiness above his shipboard station when Miss Ellen Fitzgerald, a young lady in the After Saloon, accepted his proposal of marriage. She was travelling with her parents so they must have approved the match. Robert Saddington thought them 'very soft', but it led him to do a swift survey of his own prospects with the shipboard ladies. He decided that the popular song of the day, *There's a Good Time Coming, Wait a Little Longer,* amply expressed his situation.

The happy couple sang the appropriately-titled duet *What are the Wild Waves Saying?* at the After Saloon concert. Robert found their performance 'low and rather uninteresting'. He had been given a double ticket by Captain Matthews and took Miss Harriet Rigg, an 18 year-old Scottish lass, as his partner. Dress was formal, so he donned a black coat and trousers and a white waistcoat. In the After Saloon, a 'very respectable company' awaited its guests. Many performers, either from nerves or to 'whet the whistle' had been drinking. Dr Sickler opened the concert on the out-of-tune piano with the overture to *The Prophets.* Robert thought him, 'like all the Germans, an excellent player, undoubtedly the best on board'. Captain Matthew's rendering of *The Beautiful Boy* was wildly encored, but the highlight of the first half was Mr Stevens, 'the grand American vocalist', who caused a sensation with the latest Christy Minstrel song, *The Old Folks at Home,* which brought tremendous cheers and shouts of 'Encore', so he gave another Stephen Forster number, *The Campdown Races* ('do da do da de').

For the Fore Salooners the interval was the highlight of the evening, when they partook of the fare offered to their wealthier brethren: wines, champagne, punch, sandwiches, tarts, pastries and biscuits. Many performers returned in the second half. Miss Fitzgerald was to have sung an aria from the *Barber of Seville,* but wisely decided it was beyond her powers and sang something else. 'But it was all the same to us', wrote Robert, 'as we heard it not.' Mr Laing, the Supercargo, impressed with a rendition of *Auld Lang Syne,* before Captain Matthews burst into the verses of the National Anthem, with everyone joining in the chorus. A 'glorious' burst of cheering greeted the last notes. Wild dancing followed before the ladies were 'deposited in their several lodgings'.

The mood on board was getting rowdier. Much to the annoyance of the other passengers fourteen 'nobby' Fore Salooners formed a social club to hold singsongs while drinking bowls of punch. By Lights Out, they were decidedly merry. One young man was using the most filthy language Robert Saddington had ever heard 'and I have heard and seen a little low life since I came aboard this vessel'. Someone fetched the Captain, who decided it was time for a crack-down. He threatened to put the young man in irons and gag him and banned the sale of wines and spirits to him and another drunk for the rest of the voyage. It was to be a rowdy night. A steward was found intoxicated and put in irons. At midnight, the Captain was called down to the Lower Cabin. The washerwoman who made herself notorious at St Vincent was making a terrible disturbance. She was kept in the After Saloon Smoking Room all night and told that she would be put in irons next time she caused trouble.

'The Poor Fellow'

Even the revellers were briefly muted by a melancholy incident soon after. The ship was making 12 knots before the wind with all her sails set. Most passengers had never seen a sea rolling so high. John Gray's cousin, Mr Ramsey, was sitting on the main topsail yardarm with another sailor when a rope snapped and they both fell. His companion managed to grab the rope, but Ramsey fell on his back into the sea and was soon a very long way astern. 'By the time his quaking companion had descended to the quarterdeck, the poor man's fate was sealed.' Four lifebuoys were flung to him. Some onlookers thought they saw him grab one. Robert Saddington hoped they were wrong and that those who thought that Ramsey was insensible when he hit the sea were right. John Gray, who had saved life at sea at the risk of his own before, ordered the lashing on the lifeboat to be cut. His colleagues doubted whether he would make much headway against the powerful wind and persuaded him that such an action would only put more lives at risk – and the weather was becoming more hazardous by the moment.

News of the calamity spread rapidly, but before the passengers could get on deck, Ramsey was hidden by the waves. Mr Gray's feelings as he surveyed the barren ocean that was his cousin's grave defy description. With a sad heart, Captain Matthews ordered the crew back to their stations. The sailors agreed that a rescue was impossible, although many of the passengers were angry at his apparent lack of humanity.

A gloom spread over the ship. The usual games carried on, but without enthusiasm. Occasionally someone would say, 'Well. I can't help thinking of the poor fellow.' The passengers collected £55 for Ramsey's dependants: the sailors contributed the £15 that had been collected at the Crossing the Line ceremony and the officers announced that they would contribute when they got paid off.

A Court-Martial

The spirit of mourning did not last long. Six nights later, the quarrelsome cook, who had behaved badly at the Crossing the Line ceremony had a fight with a passenger in Steerage. The cook was put in irons and the passenger was locked in the Smoking Room, but he broke out during the night.

Next day, the Captain presided over a court martial consisting of the Second and Fifth Officers, the Chief Engineer and the Bosun, all in full-dress uniform complete with swords. After five minutes deliberation, the cook was sentenced to 12 lashes at six o'clock next morning. As word went round the ship, a book was opened with odds of two to one that he would be reprieved.

Next morning, a 'busybody' woke Robert Saddington to remind him of the spectacle on deck, but, although he considered the cook's punishment to be well-deserved, Robert did not 'care to see a fellow human being writhing under the lash'. The officers assembled in full uniform. The prisoner was brought out and stripped to the waist. Quaking with fear and cold, he was strapped to a grating. The Captain took the opportunity offered by the solemn occasion to address a few cautionary words to passengers and crew. When all was ready, Captain Snell, an officer in the Royal Navy, stepped forward and requested a hearing. When this was granted, he pleaded that mercy be extended to the unfortunate cook. After some discussion, this was granted. Most of the onlookers considered it was prearranged, but that if the cook had adopted his usual arrogant attitude, he would not have been reprieved. He was taken off galley duties and put before the mast in place of poor Ramsey. It was thought likely that he would be 'served out' for the tricks he had practised on the sailors.

An Ill Wind

As the ship approached Australia, the winds were propitious and she ran rapidly before them, but it was an ill wind for Cecilia Cohen. Her severe seasickness had lasted for much of the voyage. Now it turned to croup, which was followed by inflammation of the brain. The exertions of both Dr Alexander, the ship's doctor, and Dr Sickler were 'skilful and untiring', but two days later, her lungs were also inflamed. At eleven that night, she died. Robert Saddington shared the belief, commonly held by the Victorians, that excessive sexual intercourse was debilitating and harmful, particularly for the young.

> This early marriage is the prime cause of her early death – poor fellow, how are his prospects blighted – his fondest affections destroyed and the object of them thus early snatched from his embrace by the icy hand of death – may we all learn from this sad instance of human frailty to set our affections upon heavenly things which pass not away.

Robert was thankful that they were spared the 'sad and mournful sight' of a burial at sea. The body was enclosed in a shell and placed in one of the quarter boats. When the ship arrived in Melbourne, the coffin was conveyed to the Jewish Cemetery.

SIX

'A Most Dreadful Affair'

Before her third Australian voyage in 1854, Captain Matthews resigned the command of the *Great Britain* to become Lloyd's Agent in Australia. John Gray, the First Officer, succeeded him. He was to become the ship's best-known and longest-serving captain. Preparations for the voyage took place in an atmosphere of war fever. A state of hostilities had existed between Russia and the Ottoman Empire since the previous year, and on 28 March Britain and France, keen to curb Russian ambitions in the Balkans, themselves declared war.

Captain Gray's first voyage in command did not begin auspiciously. The *Great Britain* sailed at noon on 29 April, but about 90 miles out it was discovered that the screw was faulty and it was decided to put back to Liverpool. The repairs would have to be undertaken in a dry dock, but because of adverse tides, the ship could not enter it for a week. Some passengers went ashore, got their money back from the company and booked onto other ships, but most resolved to stay with the *Great Britain*. When it became clear that the repairs would be extensive and lengthy, they were offered rail fares home until the ship was ready. The ship sailed again on 12 June. Amongst the passengers was Margaret (Maggie) Brown, a minister's daughter from Ayrshire, who was travelling to Melbourne to marry her fiancé. William Bray was one of 250 Cornishmen travelling in the Third Cabin. Most were tin miners on their way to the diggings. They spent much of their time drinking, gambling and fighting – and singing lusty hymns at Methodist services.

The tribal solidarity of the Cornishmen intensified the usual complaints about the food. They threatened to knife the officers if they were not better treated. Tempers became even more frayed as the ship entered the tropics. A man in Third Class, who had been served some very bad pork for dinner, took the plate to the Captain. When he asked him morosely what was wrong with it, the man flung the plate into his face. Exercising great self-control, Captain Gray did not retaliate, but it was generally believed that he would seek redress for the insult at Melbourne. A meeting of Third Cabin passengers passed a resolution which placed sole blame for the poor food on Captain Gray. One Saturday night, a large group of passengers who were well-charged with drink got belligerent in the bar. When the Captain intervened, he was knocked down and trampled on. The First Officer drew his sword and went to his aid, swearing that he would run through the first man who resisted. With the help of his fellow officers, the Captain was released from the mob and peace restored. Three of the ringleaders were clapped in irons, but groups of Cornishmen gathered threateningly on deck, so they were released.

Captain Gray's sense of diplomacy came to the fore. Rather than retreat into vituperation, as Captain Matthews might have done, he called a meeting in the Lower Cabin.

> From his expression of sorrow at their cause of complaint and from his being a promising young man, they have felt such a pity and compassion for him as to rescind all their former resolutions.

That day, Captain Gray and Captain Martin, who was going out Australia to set up a line of packet steamers for Bright Brothers, dined in the After Saloon. The passengers were so impressed by their explanations that they drank each captain's health 'Three times Three' and presented Captain Gray with an address of thanks.

There was apprehension about the possibility of encountering a Russian commerce raider. One night as the ship approached the Equator, William Bray was woken by 'awful screaming'. He started up in his bunk and was alarmed to see a strange red glare coming through the portholes. Someone told him that there was a Russian warship alongside. He rushed on deck, but found that the rumpus was caused by the preparations for Crossing the Line'.

'A Most Dreadful Affair'

The ship's troubles were compounded when smallpox broke out when she was three weeks out of Melbourne. One of the four sufferers, a sailor, died on 13 August. It was generally believed that his body was put overboard that night to keep his death as secret as possible. If it became known on arrival that there was smallpox on board, the entire ship could be taken into quarantine. When the ship arrived at Port Philip Head four days later, Captain Gray must have been tempted to hoist the white flag to indicate that there was no contagious illness aboard, but he knew the potential consequences in a colony whose quarantine laws were extremely severe. It would have been impossible to have sustained a conspiracy of several hundred people. 'So our noble, though unfortunate ship', wrote Maggie Brown, 'had to hoist a horrid yellow flag.'

Dr Hunt, the Medical Superintendent, went down to the ship's hospital and saw the three men who had been ill, who were well on the way to recovery. He ordered that they should be taken by boat to the nearby quarantine grounds, where they were to remain in tents until they had recovered 'or otherwise'. Then he undertook the medical examination of all on board, who had to declare whether they had been vaccinated against smallpox. 'Captain Gray', he declared when he had completed this task, 'I have seldom seen a healthier lot of passengers and, though I do run the risk of seeing you turned back to the Heads, I will take you up to Melbourne.'

As it was getting dark, the ship lay at anchor till daybreak. When the passengers woke, she was under way. 'It was a beautiful forenoon', wrote Maggie Brown, 'and the bay looked beautiful. I could scarcely tell you how I felt in coming so near the place I had so long looked forward to. I felt assured of a joyful welcome and I hoped all would be well.'

Captain Gray was fighting a psychological war. As the anchor dropped within sight of the city at two o'clock that afternoon, the ship's cannons fired a triumphant salvo. Soon after the Governor sent a dispatch forbidding contact with the shore until a decision was made. HMS *Phantom,* an 18-gun sloop, arrived to enforce the order, while four policemen circled the *Great Britain* in a rowing boat. The passengers waited anxiously to hear the next order. Realising the possibility of the worst, Captain Gray arranged for their mail to be conveyed home by the SS *Lightning,* which was moored close by and leaving for England next day.

The decision arrived late that afternoon and realised everyone's worst fears. Captain Gray was ordered to put back the 40 miles to the Isolation Station.

'This is a most dreadful situation', wrote William Bray.

> Six or seven hundred souls all healthy and strong in our own colonial port obliged to submit to this awful incarceration, watched like felons by the water police in boats sailing round us continuously and armed with swords and guns to shoot and kill any persons attempting to leave the vessel. ... Countenances which two days ago were lit up with cheerfulness and joy at their safe arrival are now marked with sorrow and sadness at their very trying and unexpected imprisonment, looking over on the land of promise, in full sight of Melbourne, but not allowed to put foot thereon.

Captain Gray decided to try to bluff things out and remained anchored in the bay in the hope that the authorities would reconsider their decision. Early next morning, the crew were called to their stations in case the news was for the worst. It came in an unequivocal form. At 7am, a cannon ball from HMS *Phantom* whistled over the ship. Captain Gray needed no further hints that he must comply. He weighed anchor and the passengers cast forlorn looks back at the receding city.

In Quarantine

At Port Philip Head, the *Great Britain* anchored 2500 yards off shore. HMS *Phantom* anchored alongside her with the clear authority to send 'another messenger' if it was required. The passengers remained on board for the first day, but the ship's boats plied to and fro to shore and they were free to roam over the vast hilly acres of the Isolation Station. Soldiers were stationed on the Head and the perimeter was patrolled by a dozen marines on horseback, 'fine looking, smart fellows', with orders to shoot anyone approaching the boundary fence without permission. Anyone escaping was liable to six months imprisonment and a huge fine of £300 on recapture. Those unable to pay faced seven years hard labour on a chain gang.

Maggie Brown thought it a lovely place, but found it strange to wander amongst the beautiful trees and shrubs, listening to the bird song, without James, her fiancé.

> O, how little do we know what is before us, for I fully expected that with no-one else but him would I take my first walk in Australia. The country seems very fine. I am quite delighted with it, but I believe that in town things are very flat.

William Bray went ashore with a shooting party. They bagged two small seabirds before getting caught in a heavy rainstorm, but they fortified themselves with brandy. On the way back they felt 'grubbish', so they went to the house of a settler and asked his wife for something to eat. She offered them a slice of a pie that she had baked from a nice seabird her husband had shot. They did not ask too many questions, in case she told them it was a young gull, but they liked the look of it, so they 'set to and made a finish of it' with a bottle of her home-brewed beer.

After a glass of grog, they returned to the *Great Britain*. Next day, everybody on board was ordered ashore so that the ship could be fumigated. The First Class passengers were allowed to return, but the rest had to remain and took their carpetbags and bedding with them. William Bray formed a party with five Cornish miners. They laboriously erected a tent from a canvas sail sent from the ship. By nightfall, they deemed it fit for habitation, but William was wary of further showers, so slept in a big barrel he rolled into the tent.

Next day, they finished work on the tent before collecting rations from the Government Station. The allowance was 1lb of beef,

2 ounces of figs, biscuits, an ounce of butter, some salt, a 'dust' of pepper and a choice between a pound of flour or ship's biscuit. They chose the biscuit, but found that it had been condemned and was full of large maggots. They complained, but had little expectation that anything would be done. Next time they fetched their rations, however, they were surprised to find that fresh supplies had been sent up from Melbourne.

They strolled along the shore picking up limpets. They had not brought their pots and pans ashore and were at a loss as to how to cook them, until they found an old tin bottle. One of the miners, Matthew Aver, cleaned it out with sand. Next day, they cooked the limpets in it and ate them for breakfast. Water was obtained from an underground spring that had been excavated on the beach. To prevent it from filling with sand, two large barrels were placed end to end in the well. Water was obtained by climbing down the narrow 12-foot shaft.

'In Durance Vile'

On the third day of captivity, those who had never had smallpox or been vaccinated were required to report to Dr Hunt. William Bray's arm felt painful for several months afterwards.

On the Sunday morning, passengers were allowed to return to the ship to collect more belongings. Matthew Aves picked up knives, forks, plates, a slice of roast beef, some bread and butter and a 'nice piece of plum pudding ... which came very acceptable'. William Bray rescued a hog's pudding, which his mother had made for him when he left home five months before. It had gone a little moldy, but it was 'the best luxury within our reach', so they ate it heartily.

That afternoon, Richard Opie, a 28 year-old tin miner, conducted an open-air prayer meeting. He 'very properly and appropriately' offered prayers and thanksgiving for God's 'sparing mercies ... beseeching him in his good pleasure to release us from this bondage and restore us again to our former rights, privileges and freedom.' Next day, it seemed his prayers had been answered when a brig came alongside the *Great Britain* to coal her, but it turned out to be a false hope.

On the eleventh day of their captivity, twenty large tents arrived from Melbourne. William Bray's barrel had become increasingly uncomfortable as more and more insects crept in to share it. Now it became a washtub for their clothing. That night a gale blew up and four of the new tents were swept away. After helping secure his own, William was freezing, so he put on all his clothes and slept through the storm.

There was a touching incident on the fourteenth day. A woman who had brought out her children to join her husband in Melbourne fainted when she was told that he was waiting at the perimeter fence. When she revived, she hurried off over the hills. The meeting was 'very affecting', although three armed guards watched them as they talked. The man did not dare to climb through to embrace his wife. He knew that, if he did, he would be obliged to join her 'in durance vile'.

'They are Coming for Us'

On Day 15, the Colonial Government posted an order: 'Every living soul belonging to the *Great Britain* must be vaccinated before they can be permitted to enter Melbourne.'

'That looks first rate', said Dr Hunt as he examined William Bray's vaccination mark. There seemed to be no reason to detain the ship. It was rumoured that she would be released at the end of the week, but the optimism was dampened when the letters that had been sent by SS *Lightning* were returned. Someone had decided that they constituted a health hazard. 'This is a hard and painful case to us', wrote William Bray, 'wishing to write to our friends to relieve their anxiety and not permitted to do so.' Nevertheless, he saw value in their detention. 'We are all likely to be in better condition for the diggings or in any other capacity than if we had gone straight to work on arrival.'

The tedium was having its effects. On the seventeenth day, a scuffle broke out between three men drawing water from the well. They tore at each other's hair, thumped one another and made the 'blood fly about in some style' – and all in the same cramped barrel. Some of the Cornishmen found a more constructive way to let off steam and, at the same time, keep up their mining skills. The surface geology of the grounds was a mixture of sandstone, limestone, fine sand and shell. They decided to dig down to the next strata. When they had struggled through 30 feet, the sides of the pit collapsed and buried Richard Opie, the miner-evangelist. He was unhurt, but the diggers were so alarmed that they filled in the hole. On the nineteenth morning, William Bray and Matthew Aver hiked four miles along the seashore. They found the wreck of a ship called the *Isabella Watson* and the tombstones of those who had perished when she had run ashore two years before. On their way back, they met three After-salooners who asked if they had heard the news.

'What news?'

'That the *Britain* and passengers are off to Melbourne tomorrow.'

This intelligence caused our hearts to leap for joy, and altho' having before complained of being tired, it caused each of us to say that our tiredness was gone and to walk back to the camp to ascertain any further particulars. By the time we returned it was the only topic in everybody's mouth.

Next morning all eyes were fixed on the ship for any sign of activity. Eventually a flotilla of small boats headed towards the shore. 'They are coming for us', everyone shouted excitedly as they ran down to the beach. 'Now boys, get your luggage ready', the First Officer sang out as the first boat was beached. They needed no encouragement. Bedding, bandboxes and bundles were thrown aboard. Within a couple of hours, everyone was back on the *Great Britain*. That evening she got up steam and sailed up to Melbourne.

The Battle of Melbourne

To celebrate the ship's release, Captain Gray ordered that the cannons fire a salute of 'joy and congratulation'. The 200 ships in the Bay responded with gunfire and rockets. The cannonade lasted until darkness fell. However, apprehension had been expressed that the powerful Russian Pacific naval squadron might attack the Australian colonies. When the gunfire was heard in Melbourne, alarm spread that it had arrived and was out to destroy the city. Soldiers mustered and spent several hours in their barracks awaiting news and orders. Merchants packed their bags and fled into the bush.

At his house at Toorak, some 8 miles from the city, the Governor was giving a dinner for his senior officials. The cannonade brought the guests onto the lawn. The sense of alarm was increased by the knowledge that preparations against a Russian attack were flimsy. Still in formal dress, the gentlemen galloped into town to organise the defence of the colony. Had the Russians really landed, they would have had a tough time. Thousands of people hurried down the road to Sandridge, 'determined to see what was up and by no means inclined to turn tail upon the Russians even if they were there'. The excitement was increased by newspaper sellers shouting in stentorian voices: 'Argus str'nary', 'Full particulars of the Battle of Melbourne'.

John Chatterton, who was due to return to England on the *Great Britain*, climbed the hill at Richmond with some friends. 'The whole bay was ablaze with the discharges of guns. Some of the knowing ones in the group that had gathered declared that the cannons were firing live ammunition. One old sailor with a long telescope declared that he could see our brave guard ship engaged with a Russian frigate on each side.' They decided that it was not advisable to go in to Melbourne, since the Russians would have disposed of the puny defences. It made sense to go home to bed and review the situation in the morning. John slept 'as soundly as if there were no possibility of seeing Melbourne in flames'.

Order was not restored until the first boat from the *Great Britain* reached Sandridge Pier. 'Byron's description of the excitement in Brussels before Waterloo', wrote a local journalist, 'can alone give any idea of the state of Melbourne last night.'

The city's biggest newspaper, *The Argus*, was highly critical of Captain Gray's conduct.

> Should it ever happen that an enemy should enter our port, the people, if armed, would fight like tigers. They were by no means pleased, however, at the Captain of the *Great Britain* for creating this alarm, and we think he acted indiscreetly in doing as he did.

The *Great Britain* sailed for home on 22 November 1854, with so many Third Class passengers that some were transferred to the Fore Saloon. The Russian threat was taken seriously, with full gunnery practice taking place on Christmas Day. Other shipping was viewed suspiciously. There was great anxiety about a ship flying what appeared to be the Russian Imperial Eagle, but closer examination showed that its emblem was a griffin.

Such incidents were presages of the ship's inevitable destiny. During the voyage, Gibbs, Bright & Co transferred her ownership to a related firm, the Liverpool & Australia Navigation Company and her connection with Bristol was severed when the ship was reregistered in Liverpool, but it was to be some time before she flew her new company colours. On her return to Liverpool, a six-month contract was signed with the Admiralty for her conversion as HM Steam Transport *Great Britain.* The ship underwent a refit that increased her tonnage to 3209 gross. She now had the capacity to carry 1650 men and 30 horses in newly-built boxes. The troops were to be accommodated in 1359 hammocks with 162 berths for officers. Another phase in the ship's extraordinary career was about to begin.

PART THREE: 'THE TRANSPORT POWER OF ENGLAND'

SEVEN

'Never was there such a Transport'

During the war with Russia, a vast army of over 300,000 British, French, Turkish and Sardinian soldiers was shipped to the Crimea. Only the British merchant marine could perform the huge task of transport and supply. 'Without the transport power of England', wrote Edward Nolan in his *History of the War against Russia,* 'France would have done little in the war.'

'There never was such a transport', exulted Tyndall Bright, the Company Secretary, as the *Great Britain* prepared for her first mission. 'The praises of our arrangements by the Officers remain unbounded.' Despite the mayhem he had caused in Melbourne, Captain Gray retained his command and became a lieutenant in the Royal Naval Reserve. Haywood Bright, the son of one of the owners, 'a fair energetic fellow', joined the ship as Supply Officer. In his bag were Bibles his pious mother had given him to distribute to the troops. To replace the ship on the Australia run, the owners acquired the *Royal Charter.* Her builder had gone bankrupt before little more than the keel had been laid, and Gibbs, Bright & Co. bought the embryonic ship and commissioned William Patterson to complete her. Her career was short, however, for she was wrecked off Anglesey in 1859.

On 2 March 1855, Commander Thomas Brewer, who had joined the Navy in 1812 as a 15 year-old midshipman, was appointed Admiralty Agent on the ship. Haywood Bright thought him a 'dear old muff', with 'one good quality ... He will put his name to anything.' Later that month, the *Great Britain* sailed for Queenstown on her first wartime mission. Crowds lined the banks of the Lee to watch her arrival. While she was in harbour, a gale blew her to within 12 feet of some rocks. Had she broken from her moorings, she would have been doomed. Over 15,000 rounds of ammunition were loaded aboard before the ship embarked for Malta a few days later, carrying the 2nd Provisional Infantry Battalion and an unnamed militia regiment.[1] The

1 It was not War Office practice to list militia regiments.

total complement on board was recorded as 1438 men, 68 officers, three horses, six women and eight children.

Haywood Bright was not impressed by the quality of the soldiers.

> A nastier, dirtier, more stupid set of men I never saw – to be sure they were a lot of recruits but they were more like blocks than anything else. The only thing they did was to eat and drink all day long.

Every four hours, 150 of them were turned out to keep watch, but all they did was smoke their pipes, or lie down on deck and go to sleep. 'They used to hate the sight of me', wrote Hayward, 'for I always put their pipes out and picked them up. It took me a quarter of an hour one night to kick up the watch.'

Valletta

The war had turned Malta into a vast military depot. Such was the urgency to turn the *Great Britain* round that she was at Valletta less than 3½ days. Haywood Bright bought a case of oranges and pairs of mittens for his family in the market, which was resplendent with exotic produce. One sailor, Frederick Gooley, also found Valletta a delightful spot and jumped ship.

The *Great Britain* began her return voyage on 24 March, carrying invalids from the Crimea and four grooms and seven horses 'of Lord Lucan', almost certainly belonging to the regiments who had charged famously at Balaclava. Haywood Bright was sad to see 'the poor fellows – But they all declare they will go back again as soon as they are well'. He was not impressed with Thomas Bellot, the naval surgeon in charge of the invalids.

> Such a specimen you never saw. He came on board with nothing but chickens, arrowroots and pearl barley and he applies to our doctor for all the medicines he may want and either to save trouble or something gives all his patients the same dose. Makes up sixty little powders about every other day. One of which each man receives.

After a stormy passage, the *Great Britain* arrived at Gibraltar two days later. Haywood Bright was disappointed in the Rock. 'Fancy the Malvern Hills surrounded with water and covered with houses, barracks and guns and you have Gibraltar.'

With the fleet at its war stations, the harbour was virtually empty. On her departure, the *Great Britain* towed the 84-gun sailing battleship HMS *Vengeance*, as far as the Tarifa Light. Two days out of Gibraltar, John Morrison, the Assistant Storekeeper, was found drunk on duty and transferred from the haven of the storeroom to working as a deckhand. Next day, one of the invalids, Able Seaman Henry Shepherd from HMS *Agamemnon*, died suddenly from a kidney infection. His remains were committed to the deep.

'Awful Muffs'

The *Great Britain* entered Portsmouth Harbour on the morning of 6 April. 'The people here are awful muffs as usual', wrote Haywood, 'don't seem to know their own minds for two minutes together.' But there was more method than he supposed. The ship was first required to moor alongside a hulk, where the sick and wounded were disembarked immediately. Later that day, she was ordered to a wharf to land the horses. Finally, all the hammocks and blankets were sent ashore, presumably for fumigation.

That day, orders were telegraphed to prepare with the utmost dispatch to embark 1500 troops. It was perhaps this urgency that caused Able Seaman James McKensie to take undue risks while working on the topmast. He fell and was killed instantly. The East Kent Militia arrived on 12 April. Twenty-two officers with two wives and two children and 599 other ranks with 49 women and 43 children were joined by 812 officers and men from the 1st Battalion of the Royals.

Next day, the soldiers cheered as the ship departed for Valletta. They steamed into headwinds for most of the way and the coal turned out to be bad. Haywood found the East Kents particularly obnoxious. The volunteers regarded the soldiers from the regiments of the line as their social inferiors and were always fighting with them.

As the *Great Britain* entered Grand Harbour, her screw got caught up in a buoy chain. A diver was paid 2/- to inspect it and found that a small piece had broken off one of the blades but it did not affect the ship's performance. Haywood again found his sojourn on Malta pleasant. 'We have no end of our old friends who we took from England the first time, coming on board with no end of invitations to dinner.' Yet again, a member of the crew went absent. Robert Jones, an Assistant Cook, was posted missing, presumed deserted.

Marseilles

The next port-of-call was Marseilles, to take on French troops for the Crimea. Enough supplies had been taken on board to sustain a trooping operation for over three months. Haywood wrote to his father suggesting that as they would be shipping wine for the French, they should also invest in claret and other 'light wines'.

Haywood enjoyed Marseilles. He spoke some French and got on well 'by looking savage and making a row'. He was amused at Captain Gray's encounters with the locals. 'He cannot understand a word and does nothing but grin and pull off his hat every half minute.' He went into a café and found Gray making all kinds of signs and faces to get a drop of milk in his coffee. After he got him some, they got into conversation with the Manager who invited them for a drive in his carriage. 'A fissing good trip it was.'

The *Great Britain* sailed at one o'clock on the morning of 12 May. She was carrying 1600 French soldiers, of whom only one spoke a little English. Haywood preferred them to his countrymen:

> They are much quicker, are always merry and never grumble, but appear very glad to get their victuals, so that except for their dirt they beat the English all to pieces, and now we are getting them to clean up &c &c pretty well – We have to provide them with nothing. They brought their own tins and each man has his blanket over his shoulder all day and rolls himself where he likes at night and goes to sleep in it – the Officers eat very little and drink nothing but the same wine the troops get, preferring it to any other we have on board.

After a smooth passage, the ship ran into the Grand Harbour at Valletta early on the morning of 16 May. She took on water and 110 tons of coal – only enough for three days steaming but with supplies uncertain in the Crimea, it was important to sail with full bunkers.

Constantinople

On 21 May, the ship anchored in the Golden Horn, the branch of the Bosphorus that forms the harbour of Constantinople. An exotic sight greeted those on deck. Hundreds of caiques shot across the water, while behind rose a forest of masts. *Muezzin* chanted the call to prayer from a thousand minarets, while three hundred churches reminded the traveller of the city's Byzantine past.

Those on board the *Great Britain* were astonished to find Robert Jones, the lost cook, waiting to greet them. He had hitched a passage from Malta on one of the many boats bound for The Crimea. The ship's log recorded laconically that 'he returned and commenced his duties on board ship this morning'. There is no mention of any punishment, so his gallant effort was probably regarded as wiping clean the slate.

Constantinople was a dangerous place as the sympathies of the large Greek population were entirely with the Russians. The correspondent of the *Daily News* reported that the owners of 'low dives' enticed sailors into their premises and got them helplessly drunk, stealing their money before turning them into the street. When they came to their senses, they accused the man of robbing them, which he indignantly denied.

> However, Jack is not put off in that way so away he goes and collects a number of his companions, and they make a fearful assault upon the house, breaking the windows and trying to force the doors. The Greeks watch their opportunity and sally out in large numbers with clubs and knives, and make a furious attack on the sailors. The consequence is, that these men being unprovided with any weapons are literally mowed down, and when on the ground, three of these men were killed just opposite to the house in which I was.

Both Thomas Brewer and Haywood Bright had business ashore. The Commander was trying to discover their orders. Haywood's task was more pressing. After the expenditure in Marseilles and Valletta, there was only £7 in the kitty, so he went to see William Hadfield, the Admiralty Agent for the Transport Service. In peacetime he had been the Agent for the Liverpool Underwriters Association. He proved 'very civil and businesslike' and said that he would do all in power to facilitate the *Great Britain*'s movements. A 30-day cash draft for £196 was secured.

The Black Sea

Early next morning, the *Great Britain* passed through the Bosphorus and into the Black Sea. Conditions in what was virtually a huge lake were not good for a ship designed to be driven by the prevailing winds. 'We never have a wind one way or the other for ten minutes', bemoaned Haywood. The ship had steamed for four hours when the cover of the port hotwell burst and water poured in through the discharge pipe. The cover, which should have been an inch thick, was in parts only an eighth of that. Alexander 'Mack' Maclennon, the ship's engineer, immediately stopped the engines, shut the discharge valves and pumped the ship dry. She lay to for 24 hours while he made a temporary wooden hotwell cover. The Royal Navy had gained mastery of the Black Sea, so there were no fears of a Russian attack.

The temporary job did the trick and the ship proceeded at 6 knots, arriving in Kamiesch Bay early on the morning of 26 May. To support the siege of Sevastapol, the French had created facilities that were a triumph of military organisation. Sappers and miners had erected an impressive wharf at which the *Great Britain* moored to rapidly discharge the troops. All were in a 'perfect state of health'.

Stretching before them was a city of tents, with named streets served by an excellent post office and in which Parisian *restauranteurs* were to be found.

> Pleasant little *vivandiers* might ... be seen tripping about with that light and graceful air so peculiar to the young Frenchwoman, and they were treated with all imaginable courtesy and tenderness. Throughout the dreary siege that followed the neatness and order of everything at Kamiesch were visual commendations of the French system.[2]

Once the troops had disembarked, the ship lay outside the bay awaiting orders. It was rumoured that she was to be sent to the Black Sea port of Varna to pick up Turkish troops.

The indefatigable Mack worked day and night to make a new hotwell cover from boilerplates, with cross bars taken from the cargo hatch gratings. Afterwards, he found the time and energy to give the engines a complete overhaul. Strong feelings were expressed about John Penn & Co., the makers of the engines. Had the matter got out, the owners could have faced indemnities. 'The authorities here will not know a word about the matter', Captain Gray wrote to reassure Samuel Bright. Doubtless the pliant Commander Brewer also agreed to keep mum. The ship was thoroughly cleaned inside and out. The topgallant yards, designed to beat before the trade winds, proved a hindrance and were struck. The broken propeller blade was examined. Some 18 inches had sheered off it. Mack said it did no harm and no one could gainsay him.

'I shall send the papers concerning last voyage', wrote Haywood Bright to his father, 'as soon as we come to a good post town, but we do not think it safe to send them from here, but they are all signed and made ready.' 'Things look bad here', he wrote again after a trip ashore. The Turkish troops were 'abused by everybody and seem a wretched set of men'. French morale was high and they were confident of taking the city, but Haywood took a different view after climbing the heights above Sevastapol. 'I could only see one small breach in the walls ... and the houses had glass in the windows.'

Haywood had two cousins serving with the British force at the siege, the splendidly named Captains Brooksbank and Robert Onesophorus Bright of the 19th Foot, who visited him on board. Next day, he returned the compliment and stayed in the British camp until the ship sailed.

---

2 Nolan's *Russian War.*

'A Scene of Desolation and Riot'

At 8am on 31 May, Commander Brewer received orders for the *Great Britain* to transport 1600 French troops, 30 officers and 27 horses to Kertch, at the entrance to the Sea of Azov on the other side of the Crimean peninsular. This ancient town, the former Tartar capital, was the base from which the Russians had been supplying Sevastapol. An Allied expeditionary force had captured it on 25 May.

Kertch was reached in a day's sailing. The ship's engines and the new hotwell cover were in 'capital order'. Haywood embarked with only an hour to spare, but the army liaison officer, Captain Boyce, missed the boat because he had ridden off to Balaclava three hours before the orders were received. The French commanding officer refused to disclose the names of his men, probably because in the haste with which the force had been assembled, he simply did not know them. Haywood persuaded him to sign a paper saying that they had been fed on board.

After the troops had disembarked, the ship lay in the outer harbour for three days as orders were awaited. Haywood went ashore on 5 June to try to buy fresh meat. The French General d'Autemarre had captured 500 oxen and sheep and had allocated half to victual the fleet. As the party from the ship landed, in the heat of a Crimean summer, they were met by a heavily-armed patrol who told them that no sailors were allowed in the town without an officer, presumably to reduce the risk of looting. So they ordered the hands 'to stay in the boat and went to look about us'. General d'Autemarre had given his troops permission to loot, not only from the houses, but also from the persons of the remaining inhabitants, who had understandably fled. The fine houses and 'fissing' (his favourite superlative) furniture impressed Haywood. Grain was scattered everywhere. His admiration for their allies evaporated when they could find nothing to buy, 'as the French plunder everything they can lay their hands on – While our own sailors are not allowed to touch a single thing', but he could not resist picking up a few small items himself. Mosquitoes and flies infested the debris. His newfound contempt caused him to squarely apportion the blame – the 'last a legacy from the French'.

When they returned to the boat, they found that some of the crew had gone off to an abandoned wine cellar, 'where the French were amusing themselves by trying who could broach a cask fastest'. Haywood had never seen such 'a scene of desolation and riot. With the English everything was quiet and orderly. I did not see an English man take anything or do anything but what he would do in London. But I did not see a French man sober.'

'Ain't that swell?'

Commander Brewer had sought out the Allied fleet commander Rear-Admiral Sir Edmund Lyons, who told him that they had taken 300 enemy vessels when they captured the port. Haywood greeted this news with derision. 'All the prizes I have seen are about the size of our lifeboats.' In fact these flat-bottomed vessels had been crucial to the Russian war-effort by conveying supplies across the Sea of Azov for the garrison at Sevastapol.

Two days later, orders were received for the ship to carry soldiers and horses for an attack on Anapa, a town of great strategic importance across the Straits of Kertch. 'Am I not lucky', Haywood wrote to his father, 'coming in for all these interesting places? If the expedition to Anapa succeeds, we shall be entitled to prize money. Ain't that swell?' An air of urgency prevailed and 27 horses were loaded aboard by nightfall. There was no fodder on the ship, so the army agreed to provide it. Nevertheless, the troops remained on shore and it was rumoured that the fleet was not ready to sail. It transpired that the success of Admiral Lyons in sweeping the Russians from the Sea of Azov had made the defence of Anapa untenable and it had been abandoned without a shot being fired.

Disappointed at being deprived of his prize money, next day Haywood managed to buy a bullock for 50/-, but try as he might, he could not lay his hands on another. All the talk ashore was that the Allies would fire the town when they withdrew because it was impossible to remove all the stores and they wanted to deny them to the Russians. The rumour was true and Kertch was burnt on 12 June. Hayward expressed no regret at the destruction of the picturesque town that he admired, but was thrilled by the 'most splendid sight' of half a mile of houses burning at once.

With the abandonment of the Anapa expedition, the ship carried 28 officers and 655 men back to Kamiesch. Haywood obtained 143 names for his victualing returns and got the Commanding Officer to sign for the rest. 'I hope these certificates will do as well as if the names were in the Blue Books', he told his father, 'but we could not manage it any other way.' At Kamiesch and Kertch, Haywood sold the wine that he had bought in Marseilles, although he let his cousins, Bob and Brooksbank, have what they wanted for nothing. He made a profit of 8/- a case, so he regretted not bringing more. The authorities frowned on such enterprises. 'It may be as well to keep them quiet', he advised his father.

Security was lax. On 14 June, Haywood recorded that the French were due to attack the Malakoff Tower, a key work in the Russian defences, that night. He worked out that their next mission would be to take the wounded from the expected action to Constantinople. The ship's engines were in good order, but with only 23 days supplies left for trooping and the Admiralty lease nearing its end, such a voyage must be a prelude to returning home. The ship's condition made it a necessity. Her bottom was encrusted with marine life: a particular hazard in Crimean waters. 'I should recommend you', he told his father, 'to have her cleaned before you make another engagement with the government.' Most army officers serving in the Crimea had bought their commissions. This meant that, within limits, they could leave the battlefront once their predetermined obligations were fulfilled. Captain Boyce was determined to go home, as 'soon as he can get an opportunity, for which he is looking very sharp'. The expected return of the *Great Britain* must have appeared a godsend.

Contrary to expectation, the assault on the Malakoff did not take place that night. At 1am, those listening out for it on the *Great Britain* were astonished when a dispatch arrived, informing them that it had been decided to reoccupy Kertch and ordering them to return there immediately. The order came as a blow to Boyce, but he determined to leave anyway. Heywood's budget was again running low and the company was responsible for the Captain's expenses, so he was given a letter of credit for £30 drawn on the reliable Mr Hadfield at Constantinople. He also carried important papers from Heywood to his father. To guarantee their safe arrival, duplicate copies were dispatched by another route.

The *Great Britain* was under way within the hour. At daybreak, they encountered the returning British fleet off Balaclava. Admiral Lyons hailed them and ordered them alongside his flagship, HMS *Royal Albert.* He expressed surprise at their mission, but allowed them to proceed 'with all dispatch'. The meeting between the ships was an impressive sight. The *Royal Albert* represented Britain's maritime pride at a time when her naval might was unchallenged. She had been launched at Woolwich in the previous year before 60,000 cheering people. Her design was based entirely on the principles that Brunel had pioneered with the *Great Britain.* Although she was 50 feet shorter, her burthen was 300 tons greater. She was armed with 131 guns, including a 5-ton 68-pounder on her forecastle, which could hurl shot a distance of three miles.

Lack of information is often the lot of those closest to events. Haywood suspected that the decision to reoccupy Kertch was another manifestation of the bungling that had characterised the war. Realising the paradox that the people back home probably knew more than those on the spot, he asked his father to send him the accounts from the newspapers.

> I cannot understand why we burnt Kertch. All our forces left it one night, setting fire to everything, including tons of provisions. The Cossacks came into the town that night. The English land again next day and again took possession and still hold the place, but having burnt everything are nearly starving. Why we should burn everything and then keep the ashes I don't know.

Next day the ship embarked 1245 Turkish troops. They were back off Kamiesch at 11am on 18 June to find that the long-expected assault on Sevastapol had taken place early that morning. It had been beaten back, but they were still 'firing away like fun'. The Turks were ferried ashore in the ship's boats.

It had been intended that the French and British make concerted assaults on the Russian strong points of the Malakoff and the Redan, but the French had attacked too soon. The rumours of an impending assault had reached the Russians. Although the cause was hopeless, the British commander, Lord Raglan, felt honour demanded that his attack proceed. Although they managed to enter the town, they were repulsed and hundreds of men died needlessly. Haywood was anxious about his cousins and went to seek them out in the trenches. He was relieved to find Brooksbank and sat on a rock to hear his account of the disaster.

> Brooksbank was among the poor fellows in the town. After being shot at all day, they crept out after dark and got to their own trenches in safety – He seems to have run several very narrow escapes, but seems all right and none the worse – Bob was in reserve and did not go into action – Nobody seems to know what the next move will be. This affair seems to have disheartened our fellows not a little. Hardly a regiment escaped without a loss, and some poor fellows that I dined with when last we were here are no more.

Haywood almost became his family's only casualty. Ten minutes after he had left, a big roundshot lit on top of the rock on which he had been sitting. 'Don't be alarmed', he reassured his sister, 'for I was not hit and the trenches won't see me again I promise you.'

Morale was becoming lower and drunkenness increasing. An Able Seaman, Auguste Bortlemain, went absent from a party that William Lawson, the Fourth Officer, had taken ashore to fetch water. He turned up 19 hours later 'inebriated and unfit for duty'. He had probably joined the ship's company in Marseilles and had been commiserating with his compatriots after their repulse on the Malakoff. Two of the cooks, Matthew Reagan and Peter Vaughan, also absented themselves, but returned before the ship sailed again. Even Haywood Bright confessed that the conditions were getting him down. 'The weather is awful hot, nearly kills me – I can do nothing but sleep during the day, but with flies, flies, mosquitoes, &c, &c, it is not much sleep one gets. The flies are a regular plague here, if you pour a glass of sherry, you have some in it before you drink it.' At least he could feel that he had done a good job. 'I think the voyage has improved him very much', wrote John Gray to his father, 'and, as you remark, he has seen a little of the world and sea life and at the same time rendered his kind and efficient services in the stores department.'

When the awaited orders arrived, they brought only amazement and dismay. The ship was to proceed to Constantinople where Commander Brewer was to place the ship at the disposal of Rear-Admiral Grey for the transport of Turkish troops. As the ship left Kamiesch next day, she was in collision with a small brig and carried away her bowsprit. Haywood exonerated Captain Gray from any blame. 'It is impossible to take a big ship like this in and out of harbours when they are crowded like a swarm of bees.'

Another mishap occurred as the *Great Britain* arrived at Constantinople. She carried away the jibboom of another small brig. It could have proved a serious business, Haywood noting that the 'charges here are very great'. William Hadfield advised that it was better to settle things quietly rather than to let them be reported to the British Consul, so the captain of the brig was paid £20 on the spot. A letter was also written to Captain Green, the Admiralty Agent in Kamiesch, asking him to settle things as best he could in regard to the first accident. Mr Hadfield reassured Captain Gray that the *Great Britain* had caused less damage than any other ship in the Transport Service.

Cholera

On 1 July, it was reported that Lord Raglan had died of Asiatic cholera. The epidemic had raged through the lines at Sevastapol, and the company of the *Great Britain* was not spared. Two stokers and two Able Seamen went down with it. The disease probably originated in the water brought aboard by Fourth Officer Lawson's party.

The presence of cholera brought a deadly hush over the ship and an increase in drunkenness and insubordination. Able Seaman William Clark went absent during working hours to sample the dangerous pleasures of life ashore. He returned with a bottle of spirits concealed in his shirt. Charles Chapman, the Chief Officer, noticed it and attempted to take it off him, but he resisted and raised his hand to strike him.

On 4 July, the cholera claimed its first victim when one of the Able Seamen died suddenly. On the same day, Auguste Bortlemain went missing again together with a seaman called John Davies, who failed to return and was posted as a deserter on 8 July. Davies returned two days later and, in the words of the ship's log, was 'suddenly seized with an Attack of the Asiatic Cholera'. The ship's doctor had more insight and recorded the malady as 'drunkenness'. He was back at work six days later.

Either through the intervention of Captain Gray, or through changed priorities, the authorities became convinced that it was a bad idea for the *Great Britain* to engage in further trooping activities. Her orders were changed and, on 8 July, she crossed the narrow straits between Europe and Asia to Scutari. Her next assignment was to convey invalids back to Britain. Haywood spent £432:6:10d on stores from a local merchant, paying with credit drawn on his father.

It is symptomatic of the attitudes of the military establishment that, as a disease ship, the *Great Britain* was regarded as unfit to transport combat-ready Turkish troops, but adequate to carry British invalids. The British Military and Naval Hospital at Scutari was housed in a Turkish barracks so vast that it could accommodate 6000 patients.[3] On the ship's arrival, a team of workmen came aboard to erect bunks for the invalids. Haywood went ashore but slipped on a pavement and cut his knee badly. The wound festered in the intense heat, but there were no long-term ill effects.

At first, the short trip across the straits seemed to have had a beneficial effect. 'The cholera seems to have left us altogether since we came here', wrote Haywood. His optimism was premature. Later that day, Able Seaman William Hellman, aged 23, died. His remains were transferred ashore on the following evening and interred at the Naval Burial Ground. Eight days later, a stoker, Henry Abernethy, aged 50, died. His body was taken to the English Burial Ground, on the shores of the Sea of Marmara, a few hundred yards from the mouth of the Bosphorus. A visitor left a description that conveys the full horror of this awful place.

> At the southern extremity of the ground are single graves, neatly defined and turfed, where those who died when the army halted here in the spring are laid. But the press of mortality no longer admitted of such a decent burial. To those accustomed to see the departed treated with reverence, and attended solemnly to their last habitation, there was something horribly repulsive in wholesale interment, while the dead far outnumbered those who stood round the grave. A pit often ten feet deep, and fourteen square, received every afternoon those who had died during the previous

3 Scutari was the hospital where Florence Nightingale and her nurses were based.

> twenty-four hours ... There is no time for ceremony; each poor corpse, huddled and doubled up limply in the case of recent death, or stiff and statue-like where it is no longer cold, is handed down nameless, unknown, and void of all the dignity of death, to its appointed station in the crowd. One row being laid, the next comes, and the feet of all those who deposit them necessarily trample on the forms below, leaving muddy footprints on the blanket shrouds ...

That night, another stoker, Patrick McGrady, aged 23, died suddenly and was buried at sea. The victims had been so terrified to discover that they had cholera that the ship's doctor considered that they had 'half killed themselves'.

After a period of uncertainty, orders arrived on 17 July to proceed to Portsmouth. Over the next two days the infirm were brought down from the hospital: eight officers and 149 men, under the charge of Major Anderson of the Royal Artillery. Three war widows and a soldier's wife also embarked. On her passage home, the *Great Britain* called at Malta and Gibraltar, where four more soldiers' wives came on board with eight children. She arrived back at Spithead on 8 August.

EIGHT

'The Very Genius of Stupidity'

The ship did not return to Liverpool for the refit urged by Haywood Bright. The need for her services was too urgent and another lease with the Admiralty had been signed even before her return to Britain. On 13 August 1855, Commander Brewer wrote to the Admiral Superintendent of Portsmouth Dockyard advising that the *Great Britain* had materially 'lost her speed in consequence of accumulation of matter on her bottom and slight damage to her screw – To rectify these defects it will be advisable to place her in dock – and request your directions accordingly.' His posting with the ship ceased four days later. He reverted to the life of narrow means that was the lot of a half-pay officer, and things were not improved by the arrival of a large messing bill, which he claimed was not his responsibility to pay in full. Haywood Bright also left the ship to become the company's agent in Jamaica for the next four years.

Balaclava

The ship's turnaround was extremely rapid. Within eight weeks of Commander Brewer's letter, she was in Balaclava Harbour, having undergone her refit and carried troops to the Crimea. They were probably intended to reinforce another assault on Sevastapol, but the fortress had fallen on 8 September.

There were even more transports at Balaclava than at Kamiesch, but in contrast to the French supply port, the scene was one of 'utter disorder'. Some ships were anchored in the harbour; some were moored below the little town. Others were left to beat about outside the harbour, perhaps never to land their stores or to land only a portion of materials or equipment that was useless without the rest of it.

> Vessels were frequently ordered off to Varna, Constantinople, Malta or somewhere else, carrying undischarged cargo to and fro over the waters of the Black Sea and the Bosphorus, as if the very genius of stupidity and folly presided over all. Many of the vessels within the harbour were injured by knocking against one another

> – so helpless was the disorder in which they were permitted to lie about wherever they could get a berth. There was no wharf – nothing that could be called a landing-place; the munitions and material were piled in incongruous heaps, as chance ordered. Confusion reigned paramount from the very first day. No guiding hand was found, on land or sea, to save the English nation from the disgrace and disaster resulting from this state of things and to preserve the unfortunate army from the direful consequences.

This censure is confirmed in a letter written by Rear-Admiral Sir Charles Freemantle, who was in charge of port arrangements. On 6 October, he complained that the crowded state of the harbour was making the landing of supplies and troops extremely difficult.

> I mention this to shew what dangers ships coming to this port during the Winter season will encounter, and I wish to prevent very large transports from coming here, the *Great Britain* has just left for Sookoom Kali with 1800 Turks. She is unmanageable except in a calm.

The latter statement strains credulity. The *Great Britain* was noted for her manoeuvrability and Captain Gray was an experienced seaman whose navigational skills at Constantinople had been lauded by William Hadfield.

Freemantle's letter reveals the *Great Britain*'s next mission – to transport Turkish troops of Omar Pasha's army to Souchoum Kaleh in Georgia in an attempt to relieve the Turkish city of Kars, which was about to fall to the Russians. While she was in the Caucasus, she picked up British sick and wounded who had been serving with the Ottoman Army: 20 naval and army officers and 28 sailors, four soldiers, a bandmaster, six women and six children. At Scutari a further nine officers and 80 men embarked as well as two escorts, four servants and a solitary prisoner-of-war. She arrived back at Spithead on 7 November.

The British Foreign Legion

The turnaround was again swift. On 10 November, the *Hampshire Telegraph* reported that the *Great Britain* would shortly embark the 1st Regiment of the British Swiss Legion. At the outbreak of the Crimean War, the British government put an Enabling Bill through Parliament to recruit a Foreign Legion, but the move was controversial. For historical reasons, many Britons were deeply suspicious of the recruitment of mercenaries by the Crown.

Great difficulty was experienced in recruiting for the Legion, not through lack of volunteers, but from the opposition of foreign governments. The recruiting sergeants operated under great difficulty and had to resort to all kinds of tricks to get their men. In some German states, they incurred heavy penalties for opening offices, while in the USA, opinion was so incensed by the recruitment drive that diplomatic relations were severed and war threatened. In a bold move, the British Government established recruiting posts along its French ally's frontiers with Switzerland and Germany. The response was particularly good in Switzerland. The Swiss were regarded as being amongst the finest mercenary troops in Europe and many experienced soldiers enlisted. On 20 March 1855, a number of appointments were announced of officers in the British Foreign Legion who had served hitherto on the Swiss Army. On 9 August, the Queen and Prince Albert reviewed 3500 men of the Swiss and German Regiments in Hyde Park. 'These foreign mercenaries', wrote Nolan, 'were most anxious to see Her Majesty and made demonstrations of loyalty which her own subjects could scarcely have surpassed.'

The Swiss were deemed ready to embark for Smyrna in Turkey. On 16 November, 1350 men of the regiment's two battalions, under the command of Colonel Dickson, arrived at Portsmouth in separate trains from their headquarters at Shorncliffe. 'They are a remarkably fine body of men', enthused the *Hampshire Telegraph*, 'young, healthy and apparently well disciplined'. Cheering crowds lined the route as the troops marched to the Dockyard preceded by a military band playing such lively tunes as *Three Cheers for the Red, White and Blue* and *Tell those Noble Wounded Men.*

The ship sailed on the following afternoon, arriving at Smyrna three weeks later. The Swiss were billeted in a large Turkish barracks that could accommodate 2000 men. Since March, the building had been a British civilian hospital, which was considered the best organised medical facility that had been established in Turkey during the war. Inexplicably, it was decided to close down this exemplary institution to house the Swiss. They were not there for long. Within two weeks of their arrival, they were transferred to Constantinople before briefly seeing action in the Crimea before the armistice was signed on 28 February 1856.

After disembarking the Swiss, the *Great Britain* proceeded to Scutari, where she took on seven officers, five medical staff, three women, four children and 140 army and 14 naval invalids. She sailed for home on 11 December and called at Malta before arriving back at Portsmouth on the 31st. Half a dozen of the invalids were carried to the Military Hospital in cots, others went in horse-drawn omnibuses, while the remainder, about 90 in number, were able to walk. The ship's services as a troop transport were no longer required and on 2 January 1856, she returned to Liverpool. In the Mersey Estuary, she ran into the port side of the Spanish screw steamship, *Habana*, bound for the Cuban port after which she was named. The *Great Britain*'s bowsprit and figurehead were damaged.

On 16 January, the Russians accepted terms for negotiating a peace treaty. It appeared that the war was over, but in order to impress the enemy with their serious intent, the Allies continued their military build-up. On 28 January, *The Times* announced that the *Great Britain* had been taken back into Government service and would convey troops to Malta when her repairs and refit were completed. On 9 February, she embarked 530 troops, composed of drafts from various regiments. Next day, she sailed for Queenstown, where she picked up additional detachments, a total of some 1150 men and 63 officers. After disembarking her disparate human cargo at Valletta, the *Great Britain* received orders to proceed to Genoa, where she was to embark the 1st Italian Regiment of the British Foreign Legion. The entry of the Kingdom of Sardinia into the war on the Allied side had opened up a fruitful recruiting ground for the Foreign Legion. At first men were slow in coming forward, but when winter inhibited work on the land, the trickle grew to a torrent, which was boosted by the hope that the recruits might be sent to a part of the British Empire where they might settle when their service was over. Thus three regiments were recruited in as many months.

The Italians were not an easy body of men to handle. Lord Palmerston, the Prime Minister, was obliged to answer allegations in the House of Commons that agents were at work, encouraging them to mutiny. Nevertheless, on 2 March 1856, the 1st Regiment marched past its commanding officer, Lieutenant Colonel Sir Coutts Lindsay, at Susa. The *Times* correspondent was impressed by their appearance and steadiness under arms, although the effect was marred by the fact that they had not received their full-dress uniforms. They greeted the announcement that they were to embark on the *Great Britain*, which had moored off the Lighthouse Mole at Genoa on the previous evening, with great enthusiasm. At 4am on 6 March, a special train left the regimental headquarters at Chiavasso and arrived at Genoa in the afternoon. From the station they marched to the quayside. Some progress had been made with the uniforms. The soldiers were wearing greatcoats with cross belts and had knapsacks. Each man was carrying a blanket and part of a field kitchen. The regiment was drawn up opposite the ship and, according to *The Times*, everyone was impressed by their 'soldierlike appearance'. The embarkation was carried out in a large barge, which could carry 400 men, and several smaller ones. Thirty-six officers, 100 NCOs, 20 drummers and 864 privates carried the tents in which they would be bivouacked on Malta: there was no available barrack space on the crowded island. 'By five o'clock they had deposited their arms and accoutrements and commenced studying the novelties of their temporary lodgings.' The accusations of sedition still rankled. 'The cheerfulness with which the men went on board', wrote *The Times* correspondent, 'proves that all attempts to seduce them from their duty have completely failed.'

Water was at a premium on Malta, so every tank on the *Great Britain* was filled. It had been proposed that some 40 oxen – intended as a means of transport for the regiment – be towed behind the ship in a small vessel, but this idea was wisely abandoned and they were taken on board. When the ship sailed on the morning of 7 March, with troops, equipment, water and oxen aboard, she was deep in the water, but she still towered over everything as she left port with a fair wind and a smooth sea. She was out of sight in two hours and arrived in Valletta five days later.

After disembarking the 1st Regiment, the ship returned for the 2nd Regiment, which arrived from Susa and marched to the Lighthouse Mole. The strong wind from the northeast, bringing freezing rain and sleet, known locally as the *traumatana*, penetrated their clothing, but the men's unflagging cheerfulness cannot have been diminished by the knowledge that their chances of dying in the Crimea were reducing by the day. The rough weather meant that only the large barge could be used for the embarkation, but everyone was on board before dark. Next day, the weather had improved and the *Great Britain* departed. Forty officers, 20 drummers and 975 privates, together with three wives, seven children and seven female servants, landed at Valletta on 24 March.

Around the time that the 2nd Regiment was embarking, an order from London suspended further recruitment. As a result the troops that had been raised for the 4th Regiment were incorporated into the 3rd. They were regarded as the elite of the Legion, 'small, active and good looking'. Unlike their predecessors, they had been issued with uniforms and looked very smart in their grey kepis and black and grey trousers, but only a few had been issued with outdated muskets.

On 3 April, just eight days after she had previously left Genoa, the *Great Britain* was back to embark them. Eleven hundred men were taken aboard on a fine day. The only drawback to the prevailing 'good humour' was the CO's 'disagreeable duty' in having to refuse passage to a number of soldiers' wives who had arrived at the quayside.

As the order on this subject is imperative and unmistakeable there was no alternative but to refuse one and all, and the men being thus convinced that at least there was no partiality in the execution, soon became reconciled to a hardship which they saw all must bear alike

Local Friction

Relations between the Maltese and their would-be defenders were wearing thin. 'Like all southern peoples,' *The Times* noted, 'the Italian soldiers are much given to noisy exclamations; they swear frequently and at times break out into blasphemy.' The Maltese, who were themselves 'not very nice in their oaths, still do not like to hear the names of their favourite patron saints taken in vain, and accordingly seem to have made up their minds from the very beginning to show the soldiers of the Legion how much they disapprove of their behaviour'.

A number of the legionaries had served with the short-lived Roman Republic that had overthrown Papal power during the revolutionary year of 1848. This caused great offence in devout Malta and the mercenaries were denounced from the pulpit. The trouble escalated when a soldier of the 1st Regiment, returning to his encampment at Fort Manoel the worse for drink, used profane language and was upbraided by a Carmelite friar. In response, he boxed the mendicant's ears. He was arrested and jailed for two months. Relations worsened. A number of the Italians paraded provocatively through the streets, singing 'songs of liberty' and shouting insults at the natives. An Inspector of Police who tried to pacify them was stabbed to death. The Italians were then stripped of their ammunition. The violent clashes were renewed on the afternoon of 8 April as the *Great Britain* was arriving at Valletta with the next contingent. Most shops closed and HMS *Hannibal* was towed into position to train her guns on Fort Manoel.

By this time the war was over. A peace treaty was signed between the powers in Paris on 30 March, although it was not ratified until 27 April. With the close of hostilities, the Foreign Legion was disbanded, although some German units were retained for service in Cape Colony. So ended a curious and forgotten episode of British military history, in which the *Great Britain* played a significant part.

'The Annual Menace'

The end of the war posed the huge logistical problem of bringing home the vast scattered armies and their equipment. On 13 April,

Thousands cheer the launch of the SS *Great Britain* into Bristol's Floating Dock on 19 July 1843. (Courtesy SS Great Britain Trust)

The SS *Great Britain* at Blackwall after the visit of Queen Victoria and Prince Albert, 2 April 1845, by R B Spencer. This shows the ship in her original configuration, with six masts. (Courtesy N R Omell gallery)

(*Above*) The *Great Britain* is towed off Dundrum beach in August 1847, from *The Illustrated London News*. (Courtesy SS Great Britain Trust)

(*Left*) In the foreground, table ware from the Saloon of the *Great Britain*. The wheel in the background was for playing a gambling game but it is unlikely that it was actually used on the ship. (Courtesy SS Great Britain Trust)

Looking aft along the original promenade deck of the *Great Britain*, with cabins ranged along each side, from *The Illustrated London News c*1845. (Courtesy SS Great Britain Trust)

Fanny Duberly in the Crimea, with her husband Captain Henry Duberly of the 8th Hussars, before her voyage out to India on the *Great Britain* in 1857. (Courtesy of the Director, National Army Museum, London)

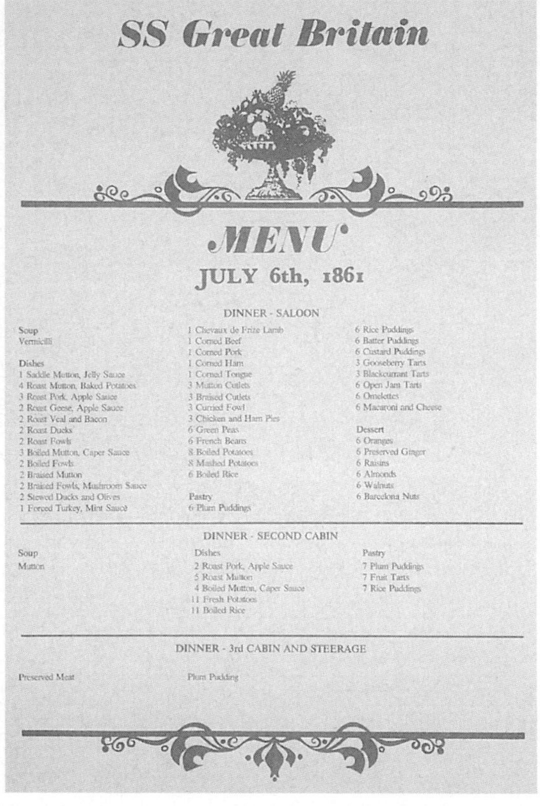

SS Great Britain

MENU

JULY 6th, 1861

DINNER - SALOON

Soup
Vermicilli

Dishes
1 Saddle Mutton, Jelly Sauce
4 Roast Mutton, Baked Potatoes
3 Roast Pork, Apple Sauce
2 Roast Geese, Apple Sauce
2 Roast Veal and Bacon
2 Roast Ducks
2 Roast Fowls
3 Boiled Mutton, Caper Sauce
2 Boiled Fowls
2 Braised Mutton
2 Braised Fowls, Mushroom Sauce
2 Stewed Ducks and Olives
1 Forced Turkey, Mint Sauce

1 Chevaux de Frize Lamb
1 Corned Beef
1 Corned Pork
1 Corned Ham
1 Corned Tongue
3 Mutton Cutlets
3 Braised Cutlets
3 Curried Fowl
3 Chicken and Ham Pies
6 Green Peas
6 French Beans
8 Boiled Potatoes
8 Mashed Potatoes
6 Boiled Rice

Pastry
6 Plum Puddings
6 Rice Puddings
6 Batter Puddings
6 Custard Puddings
3 Gooseberry Tarts
3 Blackcurrant Tarts
6 Open Jam Tarts
6 Omelettes
6 Macaroni and Cheese

Dessert
6 Oranges
6 Preserved Ginger
6 Raisins
6 Almonds
6 Walnuts
6 Barcelona Nuts

DINNER - SECOND CABIN

Soup
Mutton

Dishes
2 Roast Pork, Apple Sauce
5 Roast Mutton
4 Boiled Mutton, Caper Sauce
11 Fresh Potatoes
11 Boiled Rice

Pastry
7 Plum Puddings
7 Fruit Tarts
7 Rice Puddings

DINNER - 3rd CABIN AND STEERAGE

Preserved Meat

Plum Pudding

(*Above*) Players and sponsors of 'The XI of All England', the first cricket team to tour Australia in 1861-2. The captain, H H Stephenson, is seated in the centre. Behind him is the Spiers and Pond agent, Mr Malon. (Courtesy MCC)

(*Left*) Shipboard dining: and inadvertent study of wealth and poverty. Menu for 6 July 1861. (Courtesy SS Great Britain Trust)

(*Above*) This sketch by a German passenger, dated 1863, shows the awnings rigged over the weatherdeck when the *Great Britain* was in the tropics. (Courtesy SS Great Britain Trust)

(*Right*) John Gray, the longest-serving captain of the *Great Britain*. (Courtesy SS Great Britain Trust)

The only known photograph of crew members of the *Great Britain* during her career as a liner, taken on a homeward-bound voyage from Melbourne in 1874, taken by J Rowland. (Courtesy SS Great Britain Trust)

Another photograph, taken by J Rowland on same voyage in 1874, showing First Class passengers relaxing on the Saloon deck. (Courtesy SS Great Britain Trust)

(*Above*) The only known photograph of the *Great Britain* as a sailing ship after her conversion in 1882. (Courtesy San Francisco Maritime Museum)

(*Right*) Poster for the *Great Britain*'s only voyage to Brisbane in 1873. (Courtesy SS Great Britain Trust)

LIVERPOOL & AUSTRALIAN NAVIGATION CO

STEAM FROM LIVERPOOL TO AUSTRALIA.

THE CELEBRATED AUXILIARY STEAM-SHIP

GREAT BRITAIN,

3209 Tons, and 500 Horse-power,

CHARLES CHAPMAN, Commander,

IS APPOINTED TO LEAVE THE RIVER MERSEY,

FOR MELBOURNE AND BRISBANE

(Landing Passengers and Cargo at Melbourne, and proceeding without delay);

TAKING PASSENGERS ALSO FOR

SYDNEY, ADELAIDE, AND NEW ZEALAND,

ON SATURDAY THE 25th OCTOBER, 1873.

This magnificent and far-famed Ship **has made the passage out to Melbourne in the unprecedented short time of 53 days.** She affords an opportunity for Passengers to reach Australia in almost as short a time as by the Overland Route, *viâ* Southampton, without incurring the very heavy expenses attendant thereon, and avoiding entirely the discomfort of frequent changes. Her Saloon arrangements are perfect, and combine every possible convenience, Ladies' Boudoir, Baths, etc.; and her noble passenger decks, lighted at intervals by sideports, afford unrivalled accommodation for all classes.

FARES,

Including Steward's Fees, the attendance of an experienced Surgeon, and all Provisions of the best quality.

	TO MELBOURNE.	TO BRISBANE.
AFTER SALOON.. POOP	60 and 70 Guineas	66 and 76 Guineas
AFTER SALOON.. BELOW	55 „ 60 „	61 „ 66 „
SECOND CLASS (on Deck)	25 „ 30 „	28 „ 33 „
THIRD CLASS	18 „ 20 „	21 „ 26 „
STEERAGE	15 „ 16 „	18 „ 19 „

Children under Twelve Years, Half-price. Infants under Twelve Months, Free.

In accordance with the Passengers Act, Wines, Spirits, and Malt Liquors will be supplied on board at very moderate prices.

Passengers booked to be forwarded from MELBOURNE, by the first opportunity, to SYDNEY, ADELAIDE, and HOBART TOWN, also to HOKITIKA, OTAGO, and LYTTELTON, at an extra charge of 6 Guineas Saloon, 3 Guineas other Classes. To AUCKLAND and WELLINGTON, 8 Guineas Saloon, 4 Guineas other Classes. To LAUNCESTON, 4 Guineas Saloon, and 2 Guineas other Classes —for which separate Forwarding Tickets will be issued in Liverpool.

The *Great Britain* marooned in Sparrow Cove in the Falkland Islands, photographed by Karl Kortum in 1966. (Courtesy Karl Kortum)

The *Great Britain* secure on her pontoon and on her way home in May 1970, photographed by Ewan Corlett. (Courtesy Revd Ewan Corlett)

the *Great Britain* left Valletta for the Crimea, where she embarked a brigade of the Sardinian army commanded by General Fanti.

Typhus was raging in the east. The authorities in Piedmont had been more active than the British in their preventative measures, establishing an isolation camp at La Spezia. 'By the time the troops arrive', prognosticated *The Times* correspondent gloomily, 'we shall no doubt have the annual menace of cholera in addition.' On 28 April, the *Great Britain* disembarked the brigade into five days quarantine in the camp before returning to Malta.

On 24 May, William Howard Russell, *The Times* War Correspondent in the Crimea, reported that the *Great Britain* had carried the 30th and 55th Regiments of Foot from Balaclava. Both had suffered cruelly in the fighting, losing half their strength, killed, wounded and missing. The ship was in Marseilles on 4 June, probably to drop off high-ranking passengers to take the train back to England.

On her return to Britain, the ship was restored to her owners. She had transported over 25,000 British, French, Turkish, Swiss and Italian troops. The range and mobility that the Royal Navy's Auxiliary Transports had given the Allied cause had made a vital contribution to the victory.

The Young Doctor

At the end of the war, the *Great Britain*'s owners spent some of the handsome profits they had gained from her leasing on a refit under Captain Gray's direction. Her four masts, including Brunel's 'Monday' and 'Saturday', were replaced by three massive square-rigged ones and a huge bowsprit. The mainmast was probably the largest ever built. It consisted of four oak trees banded together. It rose 95 feet above the deck and weighed 18 tons. Another new feature was the stern frame that was designed to lift the propeller from the water when the ship operated under sail alone. The shaft was withdrawn from the screw, 'telescope fashion', by an engineer with a team of five men operating from a small chamber below the waterline. They communicated with the deck through a speaking tube with a bell attached. The screw was pulled up, with a slider running from the frame, by a chain from the capstan.

On 16 February 1857, the ship sailed again to Australia. The position of Ship's Doctor had been taken by 21 year-old Samuel Archer, who had recently qualified at University College Hospital. Although there were 469 passengers, only 16 were in the After Saloon, so he was able to occupy one of the best staterooms. A keen naturalist, he kept a shipboard journal, which evinces more interest in the wildlife he observed than in his fellow passengers, so he may not have been the most sympathetic of doctors.

On the return voyage, the ship called again at Mindelo. Samuel was relieved to see land after the long passage from Melbourne, but the joy was short-lived when the Health Officer came on board and told him that there was smallpox on the island. Six months before, two-thirds of the inhabitants had died in a cholera epidemic. All that the survivors could do was to make a heap of the corpses outside the town and burn them. Afterwards they built a stone wall around the site of the funeral pyre. Next morning, Captain Gray went ashore with Samuel Archer and the Purser to call on the British Consul. Samuel came to the conclusion reached by Robert Saddington four years before. 'Mr Miller is a very gentlemanly fellow who has been out here for twenty years and how a man could remain in so miserable a place I cannot conceive.'

The English papers had just arrived and they read of the mutiny in India and the number of merchant ships that the Admiralty had requisitioned as troop transports. It cannot have failed to have cross their minds that the *Great Britain* might be taken back into the Transport Service on her return to Liverpool.

There had been no rain on the island for nearly five years, but that morning, after leaving the consulate, Samuel Archer walked on the beach with a friend and was caught in heavy showers. He was relieved that the heat was less intense, and he could wear his greatcoat with its capacious pockets in which he could put the shells he collected as he indulged his passion for Natural History. After a short rest, they decided to climb the mountain. They edged along a ridge with a sheer drop on either side, but were 'so glad to be ashore after seventy days of water that we did not think of it'. From the summit they had a fine view over the pretty bay to 'the island of Antonio while all around were craggy mountains and plains of lava unrelieved by a single tree. Not a human being was in site [*sic*].' Heavy clouds were gathering, so they decided to return. When they got back to the beach they were in an awful mess. Samuel's white trousers were soaked and covered in sand and clay, so that he 'much resembled a bricklayer'. Next morning Samuel went ashore again, but returned when he met a passenger who told him that one of the men coaling the ship had been struck by a winch-handle, which had fractured his skull. He returned on board to treat him. The coaling was completed that afternoon and the ship got under way again at six o'clock.

On her return to Liverpool, the *Great Britain* was indeed requisitioned as a troop transport, and on 24 September, she embarked for Queenstown.

NINE

'Our Kingdom of *Great Britain*'

The reinforcement of the army in India was proceeding apace. As the *Great Britain* entered Queenstown harbour on 25 September she passed the Steam Transport *Italian*, carrying troops to India. In the harbour were HMS *Hawke* and HMS *La Hogue* and the troop transport, SS *Austria*. Next day, Government Inspectors came aboard to inspect the accommodation and supplies and declared themselves 'highly pleased'.

Samuel Archer spent the ten days before the troops embarked on sightseeing and visiting, making an excursion to kiss the Blarney Stone. He also pursued his professional interests. He found the South Infirmary in Cork City 'very dirty and bare looking'. At the Pauper Lunatic Asylum, his progressive attitudes came to the fore. He liked the building, 'but there seemed to be very little attention paid to amusing the people. The place was exceedingly clean but the walls were quite bare: not a plant nor a picture in the whole place.' His duties on the outward passage to India would be restricted to the crew. Each of the regiments due to embark had a number of surgeons as part of its complement.

On 5 October, the baggage of the 8th Royal Irish Hussars was brought down river and stowed away as quickly as possible. After lunch, the soldiers arrived in two batches, together with a detachment of the 56th Regiment of Foot. The scene was one of confusion and bustle, Samuel Archer noted that 'some few' of the men had 'seen a great deal of service'. This was something of an understatement. The regiment had charged with the Light Brigade at Balaclava. On receiving the inexplicable order to charge, a number of the troopers had lit their pipes, 'as if conscious that soldierly etiquette was no longer of any account, and that they might as well take with composure the desperate task before them'.

Amongst those joining the ship with the 8th Hussars was Mrs Fanny Dubely, the witty and vivacious wife of the regimental paymaster, Captain Henry Dubely. She was a talanted amateur artist and, as befits the wife of a cavalry officer, a fearless horsewoman. She had gained a special dispensation to accompany her husband to the Crimea and had watched the disastrous charge from the opposite side of the legendary valley of death from her husband, who was on Lord Lucan's staff.

At four o'clock, the *Austria* departed, carrying the 94th Regiment of Foot to Kurrachee. The soldiers gave three cheers as they passed the *Great Britain*. That evening, Samuel Archer took Dr Taylor of the 56th ('who seemed a very pleasant fellow') and the Major in command on a tour of the ship.

Next day at 3pm, the 17th Lancers, who had also charged at Balaclava, came down river to join the ship. Their regimental band played *Cheer Boys Cheer* and the band of the Hussars also struck up as they came alongside, 'the men hurrahing in fine style'. All the troops were on board by seven, but there was no room below to store their baggage, so it was scattered over the decks in great confusion. Samuel Archer admired their 'handsome' uniform. He preferred it to the Hussars' blue with yellow facings that reminded him of the Artillery. The regiment's Senior Surgeon, Mr Mockler, was 'a very curious old fellow. I should think the oldest man in the ship'.

That evening, the wind began to blow so strongly that another anchor was put out. Despite this, as it grew to hurricane strength, the ship was dragged up the estuary and nearer the shore. The main topsail was blown overboard. The waves crashing against the sides threw spray as high as the mainmast and water came tumbling down the gangways saturating the unfortunate soldiers on the lower decks. 'Anything like the way the British soldiers were sick cannot be described', wrote Mrs Dubely. Even Captain Gray was a sufferer, which made him highly irascible. She did not get up for two days and then was under the care of the doctor.

> I was so weak and exhausted. The fact is that the Crimea has done me up and I am too old and shaken to bear much more. My pluck is coming back now, but generally I sit by myself and cry ... It is like dying and being transferred to another existence.

She was just 24.

Next morning the wind had abated and steam was raised, but it was still too windy to sail, so another miserable day was spent lying in the harbour. At four o'clock next day, the anchor was weighed at last. The men cheered heartily and the two regimental bands played popular airs. The wind rose to gale force again that evening. 'The decks below and above were in a beastly state from the men being sick', wrote Samuel Archer. He was alarmed when a lot of water was shipped. 'The old vessel looked and was in a very uncomfortable condition.' He stood in for Dr Taylor, who was so sick that he could not get up. Next day the weather improved and he went on a tour of inspection with Assistant Surgeon Cleary of the 17th and supervised the scattering of lime chloride to sterilise the vomit-covered decks.

With the improvement in the weather, most on board recovered, but two men were unable to rally. 'One, they say, will never recover so long as the ship is in motion', wrote the sympathetic Mrs Dubely. 'Fancy allowing him to come out.' The ship was overcrowded for such a long voyage. This led to chaos at dinner. A small group of officers arranged to dine an hour later at 5 o'clock. Fanny Dubely was gratified that champagne was served at table on Wednesdays and Sundays. A week into the voyage, the claret was opened. 'The soda water they keep for the Tropics. The tea I cannot touch – and generally breakfast by myself on sago or something like that.'

She was cheering up and recovering her humour. 'Given at our Palace on the Port side of our kingdom of "Great Britain", supposed to be off the Cape', she wrote to her sister in Alresford. 'I find it pleasant enough acting Queen. My reign is absolute.' Fanny enjoyed listening to the regimental bands on deck each afternoon. 'They have an admirable collection of Opera and some lovely valses.' The seats had been removed, but Colonel Morris of the 17th gallantly presented her with a very comfortable chair. Captain Gray, ever a ladies' man, often came and sat with her. She found him very jolly and 'most kind and attentive'.

In the evenings the men sang on deck. Samuel Archer was impressed by the quality of their voices. As the ship entered tropical waters, the men were issued with smocks and trousers made of duck.[1] The East India Company had thoughtfully provided a library of 500 volumes on board. 'A thing Government would not have done', Fanny declared. Samuel Archer was a voracious reader. He devoured a novel called *Margaret Maitland* and began Charles Reade's bestseller, *It's Never too late to Mend.* Four days later he sat in the crossyard reading *Oliver Twist.*

Sao Vincente

The ship bunkered at Mindelo. The indefatigable Mr Miller came aboard at the entrance to the bay and went ashore with Captain Gray to find a pilot, but the man procured was not very competent. As the *Great Britain* steamed into the harbour, she collided with an American ship and lost her foretopmast stunsail boom. As she anchored, immense numbers of fish teamed in the clear waters and leapt at the biscuit and refuse thrown overboard. Some enterprising natives came alongside in a boat, bringing fishing rods and lines which soon sold.

1 Strong twilled sailcloth.

After dinner, Samuel Archer went ashore with the Reverend Mr Bull, Regimental Chaplain to the 17th and two medics in a boat rowed by two black boys 'dressed in very ragged shirts and an apology for trousers'. The old town was as depressing as ever. Some black soldiers stood outside a miserable guardhouse.

> Black people swarmed in every direction ... We went into several shops in most of which nothing but drinks of several kinds were sold, but in one place there was a large quantity of ground nuts brought from the African coast which are very much used by the people here as food. We saw two billiard rooms and at one ... bought a bottle of Limonada Cabosa for which we paid half a crown.

Samuel spent his time ashore collecting marine specimens from rock pools and set up a small aquarium in his cabin.

'I never saw so barren a rock as St Vincent', wrote Fanny Dubely.

> It was like walking on cinder. Not a tree, no grass – not even a goat. Only two or three ponies belonging to the Consul. I did not even see a dog. Three large burying places and a tall monument to a Captain Cole RE who died at sea.

Unlike most visitors, Fanny's artistic soul led her to find a rare beauty in the local people.

> The natives are bronze colour and mostly either entirely naked, or else the women with their one garment tucked in round their waists. I never saw such perfection of grace in form of movements. If all the young women had been struck into bronze just as they stood, they would have made statues perfect in graceful outline. They all wear strings of beads round the neck. One of the officers of the 17th purchased one for me ... It is very difficult to induce them to part with their necklace.

On 20 October, a Sardinian steamer came into port. On board was the Prince Bonaparte, whose brother Jerome the Dubelys had known well in the Crimea.

> He was dying of decline[2] and sent for our doctors. They ordered him ashore to Mr Miller's, our consul ... His gratitude at getting ashore was wonderfully great, but it came too late. Next morning the Consul's flag hung half mast high.

The *Great Britain* departed next morning.

---

2 Tubercular phthisis.

On 25 October over 70 men who had charged with the Light Brigade were given an extra glass of grog to mark the third anniversary of the action. Regular shooting practice maintained military alertness. On 26 October, the 8th tested their new carbines by firing at bottles and at a barrel hanging over the stern. Their aim was good, the line being severed and several bottles smashed. Marine life also provided targets. One evening a school of porpoise was fired upon. One appeared to be wounded and plunged down headfirst. As the ship moved southwards, the stern became crowded with Cape Pigeons and albatross. The regimental cornets were always taking potshots at them. 'One comfort is', wrote the witty Mrs Dubely, 'that as long as we have coals on board, even if one is shot we shall not be becalmed like the Ancient Mariner.'

Boredom was setting in and the heat making people more irascible. A private in the 56th was court-martialed in the saloon for threatening a sergeant. The tribunal was presided over by five officers in dress uniform. The sentence of 50 lashes was announced next day, but it was later commuted to six weeks hard labour.

Fanny Dubely was tiring of the monotonous seaboard fare. 'Our provisions are getting very nasty – nearly all salt – in fact the ship is badly found in everything but liquor.' She could not wait for their arrival in Cape Town. 'The very thought of being on <u>land</u> – to say nothing of on <u>horseback</u>, seems too delightful to contemplate.'

Boredom may have been the cause of a fight on deck on 5 November. A dragoon climbed the rigging to get a better look, leaned over too far and fell into the sea. The ship was travelling at a good 9 knots, so he passed the stern 'like a flash of lightning'. The day was fine but there was a heavy swell. The cry of 'Man overboard' surged up from every throat. Colonel Morris of the 17th threw a lifebuoy and the man swam to it. The engines were stopped immediately. The Captain rushed on deck and took immediate command. 'Lower away the gig! Cram down the helm – Gentlemen – for God's sake lend a hand and cram her down!' Fanny Dubely watched the gig go over the side 'like a live thing'. The five hands pulled admirably, but the man was already a mile astern. 'We now and then lost sight of the boat, men and all', wrote Samuel Archer.

> as they sank into the trough of the sea. Then again they would rise to the top of the wave so that we could see the keel. It gives one a very good idea of the vast extent of the sea when you see a small boat tossing about on it ...

Fanny Dubely could barely discern the man's head.

> Such a speck in the boundless sea – more than 3000 miles from land and all his hope in the receding ship. The men pulled as for their own lives – and at last he was caught, floating on his chest on the buoy senseless, and full of salt water – when he came on board he had two fits and was playing Hi Cocklorum[3] on deck in the evening.

With his tight schedule, Captain Gray cannot have been pleased that a valve in the air pump had given when the engines were stopped abruptly. Several hours were also lost while the screw was raised for repair.

Cape Town

Apprehension about the news from India increased as the ship neared The Cape. As she entered port on 17 November, another large steamer was seen to be berthed. It was thought that this might be the *Austria*, which had preceded them out of Queenstown, but when the pilot came on board, he revealed to loud cheers that it was the P&O liner *Himalaya*,[4] which had arrived from India two days before with the tidings that Delhi had fallen to the British and Lucknow had been relieved by General Havelock's column.

The necessity for a fast turnaround meant that the stay in port would be just two days. Samuel Archer went ashore with the Reverend Mr Bull. Cape Town reminded him of home, but there were such surprises as the curious conical headgear worn by the Hottentots over their long black hair and the exotic ostrich plumes sported in their hats by the hansom cabbies. After buying souvenirs they went into a large Lutheran church, where it transpired that the five-yearly Synod was taking place. A venerable old man with a long beard led in a procession of nearly 100 ministers from all over Cape Colony. The congregation rose as the Colonial Governor entered in full uniform before the service began in Afrikaans. After a walk round the Botanical Gardens, they adjourned to a hotel for lunch, which was followed by the most delectable oranges Samuel had ever tasted, 'so juicy you could hardly peel them'.

The Dubelys hired a barouche and four and drove into the countryside, 'half desert, half tangled foliage', which Fanny found a joy. At Constantia, she picked oranges off the trees and gathered

---

3 The term is not in the O.E.D., but it certainly implies that the man had recovered!
4 The SS *Himalaya*, built in 1853, was the first ship to be commissioned that was comparable in size to the *Great Britain*. She survived in Portsmouth Harbour until the Second World War when she was sunk by German bombers. Her sunken hulk remains there.

handfuls of arum, oleander, lilies and roses. She was delighted when a little Cape Fox stole across their path. Yet even this paradise was flawed. 'The Fleas here', she complained, 'laugh the Turkish fleas to scorn.' Next day they rode around Table Mountain and admired the glorious view over the 'vast plain, dotted with white English homesteads'. She hated leaving this beautiful land. 'Our ship goes out again in a few hours', she lamented, 'and we shall have seen the last of the Cape – a place I shall never forget.'

'Se Serrer'

Late on 18 November, the ship embarked on the last leg of her long journey. The weather had turned and a gale was blowing. The wind intensified as she hit the heavy swell of the open sea. 'It wasn't no use having dinner that day', Captain Gray was heard to remark, 'for 'twould all be wasted.' It was the worst night of Samuel Archer's life.

> The ship rolled more heavily than I had known her to do before, the cabin creaked as if it was coming to pieces. The men were practising the double shuffle overhead to keep their feet warm and to add to my misery I had a frightful toothache all night. I had to get up several times just to make bottles etc secure and just as I was going to sleep to see Mr Hodson who had cut his foot on a piece of glass. It was no use going to bed again so I went on deck and found that the sea was going down and the day very fine and clear ... The old ship was still rolling and several times the bridge boats were in the water, but she did not ship much fore and aft.

Captain Gray steered well clear of the treacherous coast where, five years before, the troopship, HMS *Birkenhead*, which had helped to pull the *Great Britain* off Dundrum Beach, had been wrecked with the loss of 485 lives.

As the ship re-entered tropical waters, the weather turned to an 'unutterable calm'. Captain Gray was unperturbed. The fierce winds had driven the ship before them, so he had 40 tons of surplus coal to steam away. As the sun grew more intense, prickly heat covered everybody with spots and irritation. The stokers suffered terribly. Poor Colonel Morris, who had received a sword cut to his head during the Charge at Balaclava, was in great pain and Fanny Dubely thought he would not be able to stay long in India.[5] She was already

---

5 With the remnants of the 17th Lancers, Colonel Morris had charged a mass of cavalry beyond the Russian guns and driven them back in disarray. He died in India from the effects of the heat on the iron plate in his head.

anticipating their social life. 'As soon as we land, Henry will leave his card with Lord Elphinstone and Sir Henry Somerset, which will get us into Government House society. The only society I fancy into which I will care to go ...'

Yet the sensitivity to suffering that the traumas of campaign life had given her had not deserted her. One afternoon, as the band was playing, one of the doctors came on deck and ordered them to desist, since a trooper of the 17th was dying of rheumatic fever. 'It has gloomed us all', wrote Fanny, 'being our first casualty since we left and one's heart begins to "se serrer" with the old Crimean feelings at the first approach of Death.'

The evening before landfall, a farewell dinner was held. A princely subscription of £130 had been raised to buy Captain Gray an inscribed silver salver on shore. In response, he ordered extra grog all round. He was lifted on top of the meat safe while the officers and men toasted various shipboard personalities three times three. Samuel Archer was quite taken aback when he was also lifted aloft. He had had little to do with the soldiers and was surprised they even knew his name. To Fanny's mock horror, her health was proposed with great gallantry by Colonel Morris. Amidst loud cheers, he raised his glass to 'The Lady whose silver voice and merry laugh has cheered us all – and whose unfailing kindness of heart has made friends of all.'

The Apollo Bunder

Land was espied next morning at dawn. Fanny Dubely, recovered from the euphoria of the dinner, found the sight depressing. 'The "Indian shore" lies close to us – red – arid, burnt looking, uninvitingly shadeless – sandy.' The waters teemed with small fishing boats and Captain Gray frequently had to alter course to avoid stakes to which fishermen had attached their nets. A small two-masted native vessel scraped along the ship's side and left one of her sails on the jib boom. Samuel Archer could not conceive of a narrower escape.

Off Kanery Rock, ten miles from Bombay, a signal was hoisted for a pilot. Three boats raced out to claim the privilege of bringing in the great ship, but the harbour was so crowded that she had to anchor a mile offshore. The Colonels of the 8th and 17th came on board with other officers and officials who had preferred to make the long journey via the overland passage at Suez.

Next morning, Samuel Archer got up early and hailed a dinghy to go ashore, eager to collect his mail. He landed at the Apollo Bunder, a stone pier where large numbers of boats crowded.

> ... dinghies, bunder boats (which have a sort of cabin at one end), canoes (which are just like those represented in books as belonging to various savages) and larger native boats with two masts. The steps were filled with people in different costumes and speaking several different tongues. Some squatted in extraordinary postures, others standing or sitting and all and all chattering like so many monkeys. The Parsee with his curious headpiece. Mohammedans with Turbans of different colours and shapes. Hindoos with stripes of red and white paint to denote what God they worshipped. Coolies with bare heads shaved almost clean & women with silver bangles round their ankles and wrists and large rings through their noses, ears and on their toes and fingers. To a stranger it was a most amusing and interesting sight.

At the top of the steps, he was mobbed by drivers – 'Palanquin[6] Sahib', 'Buggy Sahib', but after asking the way from a Parsee who spoke good English, he decided to walk the short distance to the Post Office. He crossed the drawbridge and moat into the old walled city, which reminded him of Marseilles with its whitewashed houses, whose projecting eaves provided shelter for crows, kites and pigeons. At the Post Office, he found that letters could not be collected until ten, so he returned to the ship. Fresh supplies had been brought on board and he ate a hearty breakfast of eggs, bread and butter and coffee with fresh milk.

Shortly after ten, he went ashore again with the Reverend Mr Bull and some officers of the 56th. After arranging to meet for tiffin at the Bristol Hotel in Apollo Street, he went again to the Post Office with Mr Bull. After collecting their mail, they admired the monuments in the Cathedral to British officers who had died in India. They paused to sample the 'capital' strawberry ices at Morina's Confectionery in Meadow Street and were at the hotel before two. There was a fine billiard room and many English people around. When their friends arrived they sat down to a delicious buffet of several cold joints, scalloped oysters, cutlets and sausages, followed by curried prawns and rice and Bombay Duck, which Samuel found a 'most excellent dish', and finished with cheese and salad, all washed down with iced beer at a total cost of 2/6d.

Mr Bull went to call on the Bishop, so Samuel joined three officers who were seeking to buy ponies and camp beds. At the regimental agents in Colabawallah Street, he bought a cover for his cap and some cheroots. Then they visited several cabinetmakers and saw the most beautiful carved chairs, but no decent beds. They hired two

---

6 A covered litter for one, usually carried by four or six bearers.

buggies to visit the native town and, *en route*, inspected ponies on sale on the Esplanade, but did not buy any. The native quarter was even more 'curious' than the town within the fort. The people looked 'squalid and dirty'. The shops had no windows and the shopkeepers squatted on their haunches among their wares 'in what appears to an Englishman a most unnatural posture'.

He was fascinated that each street was dedicated to a particular commodity: one to spices, another to silver bangles, a third to the copper pans which were used for cooking and water carrying.

> It is quite a picturesque sight to see a Hindoo woman carrying two or three of these on her head, shining in the sun, her ankles and wrists manacled with glass and silver ornaments which make a pleasant jingle as she steps and herself draped in a silk scarf wrapped around her.

Not finding what they were seeking, they drove out into the country, passing small mosques and Hindu temples and grotesquely carved and painted houses. Samuel was overwhelmed by the luxuriant vegetation. Graceful coconut palms towered above their heads. Beneath grew paw paws, mangoes, oleander, pomegranates and many other plants, which he could not identify.

As it was getting dark, they returned to Bombay and watched the sepoys parading on the Esplanade, fine, tall, well-drilled men. That he expressed no apprehension about the very caste of soldier that had begun the Mutiny is indicative of the level to which order had been restored. He went down to the Apollo Bunder with the intention of returning to the ship, but on the pier he met Assistant Surgeon Rudd of the 8th, who was conveying sick hussars to the Colabar Hospital, which he said was only half a mile away, so despite feeling tired Samuel decided to go with him. Although he rode in Rudd's palanquin for most of the way, the half-mile seemed endless and turned out to be more like 2½. After inspecting a ward and taking a glass of wine with the surgeon, they took a buggy back to the hotel.

When they arrived it was past seven and already dark. Five army officers from the *Great Britain* were there and they all decided to stay the night. The hotel was very crowded, so they were put into a large room known as the Barrack, which contained seven four-poster beds. At dinner, Samuel tried pomfret for the first time and found it delicious, as was the curry ('which is universally eaten') and the banana pudding. For dessert there was a variety of fruits including persimmons, something else he had never eaten before, all washed down with 'most refreshing' iced champagne.

After dinner, they went for a drive in the cool evening and were entertained by a loquacious and amusing Parsee driver. The streets were almost deserted, so they returned and retired early. Samuel spent a torrid night. The beds were mere mattresses with a pillow covered by a sheet, surrounded by a gauze mosquito net.

> One or two fellows managed to get inside and though they did not bite they greatly annoyed me by their buzzing. I at last got to sleep but it was not long before I woke with an uncomfortable sort of general titillation and on looking minutely found that bugs were running over me in every direction. Horrified, I immediately got up and dressed, determined to have the mosquitoes than the other enemies.

He tied a handkerchief over his head and passed the remainder of the night on the sofa, 'occasionally disturbed by the mewing of a large yellow cat which kept prowling about'. He resolved not to spend another night on shore.

Morning came as a blessed relief. The group got up early and visited the camp of the 8th Hussars, where everything was in a state of confusion with baggage lying about everywhere. The bug-ridden night did not deter them from returning to the hotel for tiffin. Later they went to the Bunder where the 56th had just disembarked and the first contingent of the 17th was on its way from the ship. After saying his farewells, Samuel Archer took a dinghy back to the *Great Britain.* The ship felt quite deserted, with only some 200 men left aboard. Yet the evening was not without incident. One of the remaining lancers, who had been 'somewhat out of his mind' for some time, tried to drown himself by leaping overboard. He was soon rescued. Since Cleary, the Regimental Surgeon, was ashore, Samuel was the only doctor available and had to attend him. Cleary returned at midnight. But Colonel Rose, who Samuel Archer thought 'a fidgety old fellow', would not let him go to bed in case the man made another attempt.

Next morning, the two doctors went ashore to arrange the transfer of the deranged lancer to an asylum. The Medical Superintendent lived in the suburb of Mazagoan, some three miles out of town, so they hired a buggy. The horse that drew it was possessed of singular habits. Every so often it stopped dead in its tracks. Sometimes it would fall down on its hind legs and occasionally it would wheel the buggy round in a circle. There was a ditch at the side of the road and Samuel was worried that the nag would cavort into it. At the official's house, the eccentric horse was fed and watered, so they expected its behaviour to improve on the return journey, but when they had got halfway, it stood stock-still and refused to move, obliging them to return in another vehicle.

On the following afternoon, the remainder of the 17th paraded on deck before embarking in barges. As they left, they gave three hearty cheers which the sailors returned. Samuel Archer went ashore with the officers on a small steam tug. He thought that General Sir Henry Somerset, the Commander of the Bombay Army, looked a 'feeble old man' who was 'certainly unfit for his post'. The men marched to the station with the band playing. After saying his farewells, Samuel Archer met two pals in the 8th Hussars to go to a circus. A Big Top had been erected at the bottom of the Esplanade. The artistes were European and very ordinary. 'There were several very nobby people present who would no more think of going to such a miserable place at home than they would of flying, but here there is so little amusement.' The 'Fourth Class' sat behind bamboo palisades and looked 'like so many wild animals'. He was growing weary of Bombay's charms, but things looked up on Christmas Eve when he was invited to dine in the mess of the 8th Hussars. It was a grand occasion. The regimental silver looked 'very handsome' and each officer's servant stood behind his chair.

Open Day

The *Great Britain*'s presence in Bombay had aroused great interest and it was decided to hold what was to prove the most exotic open day in the ship's long history on 27 December. Both gangways were lowered and the visitors arrived at two. Samuel Archer counted 15 boats, each carrying around 20 passengers, waiting to offload at just one gangway. 'The row alongside was fearful. Boatmen were shouting at the tops of their voices; passengers talking, laughing and calling to one another and altogether it was a perfect Babel.'

He stood fascinated to watch the people coming aboard. He was particularly struck by the 'Musselmen', with their enormous beards and moustaches.

> Men, women and children from all classes swarmed on board and all in their best. The quantity of gold and silver ornaments and jewels on some was enormous. Some of the women wore six or eight massive gold chains round their necks and gold rings in which jewels were strung in their ears and noses whilst all had heavy bangles round the arms and ankles. I went round the ship with several parties of Hindoos and Parsees and got much information from them. The gentlemen pointed out to me the different castes as they passed. The Parsee children are generally very pretty and I was puzzled for a long time to tell the boys from the girls for they all dress very much alike, but I afterwards found that the girls all wore bangles around the wrist whilst the boys never do. I was surprised to see what a small size of glass they managed

to squeeze over the hand and was told that when once on, they never come off unless broken.

The visitors were not restricted to people. On the morning of 20 January, as they prepared to leave for home, Samuel Archer showed a local physician, round the ship. In the engine room, two monkeys made a furious attack on them, but they escaped after having their hair pulled.

'Very Agreeable People'

Since she was no longer required for military duties, the agents had advertised passages for the *Great Britain*'s voyage home. Some 30 people took up the offer. They represented something of a cross-section of British India and included General Curzon Wylie, who was in the service of the East India Company; Mr Sheldon, a missionary on sick leave; two officers in the Bengal Army whose regiments had mutinied and various officers' wives and children. Samuel Archer thought that they seemed, on the 'whole to be very agreeable people'.

It had been arranged that he should take charge of a wealthy young man called Inverarity, whose distinctly odd behaviour had caused him to be diagnosed as suffering from some form of mental disturbance. His physician, Dr Arbuckle, brought him on board. After giving Samuel Archer some case notes, hints on how to handle his charge and a cash float for expenses, Dr Arbuckle returned ashore. Inverarity wanted to go with him and became very agitated when he was told he could not. Samuel pacified him by playing chess with him. At four o'clock, the ship passed down the harbour, saluting the American frigate, *Gormanstown.* Although the wind was strong at first, it was followed by a lengthy calm, which 'agreed very well with the passengers though very annoying to the Captain'.

On the first Sunday aboard, Mr Sheldon read the morning service and preached a long sermon. 'I am afraid he will get very prosy when he picks up strength', Samuel Archer observed wryly. On the following Sunday he wrote with some satisfaction that his attention had been distracted from the service by numerous shoals of flying fish and a school of porpoises.

In the evenings, Samuel Archer played parlour games with the passengers. He delegated some of the responsibility for his charge to Mr James, one of the stewards. It was not an easy task. Mr Inverarity had become enamoured of a lady passenger and wrote her a proposal of marriage. He was shocked to hear that she was already married and remained below all evening. After this incident, he was much more subdued.

After narrowly avoiding a waterspout off the Comoros, the ship berthed at Cape Town on 24 February in stormy weather. Shortly after breakfast, Samuel Archer and Mr James went ashore with Inverarity, who went straight to a bank and made out a blank cheque for £1000. The teller sent him on to the Oriental Bank, which was deputed to handle his affairs. There he was told that he could not get any money without a letter of credit. He became quite agitated, but brightened up when Dr Archer told him that he was holding funds for him. He celebrated this windfall by buying a new topper and hiring a carriage and four at Kammemeyer's Livery Stables. He had developed an obsession with driving out to the shop of someone called 'Nana Shute' at Constantia. Samuel Archer soon decided that this was a figment of his imagination.

It was the height of the southern summer and Samuel Archer was delighted in the profusion of plants that grew only in hothouses at home. At Little Constantia, they drove through an archway into a vineyard. The old proprietor invited them to taste the wines, but when Inverarity discovered that this was not Nana Shute's, he insisted on returning to Cape Town immediately.

After dining on the way back to Cape Town, they got back to the wharf at four, intending to return to the ship, but Inverarity's eccentricity prevailed again. He announced that he was going to stay for a year with Baron Lorenz, a local resident he knew and marry one of his daughters. Threats and attempts at persuasion proved useless, his mind was made up and he refused to return. In the end Samuel Archer gave in and suggested they take a cab to the Baron's house. After driving round for about an hour without finding it, Inverarity told the driver to return to the jetty. When they got there, he became vexatious, although it was he who had given the order. Samuel bought a street directory, looked up the address and they took another cab in which he waited while James took Inverarity up to the house. They soon returned when it was discovered that the Baron had no daughters! To their surprise, Inverarity was highly amused at his mistake and was happy to return to the ship.

Next day, Dr Archer left Inverarity with James and went ashore with General Curzon Wylie. They visited a barber, who was full of the news that Macomo, the 'celebrated Kaffir chief', was in prison in the town.[7] After doing some shopping, they decided to have a look at

---

7 Macomo was one of the Xhosa chiefs who in 1857, in the face of the aggressive policies of annexation pursued in the eastern Cape by the Governor, Sir George Gray, (who Samual Archer saw at the Lutheran Synod), slaughtered all their cattle and destroyed their crops in the expectation that this would cause their ancestors to rise from their graves and drive the white invaders into the sea.

him and took a cab to the 'small and miserable prison', which housed only some 20 inmates. After signing their names, they were admitted by the turnkey.

> In a cell of considerable size we found this celebrated character with one of his wives and two of his councillors. His wife was seated on a platform a little raised from the floor and dressed in a flowing print gown with a handkerchief tied over her head. She was the principle one out of ten which he had. Macomo himself, a grey, woolly headed old nigger, sat near her on the edge of the platform and looked like any ordinary nigger, but with a cunning expression in his eyes. He grinned at us and muttered something which we could not understand ... [He] is said to be a wonderful shot with the rifle.

Two days later, the *Great Britain* sailed for home. The agents had again been active and lots of passengers came aboard. Samuel Archer thought they looked a 'very rough lot'.

The *Great Britain* arrived back in Liverpool on 10 April 1857. After a refit, the owners sent her to New York for the first time in eleven years, a trip repeated in the following year. They seem to have been uncertain as to how best to use her. The Gold Rush was over and the lucrative American run appeared tempting, but it was Australia that prevailed. In the next sixteen years she made 27 voyages there, circumnavigating the globe each time. Apart from the occasional refit – she underwent an extensive one costing £20,000 in 1863 – she was continuously in service during this period.

TEN

'We're Bound for Great Australia'

Comparatively few people crossed the Atlantic on the *Great Britain*, but many thousands sailed with her to Australia. It is estimated that she carried the forebears of some 250,000 modern Australians to what a popular song of the day called *A New and Happy Home Far Away*. After the waves of immigrants engendered by the Gold Rush abated, the Government of Victoria entered into contacts with the *Great Britain*'s Agents 'for the conveyance from Liverpool of thousands of Assisted Emigrants'. Those departing under the scheme passed through the Emigration Depot at Birkenhead, where they received their warrants for travel in Steerage. In 1862-3, 23,997 passengers were conveyed from Liverpool alone. Of these, 22,409 were carried on the three big lines: 'Black Ball' (the then owners of the *Great Britain*), 'Eagle' and 'White Star'.[1]

'A Motley Company'

From surviving accounts, it is possible to build a picture of what life was like in the world in miniature contained on a great ship. 'Tis wondrous to stand a little way off and quietly look on', wrote the Chief Steward, John Campbell. 'Here on a small scale do we see all the human passions at work.'

Many passengers stayed overnight in Liverpool before embarking: The Crooked Billet Hotel was a favoured resting place. Next day they braved the exorbitant demands of those who 'craved payment in language which only "duly licensed" cabmen, "duly licensed"

1 In 1863, the three companies merged to form the Australian and Eastern Navigation Company, with a virtual monopoly on the route. Despite promising that 5000 of its shares would be issued in Australia, the five directors suborned most of the issue to themselves and their families. After a two-year enquiry, the General Purposes Committee of the Stock Exchange refused to set a settling day for transactions in the shares of the new company. The inter-related Liverpool shipowners were adept at passing vessels between each other, so, after the failure, the *Great Britain* passed into the ownership of the Eagle Line.

porters and "duly licensed" runners can employ. By-and-by Liverpool may be able to boast a corps of "duly licensed" pickpockets.' To those embarking, the ship seemed like a small town, 'well lit up in all directions'. The scene was one of confusion, the decks crowded with passengers, some looking for their berths, others for a missing box, 'all wearing an anxious and unsettled look'.

'The first entrance to the enormous ship quite bewildered me', wrote an Irish nun, Mary Mulquin, 'so you would imagine you would never get through its mazes.' Once they had penetrated this labyrinth to their cabin in the ladies' section of First Class, the nuns met their stewardess. 'She promised to be all attention to us, and indeed she did not lead an idle life, having 40 beds to make up daily beside all the other items of Ladies Toilette.'

The sight of his fellow passengers intrigued a traveller in 1862. 'How various their countenances!' he thought, before his attention was diverted to the ladies' shapely ankles. He was interrupted in this reverie when an elderly gentleman tapped him on the shoulder and asked him 'in a tone ... which should have charmed the admirers of thorough bass', whether he had seen 'a couple of blankets, an endless towel, and a copy of *Punch* flying about the deck'.

> With his unaccustomed hands he had put the labels on his traps, sticking a 'Wanted on the Voyage' on a brand-new and very beautiful warming pan (a present to a maiden aunt in Australia) and a 'Not wanted on the Voyage' on his bedding. Let 'intending emigrants' remember the serious dilemma into which this ancient traveller was plunged through his own carelessness. Passengers ought to mark everything, young children and brandy bottles not excepted.

The diversity of characters was remarkable. 'What a motley company we are', wrote a traveller from Melbourne. 'Here youth abroad for a revel. There age returning with hard-won gains. Sea captains and land captains, soldiers there, fresh from Maori warfare, or browned by Indian suns. Priests, parsons and doctors – soul curers and body curers, who in some instances might be admonished to "heal themselves". Some had chased fortune from California to Victoria and wrenched from her reluctant hand their gold. An American who had fought and bled for the North during the late unhappy struggle ... Here an ex-squatter and share broker and worthy Hebrews ... Children we have too ... who are bearable enough in the day time, but are given to make night, or rather morning, hideous by their howlings.'

Although the registers show that the majority of voyagers were English, the tendency to travel in groups could give the opposite impression.[2] 'Most of the passengers here are Scotch and Irish', wrote Thomas Dunn, who travelled in the Fore Saloon in 1870. 'At our mess table out of 15 who sit down only three are English. Indeed the mother tongue is very imperfectly spoken on board.'

> We have also a sprinkling of Welshmen, Germans and a few colonials. On the whole, we agree very well together.

Some were forced to the colonies by their families because of lack of opportunity at home. One such was Daniel Higson from Preston, who left his parents and his Esther, his sweetheart, in 1869. 'I am determined to get back as soon I can', he wrote. 'The only comfort I can find is in that thought. When I get home I will not leave it again I will not leave it again if I can help it. Oh, if only they knew how miserable I am they would not oppose my coming home ...'

Others were 'remittance men' sent to the colonies by their families because of some disgrace. The regular income for their support could only be cashed *in situ*. 'Some of these young men might have been different', wrote Maggie Brown in 1854, 'who had bright prospects before them at home and very likely the flowers of the family to which they belonged, but had got so dissipated that their friends would not insist on their staying at home. The youth who possesses the finest face on board this ship belongs to that class. He is a young Englishman, a medical student and as gentlemanly a lad as ever I spoke to, poor fellow. I often feel very sad when I look at him.'

Another such unfortunate was 'Paddy', a 19 year-old Irishman, whose wealthy family sent him out to 'learn a little common sense'. A fellow passenger, Robert Tindall, was scathing about him.

> A thorough little cad, who has a certain wit about him, which has made him the centre of attraction to an admiring audience, consisting chiefly of the riff raff of the saloon – Drinks to a great extent, in fact at the beginning of the voyage was seldom sober, insomuch that the skipper had to stop his liquor.

For many, it was not their first voyage. A Shropshire farm worker, William Griffiths, who sailed to Melbourne in 1859, estimated that about a third of the passengers had travelled before. Some had returned home for a visit, or to collect their families. Wives were taking their children out to join their husbands and there were parents whose successful offspring had sent for them. For others, the voyage

---

2 It was customary to mark those passengers on the registers who were not English with S for Scottish, W for Welsh, or I for Irish. All other nationalities were lumped together under OP for 'other parts'!

represented an opportunity to redress previous failures. John Gilchrist, a Highlander who sailed in 1873, was 'one of that sort generally considered a black sheep'. He had tried farming in South America for six years, but failed. Now he was going to give it another try in Australia.

'Tis Hard to Leave One's Native Land'

Shortly before the *Great Britain* cast off, the Reverend Mr Buck of the Liverpool Mission to Seamen came on board. He was listened to intently as he preached on the text: 'Let us therefore, come boldly unto the throne of grace, that we may obtain mercy, and find grace to help us in our time of need.'

> The preacher's allusions to the homes we have left, and the 'old familiar faces' that we may never see again, brought tears to many eyes. Those among us were to be pitied, who could hear hallowed word 'Home' mentioned without the slightest emotion.

The ship possessed a German band that played as preparations were made to sail. *The Girl I left behind Me* was a popular choice. As the engine got under way, the boatswain piped his men to hoist the gangway. The gaskets were untied and the sailors sang merrily as they swung round the capstan to pull the 'ponderous cable' aboard. A favourite song when leaving Liverpool was the crew's own shanty, sung to the tune of *Cheer up Sam.*

> We're bound for great Australia, where the money goes so free,
> In the noble ship 'Great Britain', the Mistress of the sea;
> With her thousand yards of canvass, and men so stout and brave,
> As ever went aloft, or sailed upon the Atlantic wave.
> Then cheer up all, and don't let your spirits go down,
> For there's many a girl that we all know well, a waiting for us in town.

A lady passenger was touched by a line in another shanty. "Farewell and we're away, away, away" – It made me feel that indeed I was away.'

When the anchor came into view, the Blue Peter was struck and the Union Jack hoisted on the mizzen. As the *Great Britain* passed downstream she exchanged two-gun salutes with other ships. The crew was mustered, addressed by the Captain and divided into watches. A ticket inspection took place. If stowaways were discovered, they were put ashore with the pilot. They showed great ingenuity. One was found three weeks out of Melbourne. He had, in the 'coolest manner taken up an unoccupied berth in the Second Cabin and sat regularly at their table'. When he was discovered, he was sent forward to work as an ordinary seaman. Three others were taken aboard at Liverpool by their friends in boxes, installed in their cabin and sustained with food taken from the saloon. They too were put to work when discovered. Others smuggled dogs and cats aboard. When their pets were discovered, they were confiscated and their owners were obliged to offer £5 (the normal cost of a pet's passage) for them at an auction, after which they went to the highest bidders.

After the tickets had been examined, a medical inspection took place. As the passengers walked past the ship's doctor in line, he looked closely into each face. 'I never saw such a farce', snorted a lady passenger. The Liverpool Seaman and Emigrants Friend Society took advantage of the line-up to distribute improving pamphlets from the Religious Tracts Society. 'We gave to each a packet as a farewell present', wrote one evangelist, James Duck. Small books were given to children and foreigners received tracts written in their own language.

Two tugs accompanied the ship. Once clear of the harbour, 'amid tears and cheers and waving of hats and handkerchiefs', one took off friends and relations. An hour later, the other one took off the pilot, agent, company guests, evangelists and mail. The lady who had snorted at the doctor described the scene. The Captain stood on the hen house and led 'three hearty cheers which were long and lustily continued'. A shot from the starboard bow was answered by one from the pilot boat. 'And now the last connecting link with the shores of England is broken. I need not say what feelings the thought called up.'

A shipboard poet expressed the poignancy of departure.

> Tis hard to leave one's native land,
> Where youthful days were passed
> To gaze upon that shore and think
> That look may be the last.

Those who decided to take a stroll on deck found that space was allocated according to class. Notices delineated the boundaries of each 'parade ground'. After-salooners, who were fewest in number, had the entire quarterdeck; Fore-salooners had the starboard side from the quarterdeck to the funnel. The more numerous Third Class and Intermediate passengers enjoyed the same facility on the port side, while Steerage roamed freely before the funnel. Inevitably, there were frequent complaints of encroachment.

The ship had a tendency to roll and many passengers were seasick as she hit the open sea. The lady was amused to see 'so many getting sick, they take it so suddenly. Sometimes they have not time to leave the table'. The Irish nun, Mary Mulquin, found the heaving so violent that she was thrown from one end of the Ladies' Cabin into the bathroom on her back and could not rise for some time. Sister Mary Patrick, 'thinking I was doing it intentionally, began to laugh at the disaster, but instantly was taken off her feet and pitched to the opposite side, while others were laid flat in the corridor.'

'The first signs of seasickness', she wrote a little later.

> Stomach in a fearful state, discharging every few minutes, and a breaking headache. If those at home could get a 'coup d'oeuil' of our state they would both laugh and cry; no description would suffice ... certainly we would not much care if we were confined to the deep – no breakfast – only a drink of tea – most of the ladies on deck in a similar state of suffering, the gentlemen not sick, being accustomed to sea life, while some of the fair sex are ill all the way.

At 10pm, the bell sounded the order to retire. Half an hour later, the lamplighter removed the lights from the corridors. At 11pm, the officers made a tour of inspection and ordered that the private lights in the After Saloon cabins should be extinguished. Every four hours during the night, the Mate on duty made a circuit of the ship to look for fires. 'They are very watchful', wrote a passenger, 'and surely they ought to be so where there is such a level of responsibility.'

'The main thing about the voyage was that it was uncomfortable', recalled a Fore Saloon passenger, 'little room and crowded conditions. One had to wait for the others to retire before being able to go to bed.' Once this hurdle had been crossed, most passengers experienced the shock of trying to sleep in their cramped bunks. 'By 10pm, fat people had contrived to stow themselves away in narrow bunks, long people had contrived to coil themselves in short ditto, and little people had dropped off to sleep.'

'The beds are certainly not the softest in the world', wrote Mary Mulquin. 'It strikes us forcibly that people with diseased spines could never endure this rocking of the vessel for the back becomes quite tired and sore from the hard resting place, added to the fact of being liable at every moment to be cast on the face and hands or backwards.'

'Very Intimate Friends Indeed'

The rigid segregation of male and female sleeping accommodation was highly effective, although celibate shipboard romances occurred. 'Some of the young ladies and gentlemen were very intimate friends indeed', a perceptive 14 year-old, Louise Buchan, noted. In all the extant letters and journals written on the ship there is little hint of sexual impropriety. On a voyage in 1867, there was a row between two women. 'One was married and she was for thrashing the other for winking at her husband', while John Campbell, the Chief Steward, recorded in 1872 that an Italian woman in Steerage had given birth to a daughter. 'Strange stories of her trying to conceal the birth and of her husband having been in the colonies two years now.'

Robert Tindall, a young man from a Scarborough shipbuilding family, who embarked in First Class in 1873, cast a critical eye over his fellow passengers and came to negative conclusions about the fairer sex. 'No very pretty ladies, one or two moderate looking ones.' Miss Elizabeth Buxton was aged about 24. She had red hair 'and though not good features yet has a nice expression'. She read music 'capitally' and played it very well. Her sister, Mary Ann, aged 19, was 'moderately pretty, but her looks are of the common sort, rather what I would call shop-girl or bar maid-like'. She embarked on a flirtation with James Greenlee, a young Scotsman, who soon dropped her. Robert could not 'quite call him a gentleman, but he has been quite civil to me during the voyage'. 'Oh, she would be vexed if she could but see this!' he added.

The Buxton family came from a small village in Kent. Robert guessed that they had 'not seen much of the world, or at least of good society ... This has made Miss Buxton rather shy, and Miss M.A, a flirt, as no doubt this is like a coming out for her, and she wants to try her powers of command over men.' 'However they are not bad companions for the voyage', he added benignly, 'and I like the Miss Buxtons' society.'

Flirtation was the limit of most sexual liaisons, although even this could get a lass into trouble. Miss Hackforth, the 22 year-old governess to the five children of wealthy New Zealand squatters, 'got into hot water with the Elworthys for flirting with certain disagreeable men on board'.

In 1875, the Hon Georgiana Bright was appalled, when a 34 year-old lady in the After Saloon found herself an Adonis, but she demonstrated a rare, if somewhat scathing, tolerance.

> Mrs Kenneth Ferguson and young Bertie have struck upon an immense flirtation – really it makes me feel rather angry to see a woman about the same age as I am making such a fool of herself with a boy like that – such a selfish boy as he is too. But if it pleases her it does not harm me – only I am glad to say they both have the grace to be ashamed of themselves before me.

Robert Tindall considered that Miss Cottiers, 'an elderly spinster' was not 'likely to be married very soon, judging from her face and her temper'. She was in fact just 30 years old and had a greater capacity to find a man than he credited. 'Just heard she is engaged!!!!! I can hardly believe it', he wrote on the next line.

Those who transgressed against the prevailing morality were not just subjects of gossip, but could be ostracised. Mrs Hodgson had 'an unenviable reputation on board'.

> Some say she is a barmaid, some that she is a professional singer – All the ladies have cut her, as she took up very familiarly with a very shady man – In consequence she has associated with the very worst of the men – I have not had much to do with her – she has come out in an innumerable quantity of dresses – she is decidedly the fast one on board, and has obtained the name of the 'lively woman' among the sailors.

The 'shady man' was called Marvel. This must have been a *nom de voyage,* for no-one of that name appears on the register. A tall man who was fluent in French, he had a 'bad repute' in Australia. 'I avoid him as much as possible', wrote Robert, 'without being positively rude'.

An incident of latent homosexuality occurred in 1860 when a young passenger 'gathered a fancy' to the Second Mate and hung around him during his watches. The sailors decided that he was 'moonstruck' from lying on deck at night during the hot weather. He was straitjacketed and kept in the ship's hospital until deemed to be cured.

The class-ridden nature of Victorian Britain was nowhere more reflected than in the nuances of status that prevailed among the First-class passengers. Mrs Payton, a clergyman's daughter, was travelling to Sydney, to meet her husband, a naval chaplain.

> She was only married last March and is young – she can sing pretty well and play a little – she is however very injudicious and snubs some of the passengers, so she is I am afraid generally disliked.

Robert was not himself beyond making petty social judgements. Mr White was 'no gentleman by any stretch of the imagination'. Mr Elworthy had 'been in the colonies for some time and so has rather got the colonial manners'. John Andrew, a young Mancunian, was going out to work on the Elworthy's sheep station. He was 'not a gentleman, but we just get on together with small chats at intervals'. Mr Masters, a tall, athletic and well-built American, who had been wounded twice in the Civil War, was 'not a bad fellow, though hardly a gentleman'. As a German Jew, Herr Blaubaum had even less social status than a colonial. 'This sounds rather awful, but he is not a bad fellow when you get to know him.'

Despite the deprivations wrought by the ocean, a sea voyage was regarded as good for the health. One who took such a cure was George Tangye, a characteristic Birmingham manufacturer, who had risen from humble origins to own one of the biggest engineering works in the city. Robert wished that he had 'the advantage of a good education as I cannot call him a man of polished manners', but at least he was good hearted and might be 'called one of Nature's gentlemen'.[3]

Mr W H Fox from Wisconsin did possess the advantage of an education at 'a sort of American University', but unfortunately it was not Yale or Harvard. Accent was another indicator. 'Cannot be called a lady in her manner', Robert Tindall observed of Mrs Battersby, a colonial's wife, 'drops h's, but is a good hearted and a quiet person'. One of Robert Tindall's main aversions was a man called John Dalby who had 'the most sodden appearance. He had I should say a very scanty supply of brains from nature and what he had, seem all drunk away.' He regretted to note that he was a fellow Yorkshireman, but he did exhibit one Tyke trait. 'Gives out that he is a great cricketer.'

For all his disapprobation of those who failed to pass social muster, Robert conceded that they possessed qualities lacking amongst some of the more ostensibly respectable.

> There are also a good few men who are remarkable neither for their virtues or their vices, who may sink into oblivion as far as I am concerned.

'Haul Away Joe'

Every half hour through the night the watch cried 'All's well!' just one of the many sounds that permeated the life of the ship. Edward Towle reckoned that the sailors could 'do nothing without a song'. The more aware passengers soon learnt to interpret what was going on from this regular pattern. 'I have now got so used to the different songs', wrote one, 'that I know what they are doing ... as everything they do has its own song.

> Thus I know when I am awake through the night and hear the sailors sing when they are taking in the sail and when they are hoisting and when they are expecting a squall.

The nonsensical nature of the songs amused the passengers. 'Singing such ditties they haul with a will and haul together.' A

---

3 Despite his misgivings about his gentility, Robert Tindall must have cultivated Mr Tangye, for, on his return to England, he became a Director of his firm.

favourite shanty was *Haul Away Joe*, in which a solo singer gave the first line, the company took up the next two and they all hauled away on the last word: 'Joe'.

Away, haul away my pretty little Rosy
　　Away haul away
　　Haul away Joe.
Away, haul away come rock and roll me over
　　Away (&c)

Away, haul away, come roll me in the clover
　　Away (&c)

Away, haul away, wc will cither bust or bend her
　　Away (&c)

'Jimmy Riley' was another favourite hauling shanty.

Ah, la Jimmy Riley had two daughters
　　Ah, old Jimmy Riley, Oh,
Ah, old Jimmy Riley had two daughters
　　Ah, old Jimmy Riley, Oh.
Ah, one knit stockings and the other garters,
　　Ah, old Jimmy Riley, Oh,
Ah, one knit stockings and the other garters,
　　Ah, old Jimmy Riley, Oh.
Ah, old Jimmy Riley he liked brandy,
　　Ah, old Jimmy Riley, Oh,
Ah, old Jimmy Riley he liked brandy,
　　Ah, old Jimmy Riley, Oh.
Ah, old Jimmy Riley died in Pandy,
　　Ah, old Jimmy Riley, Oh.
Handy, Pandy, drinking brandy,
　　Poor Jimmy Riley, Oh.

'A Most Disagreeable Piece of Furniture'

After the first Australian voyage, the *Great Britain* ran before the trade winds past Madeira and the Canaries until she was some 500 miles from the coast of Brazil. At around 55 degrees south, she turned to run before the strong westerlies all the way to Australia.

To save precious coal, the ship spent as much time as possible under sail, but when there was no fair wind, steam was raised and four men spent a quarter of an hour lowering the stern frame into the water. 'A most disagreeable piece of furniture', complained Samuel Archer, 'the motion is as different as possible when the screw is down to what it is up. It makes a great deal of noise in the stern and is quite unpleasant in the boudoir.'

Less experienced sailors than the ship's doctor overlooked the noise and preferred the steady equilibrium of steam to the erratic tossing of the ship under sail. Mother Mary Mulquin noted that when the screw was taken off, the swaying motion caused 'a most terrible feeling at first'. A sailing ship was not 'a pleasant mode of conveyance ... the engine began its operations the next day and we were not sorry. Deo Gratias'.

Once the fires had been banked, the sails were taken in. The First and Second Officers took charge of the fore and main masts respectively and Captain Gray of the mizzenmast. 'The Captain would never hesitate to lay his own hand to a rope in an emergency. And a powerful hand he had too.' If the wind blew up again, smoke from the funnel deposited particles of soot, known as 'blacks', across the deck, to be blown into the cabins. 'Everything seems cleaner and brighter', wrote a passenger, 'except our faces, which are totally disfigured by the smuts from the chimney.'

William Routledge, who sailed to Australia as a boy in 1866, still recalled 70 years later the large capstan in the waist of the ship that was used to raise the screw. When its bars were shipped, they almost swept the width of the deck. When the wind strengthened, the crew and passengers manned them. As a fiddler played on the capstan head, they walked the screw up to a rousing chorus of 'Hurrah! Hurrah! For we'll all get blind drunk when Johnny comes marching home.'

> The swelling canvas, the straining gear, the vessel's rhythmic sway, the tramp of the men at the bar, the lilt of the chantry [*sic*], and the crash of its chorus never failed to infect the company with its contagious good humour.

'What a Monstrous Life this is'

As the ship sailed into the tropics, awnings were rigged to provide shade on deck. For those cramped in Steerage, the heat was intolerable. 'The fierce sun of the Equator', wrote one, 'has made the iron receptacle which contains us, one enormous oven in which we poor devils are baking, sweltering and sweating all day and night.' Tar dripped off the ropes. At table, oil was substituted for butter which melted too quickly to use. Every face strained with beads of perspiration 'like window panes in a flood of rain.'

'As we are approaching the Equator my lungs are gradually getting worse', wrote the Revd James Maughan. 'I cannot respire in this frightfully humid atmosphere. My attacks of dysphasia are becoming both frequent and violent, especially at night, when I can scarcely ever lie down but I awake in agony, and then have to sit for hours to recover myself.' Some relief was found on deck, but tropical storms could force passengers below. 'It really was fearful to suffer the heat', complained one lady passenger, 'everyone using their fan to try to get a breath of air.' Even the sea compounded the vulcanic atmosphere. After dark, phosphoric glares could make it seem to be on fire.

Intense homesickness had a debilitating effect on reluctant emigrants like Daniel Higson.

> What a monstrous life this is – perspiring all night without clothes on the bed; all day reading, mauling about on deck wishing to be home and almost starving ... I always wish to be home on Saturdays and Sundays more than any other days. I looked at Father's and Esther's portraits and I wished I had one of my mother. I cried when I thought that if I were at home I should be with Esther in Ashton Road or some such other place.

'All the rest of Sunday we ... sighed for the peace of our green island home', wrote the Irish nun, Mary Mulquin, 'now doubly dear from our mixing with the unbelieving multitude around. How much more desirable is our own sweet refectory to here – we could enjoy a silent hour at our accustomed meal – better than the hurry and style of the crowded saloon with piles of every imaginable dish ...'

'Well, heaven is worth the sacrifice', she concluded.

Another Irish emigrant in 1875 poignantly recorded his progress away from his homeland.

> 6 weeks since I left Gravesend.
> 7 weeks since I was in Belfast.
> 8 weeks ago I was in Bunding.
> 9 weeks ago I was in Burtonport.
> How I would like to hear from them.

Even the heavens compounded the voyager's nostalgia for home. One evening, as the ship approached the Equator, Robert Saddington stood on deck and looked at 'an old friend with whom we must soon perhaps part for ever.

> I allude to the Polar Star, but his brightness is already getting dim and we are looking forward to the new and shining Constellation of the Southern Cross. This is the last visible link to the Northern Hemisphere, but there are still many bright and shining stars which to me will never grow dim however much their brightness be over-shadowed by New Constellations.

The continued proximity of people in a confined space had its effects as the ship neared Australia. 'What a trifle gives offence here', wrote a lady passenger. Samuel Archer noted that some of the ladies and gentlemen who had been dancing in the Saloon were inclined to be quarrelsome. 'Mr McD was disposed to be violent and Mr M was in a great passion with Mr F.' 'Indeed it is a good thing that we are near the end of our voyage', he added perceptively, 'for people are beginning to find out the failings of others.'

As Melbourne approached, much 'scrubbing and rubbing' went on all over the ship. Other signs of imminent arrival could manifest themselves. Thomas Dunn noted that 'several butterflies made their appearance on deck having been blown off the land which must have been a good distance.' The shout of 'Land on the weather bow' greeted the first sighting of the Australian mainland at Cape Otway, with its revolving light and weather station. News of the ship's arrival was telegraphed to Melbourne. The coastline was thickly covered with brush and gum trees, densely forested with huge pines. So clear was the atmosphere that individual trees could be identified from 20 miles away.

After clearance from the Health Officer, the pilot came aboard to deafening cheers and told the latest news ashore: in 1861, it was the sad fate of the explorers, Burke and Wills. In the shadow of the mountain called Arthur's Seat, the ship passed into Port Philip Bay at the pretty hamlet of Queenscliff. If the ship arrived at night, sleep was impossible 'amid the melange of singing, hurrahing and drumming on tin pails which was kept up all night and long before the sun had gained mastery over the many lights which glistened on the water, the decks were thronged with groups eager to see their new home.'

'The Quiet of an Anchorage'

Within five years of the *Great Britain*'s first arrival, Melbourne had been transformed from a shantytown into a thriving metropolis. A railway ran out to the Hobson's Bay terminus. Sandridge Pier had been built on piles and extended for 700 yards into the Bay, so even the largest vessels could now moor alongside it, although with the waning of the Gold Rush, there were some 40 ships in port where there had once been 400. When the *Great Britain* appeared, they hoisted their colours. Soon her sides were besieged with those meeting passengers: friends and relatives, reporters, agents and 'strangers of all sorts'. Some people landed and made the two-hour train journey to Melbourne. Most, with their mountains of baggage, went by tender up the seven miles of the winding Yarra.

The *Great Britain* stayed about a month in Melbourne. For the ship's company, this was one of the most pleasant times afloat. Samuel Archer found the evening after the passengers had disembarked 'delightfully quiet, and the change from a noisy ship ... to the quiet of an anchorage in a perfectly calm bay was most agreeable. No sounds were heard except the occasional bark of a dog on shore, the buzzing of some insects and the striking of the bells of the ships in port.' For the officers, a hectic round of social invitations ensued: from the captains of other ships, previous travellers on the *Great Britain* and from Captain Matthews, by now a thoroughgoing citizen of Melbourne.

Homeward Bound

Shortly before the ship sailed for home, up to half a million pounds worth of gold bullion was brought aboard under armed guard. When the passengers arrived, those of 'wild' appearance were relieved of their guns. Once again, the band played as the ship cast off on her homeward journey. Next day, she passed through the Bass Strait along the rocky coast of Van Dieman's Land. After passing the abandoned whaling stations on the islands south of New Zealand, she crossed the vast tracts of the Southern Ocean along the rim of the known world.

As the *Great Britain* passed into the polar zone, Captain Gray would remark that he would soon have the passengers in weather in which they would need warm water to open their mouths. Soon the ship was buffeted by gales, hail and snowstorms. Icebergs were seen frequently as she passed close to the Antarctic pack ice. In 1854, she passed one that was 50 miles long. In 1865, she made her way through 100 in a day. A passenger, the Reverend Dr Cairns, penned an account of these 'mountains of ice'.

> They were dazzling white, some were peaked, some round a-top, some resembled towers or castles erected on a broad platform of shining marble, some had the similitude of a huge palace in ruins, while others had the appearance of a large island, with its heights and valleys, its scooped out bays and sheer precipices. The feeling of admiration excited by such a display of the prodigies of nature was mixed with one of awe allied to fear.

In such conditions, by night or day, the 'skilful' commander stood at lookout in the bows, with the watch stationed along the deck to convey his orders to the wheel. Snowball fights took place on deck, the more boisterous passengers throwing them down into the saloon where the less hardy were huddled round the stove.

Rounding the Horn aroused anxious expectations amongst the passengers, but the prevailing winds were normally with the ship and it was generally a placid affair. On some voyages there was a cry of 'Land! Land!' and everyone rushed on deck. Glasses of every description were raised and every eye strained to see the Cape, 'a large mountain in a dazzling black cloud'. If coal stocks were depleted, the ship bunkered at Port Stanley. As passengers surveyed the austere scene, no-one can have realised how closely the *Great Britain*'s future was bound up with the Falkland Islands.

As the ship entered the tropics, steerage passengers watched theatricals in the Fore Saloon through the open skylight. Quarrels were as frequent as on the outward passage. Mary Crompton, a First Class passenger, noted another unpleasantness. 'We are beginning to see the rats. One came into my cabin the other night as I was going to bed. I jumped onto the berth and waited till Joe came down. Then he and one of the stewards had a grand old rat hunt, but the gentleman escaped through a hole. Mrs Fenwick was wakened by one biting her toe nails and Jane Cumming had a new stocking eaten by another.'

Sightings of other ships became more frequent as the *Great Britain* entered the major sea lanes. Messages were exchanged with a view to reporting positions on arrival in port. In 1860, off the African coast, a large ship passed close to her stern, but would not 'speak'. Captain Gray surmised that she was a slaver, bound for the southern States. On the next voyage home, on 25 August 1861, a small vessel, the *Atlantic*, was seen approaching the ship, flying what appeared to be distress signals. The engines were stopped and the mizzen sails banked, but it transpired that she was trying to convey the message that civil war had broken out in the United States. In the ensuing months, Yankee skippers enquired anxiously after sightings of Confederate raiders.

On some voyages, the Irish coast was the first sighting of land after leaving Australia. The ship sailed so close that passengers could wave to people on shore. 'The green fields looked so fresh to our unaccustomed eyes', wrote Louise Buchan. At Cork, a pilot boat came alongside to take off any passengers who wished to land. Off Anglesey, rockets were fired to signal the pilot aboard. 'Everybody', wrote Mary Crompton, 'got into a state of excitement and boxes kept coming up as if there was no end to them, to say nothing of bundles, bags and portmanteaux.' The After Saloon passengers were taken off in steamers. Mary was sad to leave the 'beautiful ship'. The Captain stood on his bridge and 'gave us a hearty cheer to which we all responded again and again.' The other passengers went on to Sandown Dock. A Customs inspection took place as the ship passed up the harbour. Then came the greatest discomfort of all, the 'trouble and anxiety of looking after our effects and getting on shore with them, through the motley crew of porters and other spectators'.

ELEVEN

'Up Boys and Take the Air'

Captain Gray became a celebrity in Victoria. He was 'deservedly esteemed for his tact and judgement' and his picture was in the window of every print shop in Melbourne, alongside those of Mr Gladstone and Prince Bismarck. The colonists regarded him 'as more important than anyone who had ever visited them'. Those who had come over on the *Great Britain* felt they knew him personally. 'The Greyhound of the Deep' was Captain Gray's favourite term for his ship. 'I love every plank of her. I pat her sometimes and I've promised her a rest if she will only get us home in less than 70 days.'

'What a nice man the Captain is', wrote Mary Crompton. 'He always seems to be looking for something to make his passengers more comfortable ... Among so many of course, he cannot give much time to each one, but he always has a pleasant word or smile for everyone.' Once, when a panorama was being shown in the After-saloon, a picture of the *Great Britain* and John Gray was displayed with the caption 'OUR CAPTAIN AND OUR SHIP'. The audience rose in song as the band struck up with *For He's a Jolly Good Fellow.* The Captain stood up, with tears streaming down his face and waved his handkerchief in acknowledgement. The wealthy After Saloon passengers expressed this affection in material form. 'Why that man got more presents than any merchant captain that ever sailed the salt sea', an old sailor recalled.

In 1858, Captain Gray was offered the command of Brunel's giant ship the *Great Eastern.* Gibbs, Bright & Co. sent in an appreciation, stating that they would be sorry to lose his services, but they would not stand in his way. In the event, he could not return in time to take the position, which may have been to his benefit, since that ship's career was fraught with difficulties.

The Captain ran a well-ordered ship. The previously rowdy 'Crossing the Line' ceremony was tempered to a party for the children in the First Cabin, at which they ate plum cake and nuts, with the children of the other classes reduced to scavenging for the fragments. The occasion also provided an opportunity for the Captain to exercise his sense of humour on the gullible. A passenger in 1862 was both amused and surprised at the level of ignorance that prevailed.

> Some expecting to see it [the Equator], others supposing that the ship would sustain a heavy shock by coming into contact with it and others actually proposing to go out and have a walk upon it. Our Captain told us on deck today that he was greatly afraid of the screw catching on it and thus throwing the ship overboard.

Captain Gray's jokes occasionally came unstuck. He once chafed a young man that his 'long hat' was causing adverse winds and that he would throw it overboard if no-one else did. The jocular remarks misfired when someone who had obviously overheard his repartee snatched the hat. When it transpired that the young man was a Catholic priest, the Irish emigrants in steerage sought to make the incident into a 'religious and party question'. Some of them went round trying to find out who did it with 'the amicable intention of throwing the delinquent overboard'. The Captain, as the inadvertent instigator of the incident, also had his name 'lined up'. 'I think they would have had more difficulty in accomplishing their object than anticipated', wrote a passenger. Fortunately, some of the 'better class of Irish' calmed things down. and the affair blew over.

The Captain was a firm, sensible and fair disciplinarian. In 1863, Gilbert Peterson, the Second Mate, was found drunk on duty. He was ordered to his cabin and confined there for two days before being restored to his duties. 'The Captain is very strict in cases of this kind', wrote a passenger, 'and justly so, for the discipline cannot be too strict where the lives of so many are at stake.' He was also a fitness fanatic. He climbed each of the three masts three times a week. On the first morning of any voyage, he would be down in the crowded quarters of Steerage, ordering the passengers to bring their blankets on deck and overriding all objections as he showed them how to hang their bedding in the rigging to air.

The *Great Britain*'s reputation as a healthy ship owed much to her Captain's obsessions. On occasions they could cause him to ignore the niceties in his dealings with the opposite sex. Elizabeth Joseph recorded that he came down with the doctor each morning.

> To see if we are all out of bed and ready to go on deck; if not they wait till we are ready and drive us all up. Captain came down one morning and found some of the ladies in bed: they had been sick all night. 'Now then', said he, 'get up. If you don't, upon my word, I will take you out and dress you', stamping his foot at the same time. I can assure you that they got up as soon as he left the room and were on deck in a few minutes.

One who approved thoroughly of the Captain's obsession with clean living was a negro crewmember, P A Jones, who celebrated working his passage from Melbourne in 1862 with a poetic effusion entitled *The British Seaman.*

Sweet be thy rest brave Captain Gray,
And calm thy slumber be;
Those whom thou watched o'er on the deep,
Gratefully think of thee.

Then when to warmer seas we sailed,
And skimmed the torrid clime:
A true commander's qualities
Again did brightly shine.

For well he knew the sultry heat
Might foster fell disease;
Or in mysterious caverns breed
Juvenile bugs and fleas.

So every morning soon and bright,
His voice rang loud and clear,
Through all the rooms in this great ship,
'Up boys and take the air.'

'Bring up your beds, wash out your bunk,
The port holes open free,
And let the air in fresh from off
The bosom of the sea.'

'Let pure air sweep through every port,
Lavish let water flow,
Till cleanliness throughout is found,
Around, above, below'

'Up stretch your limbs and have your berths
Perfectly clean and sweet,
That with fresh looks and perfect health,
Your friends at home you'll meet.'

Thus through the tropics did we pass,
From plague and fever free,
In glorious health and spirits now,
We skim the northern sea.

No foul or obscene language
Is heard from lip to lip.
No fighting or profanity
In this well governed ship.

Another of the Captain's obsessions was the danger of fire at sea. 'It is hard to say how many fires Gray saved by his extreme caution', the old sailor continued. 'About 12 or 1 o'clock in the morning he would rig himself out in an old canvas suit, and explore every part of the ship, and woe befall the watchman that was found neglecting his duty.'

The Captain was capable of the occasional eccentricity. In 1861, he put a party of volunteers ashore to annex the uninhabited island of Martin Vaz in the South Atlantic to the British Empire. That evening he threw a banquet to celebrate the latest addition to Queen Victoria's vast dominions. He was a strong patriot, averse to employing foreign sailors on British ships. Indeed he always thought first of his home islands when engaging his officers. In 1862, Shetland Islander Robert Peterson and his brother Gilbert were First and Second Mates. Another islander, Peter Christie, became Third Mate in 1863 and John Angus, Fourth Mate in 1864 and all four quartermasters were Shetlanders.

'Good-hearted Manly Fellows'

The relationship between passengers and crew was generally convivial. Most would seem to have concurred with the view of Gus Hatton, a passenger who was invited into 'the forecastle to join a concert among the sailors. They are a rough lot, but good-hearted manly fellows withal'.

Steerage passenger, Shropshire farm worker, William Griffiths, had a different opinion.

> Although the officers genrial are very civil and obligeing yet the crew hare the most blasphemous and some of the basest of men I was ever amongst. Here fallen nature in its basest form appears. I have just been reading through the life of that holy man of God, Mr Fletcher ... What a contrast to what I see around me.

Thomas Dunn, who sailed in 1865, did not even care for the officers, although he conceded that they had to deal with some difficult characters.

> Those in authority are far from adopting the easy style of dealing with the passengers. Sailing out of Liverpool a great many rough customers are generally on board which may possibly account for their behaviour. Still it is just possible to manage these things without being quite so brutal.

Few passengers seem to have grasped that, for many of the crew, life was hard and short. Rosamund D'Ouseley was one who did. 'We went into the Furnace Room and were unusually roasted, the men who work them seldom live more than fifty.'

Travellers' Tales

Travellers' tales abounded on board. The crew recounted anecdotes of many a far-off place, and many had served on the ship in the Crimean War. Mr Chapman, the First Officer, would tell of his visit to the Friendly Islands, whose King came out to meet him, conducted him to the palace and introduced him to the Queen, who was around seven feet tall. It was the custom to venerate her with a kiss of peace, so Mr Chapman was obliged to climb on a chair to reach her.

A man called Caughey showed Samuel Archer a sketchbook that he claimed to have got from a friend who was shipwrecked on the Pacific island of Penrhyn some years before.

> He and others were kept prisoners. The other men were killed but he was made a chief and had several wives given to him, daughters of the king. The book was full of views of the island, portraits of the wives and other natives, sketches of their dances, customs, etc. and was exceedingly interesting.

Occasional sightings of land gave relief from the prolonged prospect of the open sea and got passengers busy with their sketchbooks. On some voyages one of the remotest outposts of Empire, Tristan da Cunha, 'lifted its precipitous barren side from the blue deep'. A lady passenger heard the story of the place from the First Officer.

> A person name of Glass who had been in the Navy on being superannuated went to live at the Cape of Good Hope where he got married to a black woman. While living there he heard of the Island of Tristan da Cunha and he wrote to the Government asking permission to go and take possession of his little Kingdom. There several children were born to him, these in the course of time went to visit the Cape where they got married and returned again to their home. The old gentleman is still alive and is known as 'General Glass'. When ships call there as they sometimes do for water he comes off in a small boat to present his compliments and offer his congratulations and hospitality to those on board.

Ascension Island was another remote outpost seen occasionally in the South Atlantic. 'The only inhabitants', Samuel Archer heard as they sailed past it, 'are a few English mariners who subsist chiefly on Turtles which is abundant here.'

The Path of Duty

A large sailing ship, like the *Great Britain,* with its vast masts, yards and expanse of sail, was a dangerous place and the normal activities of the crew involved continuous risk. Men were lost overboard, or crashed down onto the deck with sickening frequency during the ship's career.

Life-saving at sea was a great tradition and the crew demonstrated considerable courage and solidarity in their attempts at rescue. A noted member of the crew was Joe Rogers, the lamplighter, who as a sailor aboard the doomed *Royal Charter,* swam ashore with a rope tied around him, thereby saving the lives of many of those on board. John Angus, the Fourth Officer, was another hero. In 1864, while the ship was in the icy waters of the South Pacific, a seaman fell overboard and sank beneath the waves. Angus jumped overboard with a rope and, diving down, pulled him to the surface. 'The poor fellow was got on board the vessel and restoratives being promptly applied he was gradually restored.' On his return to Liverpool, Angus was presented with the Silver Medal of the Shipwrecked Mariners Society. He hoped that the award would be an incentive for himself and others to persevere in the path of duty, for he considered that he had merely done his duty in assisting a fellow creature in distress. Humanity had ever been a prominent characteristic of the British seaman, and he hoped it would continue to be so. In what he himself had done, he believed he had only acted as any one of them would have done under similar circumstances.

In 1872, the *Great Britain* rescued the entire company of a small ship. She was approaching home waters on 22 December when the brig *Druid* was seen to be in distress. As the distance closed, her captain reported her to be sinking. A boat was lowered and took off her crew of seven men and a boy. The vessel was shipping grain from New Orleans to her home port of Portmadoc when heavy weather caused her cargo to shift. Part of her bulwark had been carried away and the pumps had clogged. 'Looks a fine brig', wrote John Campbell, 'a pity to leave her, but life is precious and her poor crew was glad to get on board. Brought a bag of clothes each, and that was all.' It took about two hours for the *Great Britain* to get going again. 'Such is sea life', he concluded laconically. 'A good work for a Sabbath morning.'

The almost instant decision necessary as to whether to attempt rescue at sea or not was a desperate dilemma. On a return voyage in 1859, every inch of canvas was raised when a sailor was washed off the forecastle bowsprit yardarm. A lifebuoy was promptly thrown, which he secured. Over 40 years later, a passenger, Edward Byrd, recalled vividly the Captain's awful decision and the man's cruel fate.

> Poor man! whom every now and then we could see upon the rising crest of the waves. See in that boat is the second mate & willing helpers standing ready, their eyes fixed on the skipper, waiting his decision – he looks up at the sails, upon the boisterous waves, and at his men in the boat and decides – 'No I dare not let you go – your lives would all be sacrificed before I could bring the ship about, and pick you up again.'

A collection was made for the sailor's widow.

Such desperate decisions were not always fully understood. On 3 April 1869, off the Australian coast, Captain Gray was confined to his cabin by illness and Charles Chapman, the First Officer, was in command of the ship. At 5.45pm, the ship was making about 9 knots under canvas in a slight wind when Robert Lawson, a well-known magistrate in Victoria, jumped overboard 'in a fit of temporary insanity'. He rose to the surface a few yards from the stern. A buoy was thrown to him, but he did not appear to see it and floated away on his back in the ship's wake. No attempt was made to rescue him and when the ship docked, twenty-four passengers, who included four army officers, two magistrates and a clergyman, wrote to the *Melbourne Argus* that they were 'of the opinion that steps should be taken to compel commanders of ships to rescue the life of any man falling overboard in fine weather'.

The Marine Board took Mr Chapman's Master's Certificate from him and initiated an Inquiry. At a hearing on 15 April, ten witnesses testified, who included four of the complainants and the crew-members nearest the incident. The Chairman gave the verdict that the Board was of the opinion that he did 'all in his power under the circumstances'. The body had sunk so rapidly that the lowering of a boat would have been of no avail and an unnecessary risk. Mr Chapman's certificate was accordingly returned to him.

Peril on the Sea

Although Captain Gray was renowned as a skilful commander, even he could run into difficulties. The forces of nature were strong and could overwhelm even the best-navigated ship, as the Reverend Dr Cairns realised when he contemplated the icebergs.

> Let a thick mist envelop the expanse and how might this capacious vessel, strong as she is, be dashed to fragments by collision

> with these giants of the deep. No wonder ships are lost in this southern sea, the matter of surprise is that casualties are so few.

Disaster almost occurred on the ship's first voyage to Australia after her return from India. Off the coast of Portugal, she ran into what the Captain considered to be the worst storm he had seen for twenty years. 'The wind fairly flattened the sea and the howling of the wind through the lofty spars was pandemonium', wrote a passenger. Captain Gray hove to in the comparatively sheltered waters between Capes Roca and Espichel at the entrance to the Tagus Estuary. Despite steaming into the wind all night, by next morning the ship had been driven 30 miles nearer the coast. The misery was deepened by a tragic incident. Part of a sail on the mainmast had been blown loose, so a sailor went aloft to try to furl it. He lost his footing, grabbed the billowing canvas and clung to it for a few seconds before he fell. He landed across the iron railing on the gangway and was killed instantly. The burly First Officer slung him across his shoulder 'like a bag of flour' and carried him below.

When the gale died down, the ship made fine progress in splendid weather and the sense of shock abated, but another serious mishap occurred off Madeira. The *Great Britain* was bowling along before the wind on a dark night with every available stitch of canvas hoisted. Just before daybreak, she was struck on the port bow by the American barque, *Celestia*, which ground down to amidships, tearing away the rigging. A passenger, Arthur Robinson, rushed on deck.

> It looked like a mass of tangle overhead – every yard on the foremast, except the royal, was broken and hanging in all directions and the main topsail yards on the main mast were badly damaged.

The barque had also suffered in the collision. Her foremast had broken in the middle and fallen back onto the mainmast.

Robinson ran forward to a group of sailors. They were hauling up a sailor who had been lowered over the bows to see what damage had been done to the hull. He was telling them 'in sailors' language', that there was a big bulge but no hole, adding that 'if we had been struck a little harder we would all have been in Davy Jones' locker by this time'.

> As soon as we found we were in no immediate danger a boat was lowered and the mate put off to the Yankee to see if he wanted any assistance but he would not accept any help & accordingly to the mate's account, was very abusive and said that he would not get out of the way of any darned steamer afloat.

Full steam was raised rapidly and the damage surveyed. The main yard looked as if it might fall at any moment. Perhaps conscious of the recent tragedy, Captain Gray did not order anyone aloft but called for a volunteer. A sailor came forward and swarmed up the rigging. He had just reached the end of the yard when it parted in the middle. He leapt clear into the sea just before it crashed down onto the bulwarks and was soon quite a way astern, but he was a Liverpool diver by trade and a strong swimmer. To everyone's relief he was picked up safely. After consulting his officers, Captain Gray decided to proceed to Mindelo for repairs. A number of passengers responded in the usual way to this extraordinary place and 'painted the town red on white rum'.

In 1860, what could have been a worse disaster than Dundrum Bay was only narrowly averted. As the ship approached the Irish coast, she was enveloped in thick fog. Captain Gray ordered that the whistle be blown every 10 minutes. Despite this, a collision with a barque was only just avoided. Next day, the fog was as thick as ever and the colour of the sea had changed from blue to light green. At noon, breakers were seen ahead and the ship was put astern. A sounding revealed that she was in 40 fathoms of water. No-one had any idea of their position.

At six next morning, land loomed again through the mists. It was so near that some people reckoned they could have jumped ashore from the jib boom. The Captain instantly ordered the engines reversed. As the ship moved backwards, her helmsman suddenly saw that she was heading for a rock. The engines were stopped again. Tense moments followed as the *Great Britain* drifted out of control, but she gradually moved round till her bows pointed out between the rocks. Steam was raised and she was soon out of immediate danger, although no-one had any idea whether it was the Irish, Welsh or English coast on which she had nearly run ashore.

Fortunately, most of the passengers were still abed and the Captain ordered the crew to keep quiet about the incident. At 11am the fog cleared and revealed many ships in the distance that seemed to be outward bound. At noon, the Captain hailed a Dutch schooner, but no-one could make out the reply, possibly because it was in Dutch. At 3pm they ran alongside a small fishing boat and with great difficulty in the heavy swell got one of the fishermen aboard. He told them that they were 50 miles off Holyhead and heading straight for the Isle of Man. He agreed to pilot them to Liverpool for £10, but his confidence was misplaced. At 10pm, they ran onto a sandbank. Captain Gray coolly ordered the two anchors to be released, the cannons fired and, in the words of a passenger, any 'number of blue lights and rockets besides, but all was no use for no assistance came to us. Terror seemed to look from everybody's face for the *Britain* began to labour very heavy at the bottom.'

Luckily, the tide was rising and by 2am the ship was afloat, but she struck bottom when there was a heavy swell. The Captain ordered that every possible ounce of steam be raised. He then got the maximum number of hands around the capstan, both sailors and passengers ('for the passengers were willing to do anything possible to save their lives'). Not surprisingly, the anchors were raised in record time and soon they were in deep water. Much relieved, most of the passengers retired to bed. When they woke next morning, the ship was 20 miles out of Liverpool with the pilot on board.

TWELVE

'The Goat of the Sea'

Feeding nearly 1000 people on a two-month voyage was a complicated business. For days before sailing, the *Great Britain* was loaded with livestock and stores. On a typical voyage from Melbourne in 1865, she carried 126 sheep, 4 lambs, 30 pigs, 2 bullocks, a cow to provide milk for the saloon passengers, 510 fowl, 286 ducks, 65 geese, 32 turkeys and 6 rabbits. Fodder was provided by 4 tons of mangelworzel, 4 tons of hay and 100 bushels of maize, oats, bran and oil cake. The ice store contained 3120lbs of beef, 162 of mutton, 60 of pork and 134 of veal. Sides of beef were hung in the rigging to cure. One once fell and severely injured the ship's carpenter. A bakery produced fresh bread and rolls. At the start of a voyage, the ship's fresh water tanks held 35,338 gallons and she was fitted with two condensers capable of producing 1500 gallons of fresh water a day from sea water.

A vast amount of drink was shipped aboard. On her first Australian voyage, the *Great Britain* carried 717 dozen bottles of sherry, 106 of port, 20 of hock, 25 of sauternes, 15 of moselle, 100 of brandy, 28 of Hollands, 28 of gin, 1700 of ale and 996 of porter, but, surprisingly, only 18 dozen each of whisky and rum. First Class passengers kept their drink supplies in racks above their seats in the saloon, or 'cuddy' as it was popularly known, but these racks were vulnerable to the depredations of 'suspicious' characters from the Lower Cabin. On the second Australian voyage, Fred Smith was strolling on deck when he was amazed to see a sailor with his arm thrust through a porthole into the After-Saloon. He rushed inside and told a steward who grabbed a heavy tumbler, crept up to the porthole and dashed it in the man's face. 'The suddenness of the deed and the pain resulting from it' caused him to drop a stick with a noose on the end that he had hooked round the neck of a brandy bottle. 'In another moment it would have gone, whilst the stewards would probably have been suspected.' Thieves sought drink all over the ship. Miss Augusta Jacobs, an After-Saloon passenger, was woken one night by a rustle over her bed and found that the porthole had been opened and two bottles stolen. The thief would have been disappointed to find that they contained raspberry vinegar.

All classes mingled in the ship's bar, although the Captain could order it shut 'on occasions of excitement'. As well as liquor, it stocked provisions to enhance the shipboard diet. Saloon passengers could get credit by writing their name and berth on a card, the Purser collecting the tabs weekly. Many were the complaints of drunkenness. It was generally considered that the outward voyage was more bacchic than the return. 'Some of them may well feel the want of the money they are squandering so freely when they come to experience the vissisitudes [*sic*] of colonial life', wrote Thomas Dunn. Reckless rowdiness abounded. One drunken passenger wandered into the engine room and fell into the revolving machinery, but fortunately he was pulled out before he was threshed to pieces.

A 'first rate' table was provided in the After Saloon. At her first dinner on board. Mary Mulquin was amazed to see the tables laden 'with every variety of viands' and by the huge number of courses.

> First remove – soup – some for us – then a succession of removes – waiters taking away each one's plate, as soon as finished, at the expiration of an hour or so, we had little relish for anything – and when the second course and dessert came round it was somewhere about two hours or more.

Mary Crompton thought lunch the 'pleasantest meal ... We have hot soup, cold meat, bread and cheese'. At 4pm, twelve stewards served dinner. 'It is funny to watch them bringing in the dishes: one rings a little bell which is the signal for the cook to send up things from the lower regions. Then the 12 stand in a row down the saloon passing the dishes like firemen pass buckets; on rough days they have to stand slanting and look very comical. They very seldom drop things; one spilt a cup of tea down a gentleman's back yesterday.'

Food was rationed to the other classes of passenger. Each person received a pound of oatmeal per week, ½lb of raisins, 6oz each of suet and lime juice and 21 quarts of water. Other rations, which varied in size according to class, included beef, pork, treacle, sugar, tea and coffee. The Second Cabin received cheese, pickles, jam, tripe and, when it was available, milk from the shipboard herd. For the 'poor unfortunates of the Intermediate' life was less lavish. Both sexes shared a pump with the cooks. 'Gentlemen, you are desired to go for breakfast', a voice shouted at 7.30am. One listener thought that this implied that there was nothing for the ladies. After an 'accustomed feed' of burgoo [a sort of porridge] and coffee, the women washed up at the pump. At ten, there was a rush to the butcher's shop for meat rations, which were taken to the Galley to be cooked. At 12.30pm, the Chief Steward called out the numbers of the portions, which were served with a 'liberal portion of yellow paint [pea soup].

Having tasted, those with a delicate stomach turn away with evident dislike on their countenances.' After making up their teas, the 'Intermediates' retired to their various hobbies and pastimes.

'The galley was far too small', recalled another Intermediate voyager. 'The passengers had to fetch their meals and they did so with a rush! This made it uncomfortable as coffee, tea, pea soup, barley soup would be splashed over everybody! This constant treatment made a real mess of one's clothing.' 'However', he concluded. 'The *Great Britain* with all her faults has been the best ship I have so far sailed in.' Steerage passengers were obliged to clean out their berths every morning. Unless they did so, they received no breakfast.

The mountains of ship's biscuit carried on each voyage were another source of complaint. 'Our biscuit was none the best today', wrote an Irish emigrant. 'Nearly impossible to break ... If it had not been for the butter I had, it would have been wasted.' Similar complains came from the Lower Cabin about the coarseness of the salt beef and the dish known as 'Tiger' – pudding rice boiled in water without sugar. John Chatterton found the food in Third Class adequate, but the method of service 'horrid', with several people cutting hunks off the same 'piece of meat'. On the same voyage, a poetic effusion was hung in the main gangway.

That ship of starvation
With owners so stingy,
A disgrace to the Nation
Both dirty and dingy.

When the ocean she passes
A bird of ill luck
With her meals of molasses
And oatmeal and muck.

With her biscuits no butter,
No sugar, bad tea,
Her passengers mutter,
The goat of the sea.

With her salt junk so stinking
Neck, cheek, ribs and shoulder
The mere sight would sicken
The coarsest beholder.

Not surprisingly, some passengers sought to improve their status and their diet. After Saloon passengers were given notice to produce their tickets at dinner. 'Report says that Lower Saloon passengers are in the habit of favouring us with their company.'

'There was one fault as to meals', George Townsend, a Second Class passenger recalled. 'They kept us from 5pm to 8am next morning, fifteen hours, without anything, having only a little soft bread and biscuit with butter, or jam with it. It was too long to fast and was generally complained of.'

The shipboard diet could be resourcefully enhanced. On Edward Towle's voyage, a sailor in the martingale stay harpooned a porpoise.

> The skin is like an alpaca coat. Mr Falkes, who is the enterprising caterer for our table, entered into negotiations for the purchasing of part of it. It turned out excellent. No one, I am sure, could have told the difference between it and very tender salt beef steak.

On another occasion, the Second Officer harpooned a large fish. It was strung up for passengers' inspection before the head was cut off for oil and the body flung overboard.

The *Great Britain* was a popular billet with her crew. 'She was a good ship for food', recalled A J Cross, a former steward, 'and we had butter all voyage.' He remembered fondly the old naval custom of 'Grog O!'.

> We all went to the fo'ard capstan, on which was a copper can, holding about a gallon of rum. There was a ladle attached which held a good tot. Each man dipped it into the can, and all drank out of the same vessel.

Contingencies of navigation meant that the lavish farewell banquet thrown by the Captain for the After Saloon was not announced until the last moment. On a typical menu, vermicelli soup preceded a choice of 22 main dishes, 5 vegetables, 9 pastries and 5 desserts. A lady passenger recorded the scene.

> News arrived in our part of town (for that is the nearest thing our noble ship resembles) at 4 bells, which is 11 o'clock) that we were to have the Captain and his treat at half past 12. It created great commotion, particularly among the ladies who ransacked their wardrobes to appear in their best for the occasion ... a great number of toasts were proposed and drunk with great enthusiasm.

Next evening, the Second Cabin had its treat. At 8.30pm, the Captain appeared amid 'deafening acclamations'. A 'swell' dinner followed which included roast and boiled mutton, an abundance of pastries and puddings, nuts and raisins, two decanters of very 'hot' sherry and two of 'indifferent' port. 'It was thankfully received' wrote Rosamund D'Ouseley, 'by us starving beggars who have been fed on salt meat five times a week and twice on fresh'. 'As usual', she added, 'one or two got drunk before the day was over.' Steerage was not overlooked and received a modest treat of preserved meats and plum pudding at a farewell dinner.

Other occasions were duly observed. On 19 July, the anniversary of the ship's launching, loyal toasts followed a 'sumptuous' dinner in the After Saloon. On Good Friday, hot cross buns were served to all classes. On 5 November, children from the Saloon carried an effigy of Guy Fawkes around the ship. Another great feast came on 13 November, Captain Gray's birthday. There was 'much profusion of wines, speech making followed by cheering and clapping of hands, dancing and all would up at half past 10 o'clock with a grand concert and other theatricals'. On Christmas Day, extra rations of beef and pudding were served in Steerage with a glass of rum. The other classes fared better. The Fore Saloon was treated 'to a pretty good supply of roast duck, roast pork, boiled mutton, plum pudding and tarts; for dessert we had a plentiful supply of sherry wine, tarts and small biscuits.'

The Captain's occasional visits were popular with the Fore Saloon. 'In consequence', observed Robert Saddington, 'we have a first-rate table – Cod and Egg Sauce, Salmon, Corned Beef and Pork, Potatoes, Rice, "Dough Boys" (a kind of dumpling), with soft bread and pickles. There was also an excellent Pea Soup.'

'The Feathered Harmonists'

The large number of domestic animals on board gave the *Great Britain* a rural flavour. 'On awakening', wrote Edward Towle, 'we readily could imagine ourselves in a farmyard. We hear the pigs grunting, sheep bleating, hens and ducks all noisy to be fed. A fine large hound which is fastened near the forecastle often begins to bray at the same time which completes the illusion.' 'Six pigs were slaughtered this morning', wrote another passenger. 'Their dying screams were the music that greeted us during us during dinner.'

Mal de mer was not the sole prerogative of human beings. 'Livestock very seedy', wrote the Purser on one particularly stormy passage, 'Chief Steward having to kill more than we require.' The shipboard flock of sheep was shorn as the tropics approached. 'It is a great mercy for the poor things', wrote a lady passenger, clearly unaware of the animals' impending fate.

To this cacophony was added the noise of wild creatures brought to Australia by those seeking to introduce them to a new habitat. As the ship's newspaper put it, most, if not all emigrants, cherished 'a lasting attachment to their native country, and amongst new scenes, delight to draw around them the memories and associations of home.

> Fortunate as the land of our adoption is in the possession of a pure atmosphere, rich pasture and arable lands, mines of undeveloped wealth, flowers of bright hue, and birds of gorgeous plumage, the English emigrant misses the richly varied scenery to which he has been accustomed, and the gladsome songs of the feathered harmonists which make the woods and fields of 'Merrie England' resound with a melody, scarcely equalled by any other country, and which awaken a response in some of the purest emotions of the heart.

'Acclimatisation Societies' were formed to introduce British species to Australia. Some travellers brought birds on board, hoping to sell them on arrival. In good weather, the cages were taken on deck.

In 1862, Mr Hurst of Gisborne, a wealthy settler travelling in the After Saloon, brought 36 sparrows aboard, a gift to the Acclimatisation Society in Melbourne. A beak-count found that other passengers were carrying 23 canaries, 17 thrushes, 9 blackbirds, 4 linnets and pairs of chaffinches, goldfinches and starlings. In addition, the Chief Engineer was tending 48 skylarks. Mr Hurst's sparrows were fed on oats and boiled potatoes, but this nutritious diet was of little avail, for rats killed all but one before the ship had been many days at sea. The survivor continued in good health for most of the voyage, but died shortly before the ship reached Melbourne. Eight blackbirds and thrushes met the same unhappy fate, and twenty of the Chief Engineer's skylarks perished after being deprived of the green food of their natural habitat. The greatest mortality occurred in the cold and wet weather after the ship had rounded the Cape of Good Hope. 'If those who follow us', enthused the ship's newspaper, 'endeavour to bring with them a few English singing birds, they will find the care of them a not disagreeable recreation to break the monotony of the voyage, and may be well rewarded by the sound of their familiar voices in their new home.'

The settlers' homesickness was also assuaged by the introduction of British flora. In 1862, the *Great Britain* carried a 'very fine' collection of flowers and ornamental trees, including fuchsias, geraniums, carnations, azaleas, camellias, Chilean pines and 'juvenile specimens of the Wellington Gigantica'. The plants were vulnerable to the contrasts of climate on the voyage, but due to the 'unremitting care and attention of Mr Harvie, who has charge of them', very few died. The ship's newspaper considered that great credit was due to that 'enterprising firm' Messrs Lang and Co. of Ballarat, for their efforts to add to 'the floral beauties of Victoria'.

A Wealth of Wildlife

Wildlife abounded. On the voyage to India, a Man-of-War Bird was caught off the Chagos Islands. It resembled a vulture.

> The poor brute when caught was very vicious and snapped and pecked at anyone or anything near it – constantly uttering a hoarse 'Quaa! Quaa!' something like a duck. They fly most gracefully, seldom appearing to move the wings, but soaring or sailing about the ship.

The unfortunate bird was lodged in a hen coop with the ship's duck for company.

In the southern oceans, various breeds of petrel appeared to race across the surface of the sea. There were sailors' names for each one. 'Molly Mawks'; 'Whalebirds'; 'Cape Hens'. Most dreaded were 'Mother Carey's Chickens' (storm petrels). When they flocked in large numbers uttering piercing cries, it was regarded as a harbinger of storms. White albatross, the largest sea bird, followed the ship for miles, hardly moving their huge wings. They reminded Samuel Archer of the 'restored pterodactyl' in Crystal Palace Park. The sailors, oblivious to the fate of the Ancient Mariner, occasionally caught one with a hook baited with pork and kept afloat by corks. Cape Pigeons also provided a form of sport. A lightly weighted line was trailed astern. Not seeing the thread, the birds got their wings entangled in it and were easily hauled in. Boobies, large yellow and brown birds, were so-called from their habit of alighting in the yards and allowing themselves to be knocked off with marlinespikes. Mr Chapman, the First Officer, shot and missed three times at one perched on the fore topsail boom without the bird moving. The booby then dived into the water and caught a flying fish, which it swallowed before returning to the same perch. The fourth shot brought it down.

The little fish known to the sailors as 'Neptune Birds' fluttered through the water, reminding one passenger of jenny wrens. Shoals of jellyfish abounded in the warmer waters. Samuel Archer admired the beautiful blue and pink colouring of the Portuguese Man o' War and its 'membrous' sail that rose above the water. In 1861, a passenger who touched one was stung so badly that he foamed at the mouth. Edward Towle was amused to see 'a sort of steeplechase' between two dolphins. 'They were about a mile away and came bounding towards us at a terrific speed. They would be a good match for any locomotive, and, as to their leaps, a Melton hunter would not stand a chance against them.' Another group reminded him of a pack 'of hounds in full cry'. His Midlands similes extended to a whale that spouted 'like a Chatsworth fountain'. The species was already endangered, and in 1862, the ship's newspaper lamented 'the destruction of these valuable creatures of the deep'.

In the tropics, flying fish rose from the sea in coveys of several hundred at a time. Sometimes one landed on deck after a prodigious leap, and the Menzies family was alarmed when one flew in through their porthole. It was hung out as bait to try to catch a dolphin. Schools of tuna, the beautiful blue and white bonito and blue-finned albacore rose high in the air in pursuit of the flying fish. The sailors tried in vain to catch them by dangling pieces of cloth to resemble their prey. Sharks outstripped the swiftest ship and played around the *Great Britain* 'without exhibiting the least symptom of exertion or apprehension'. They devoured empty bottles thrown to them by the passengers. Edward Towle saw one leap from the water 'as if longing for a taste of one of us'. It was much larger than 'I had any conception. Two of us could easily have found very comfortable accommodation in his interior.' In Mindelo Harbour, Samuel Archer saw a 12-foot leopard shark swimming near the surface, surrounded by its shoal of pilot fish.

> The brute opened his great mouth and snapped at a piece of biscuit. A hook was baited with a piece of pork and put over the stern but the old fellow was too cunning and would not bite. After swimming about for some time he disappeared.

On the homeward passage, the ship passed through the Sargasso Sea with its great masses of seaweed. The sailors would fish it up on deck and sell it to the passengers. 'It was very pretty', thought Louise Buchan.

THIRTEEN

'All Sorts of Games and Vices'

Felix Spiers, the young man who sailed on the *Great Britain*'s second voyage to Australia, prospered. Melbourne was bereft of smart eateries, so he opened the hugely successful Café de Paris in Bourke Street. Then, together with Christopher Pond, another emigrant with business flair, he began the world's first railway catering service, purveying refreshments to thirsty gold-diggers on the line between Melbourne and Geelong.

Soon Christopher Pond had another idea. Cricket was an obsession in the Australian colonies, even the smallest township having its own team. Spiers and Pond would celebrate their success by bringing over the famous 'Eleven of All England' to play the colonists, 'trusting to the generosity of the public to repay their outlay'. The XI had undertaken the first-ever overseas tour in 1859, playing teams of 22 players in North America and winning all their matches. The captain was George Parr of Nottinghamshire, a fine cricketer, but a poor sailor, who was convinced that the ship was about to sink. The only remedy was to maintain himself in a state of inebriation throughout the voyage.

In 1861, Christopher Pond returned to England with one of his agents, Mr Mallon, and secured the services of the XI. George Parr declined to tour because he did not consider the money good enough, but twelve cricketers agreed to go for £150 a man, provided that they travelled First Class and played no more than thirteen matches against Australian XXIIs, so that they could catch the mailboat home on 26 March 1862.

Half the players were Surrey men and there was only one northerner, Roger Iddison, 'a strong, stout, red-faced, healthy-looking man – a true type of the old-fashioned Yorkshireman.' H H Stephenson, the Captain, was 'much respected for his gentlemanly demeanour'. His custom of dressing in a black frockcoat had led George Parr to dub him 'Spurgeon', after the famous preacher. The party also included George 'Farmer' Bennett, 'an extremely useful bat', William Caffyn, 'first-rate as bat and bowler', who had taken an astonishing 16 wickets against the XXII of the USA; William Mortlock, 'unquestionably the best long-stop in England' and, the undoubted star, George 'Ben' Griffiths, 'one of the hardest hitters who ever lived. As an all-round man he had few equals in the kingdom'. In Australia he earned the nickname of the 'Lion Hitter'.

At a farewell dinner in London, glasses were raised to a thundering chorus.

> Success to the Eleven of England!
> The toast is three times and one more.
> May they all meet success o'er the briny,
> And safely return to our shore!

The XI embarked from Liverpool on the *Great Britain* on October 20th, 1861. Match practice was a problem on the long voyage. An attempt to remedy this ended in disaster when a belaying pin being used as a bat flew from the batsman's hand and broke the bowler's nose.

William Caffyn was much troubled by mosquitoes, which presumably bred in the bilges and may have been descendants of the many bugs that had come aboard at St Helena nine years before.

> These tiresome insects seem to have singled me out as their special prey and tormented the life out of me. I was quite ill for a time and had to consult a doctor. I used to get a large piece of muslin and wrap it round my head before going to bed, and also put a pair of stockings on my arms. I shall never forget the laugh that was raised when my fellow cricketers first saw me in this disguise.

Melbourne was reached in 64 days. The team donned their white hats and Messrs Spiers and Pond came aboard to present an address of welcome. A vast cheering crowd followed the team's coach to the Café de Paris.

On New Year's Day, 1862, the XI took on 18 of Melbourne before 15,000 spectators. The team took the field to the strains of 'God Save the Queen' followed by a tremendous burst of cheering. The Australian sun burnt the skin on their faces. William Caffyn bowled the first ball for an English team in Australia, but soon had to come off because of his painful mosquito bites. Despite this, the '18' were bowled out for 118. In reply, the XI knocked up 305. Caffyn was top scorer with 70. The Australians only scored 91 in their second innings, leaving the XI victors on the fourth day. A gentleman who had won a £100 sweepstake on the highest innings was so pleased that he gave Caffyn £10.

After the next fixture at Beechwood, the Lion Hitter took on eleven Australians at single-wicket cricket. He got each one out for a duck and then won the match by knocking the ball out of the ground! In Sydney, the team received another tumultuous welcome.

A New South Wales XXII was defeated by 48 runs, but the XI faltered against a combined XXII of New South Wales and Victoria – the nearest thing to an All-Australian team – losing by 13 wickets. The explanation may lie in a charge that was to dog subsequent touring teams. 'Scarcely a day passed', wrote William Caffyn. 'without our being entertained to champagne breakfasts, luncheons and dinners.'

The XI was offered £100 a man to stay another month, but had to decline because they had to be back for the start of the English season. Spiers and Pond's faith in the support of the Australian public was fully justified. They had made the huge profit of £11,000. Realising that England was open to their sort of business, they sold up and returned, building a new empire in railway hotels and catering.

Such was the success of the tour that another was organised two years later. This time the sponsor was Melbourne Cricket Club. The fee rose to £250 per man, so George Parr was persuaded to overcome his aquaphobia. The team was much stronger. It included the remarkably-named bowler, Julius Caesar, the original 'Demon Bowler', Nottinghamshire's John Jackson and Dr Edward Grace, who despite being the only gentleman-amateur in the party, shared his legendary brother's partiality to a fat fee.

Once again the party embarked upon the *Great Britain.* Dr Grace's medical skills and the strength of his batting arm proved useful when one of the party, George Tarrant, suffered from toothache. 'So I pulled it out', Grace wrote in his journal. 'It required all my force.' Later that day, he appeared 'for the first time in my white cap with the rose in the front and my canvas shoes with the red tapes which caused quite a sensation!' In Melbourne, he played a solo challenge match against six local players. They could not dismiss him and he made 106 not out. The only player who had been on the previous tour was William Caffyn, who was amazed by the progress the Australians had made. Despite this, the team was undefeated in its games in Australia and New Zealand. In Sydney, 20,000 people watched them defeat the XXII of New South Wales by a single wicket.

After the first Australian tour, Charley Lawrence, the Surrey professional, stayed on to coach the Albert Club in Sydney. After the second, William Caffyn became coach at the Melbourne Club. The seeds of Australian ascendancy may he seen in his comment that he 'never saw such painstaking cricketers as the Australians ... Even at that time there were some of them very tricky as regards pace and break'.

> A great impression had been caused by the brilliant fielding of the two English teams, and young Australians undertook to perfect themselves in that department of the game.

As a Surrey man, Caffyn was proud that 'my native county has been so closely connected with Australian cricket in its infancy'.

In 1877, the combined Australian XI defeated the England team in the first official test match in Melbourne. Five years later, *The Sporting Times* carried its famous 'obituary': 'In Affectionate Memory of English Cricket which died at the Oval on 29 August, 1882 ... the body will be cremated and the Ashes taken to Australia.'

Fundraising

The necessity for many on board to raise funds for use during the voyage or on arrival led to regular auctions and raffles. Some passengers sold handicrafts like pictures of the *Great Britain* etched on shells and sales of ladies' clothing were advertised. Indeed, anything that might bring in money was put up for sale. Even John Gray, when he was First Officer, sold 54 tickets to those keen to win his 'superb' gold watch. 'Lots of raffles going on', wrote John Campbell, the Chief Steward. 'Money getting scarce with the Loafers and Swypers, and the young men who think it manly to drink and shout.'

Edward Towle was disappointed to find that he was not allowed to collect water filters that he had brought to sell on board from his trunk in the hold. A man named Brown shipped boots and shoes and sent on 100 cases of champagne by the SS *Sarah Sands*. Despite the fact that their trip was ostensibly made for their health, the Birmingham industrialist, George Tangye and his brother-in-law, Robert Price 'brought enough knick knacks with them to set up a shop'. Robert Saddington brought knives and reckoned that a man with £40 worth of goods to sell could pay for his passage.

Some people found employment on board. William Eckersley had been an engineer on the Manchester canals. His eldest son had gone to Australia and sent back favourable reports, so Elizabeth, the mother, saved £10 each for her husband, herself and their five other children. On their passage in 1860, James, aged 16, found work in the bakery, while Mary, aged 14, became a nursery help to a doctor's family in First Class. She had worked after school since she was eight, sweeping floors and picking up spindles in a cotton mill. Crew-members used their ingenuity to raise funds. Joe Rogers, the lamp-lighter, made good money out of washing clothes, charging Rosamund D'Ouseley 15/- for 15 handkerchiefs and 3 towels.

The author Anthony Trollope turned the long voyage to good effect when he travelled to visit his son in Australia in 1871.

> When making long journeys, I have always succeeded in getting a desk put up in my cabin, and this was done for me in the *Great*

> *Britain*, so that I could go to work the day after we left Liverpool ... Before I reached Melbourne I had finished a story called *Lady Anna.* Every word of it was written at sea, and was done by me day by day – with the intervention of one day's illness – for eight weeks.

Philanthropic ladies in the After Saloon sometimes organised a school for the children on board. 'The pupils seem willing to learn', reported the *Great Britain Times,* 'and there is every prospect that before the end of the voyage, they will feel great benefit and improvement from the various lessons which they are taught.'

On some voyages, passengers produced a newspaper as 'a medium of communication between all ranks and classes'. Contributions were placed in a box near the bar, but it warned that 'all offensive items will be rejected'. The paper carried news of the ship's progress, poetry, bad jokes and tips on such useful items as making your own lifebelt. It was published by subscription on arrival in port.

'Such a Concourse of Sound'

The Victorians were adept at amusing themselves. The After Saloon was provided with a piano, which was not always in tune, and a backdrop, which could transform the room into a 'commodious' theatre or concert hall. Early in the voyage, meetings were organised for those keen to perform. Those interested in forming bands brought along their instruments. Standards varied, but the reception was unfailingly generous. Edward Towle heard a 'most execrable' flute duo, but 'the worse the performers, so much more did the audience cheer and seem delighted'.

One evening when the ship was in the mellow waters off Madeira, Edward Towle strolled the length of the deck and was reminded of a fairground. 'Such a concourse of sound was never before heard on board ship.' In the forecastle, an Italian boy was entertaining the sailors on a portable barrel organ. Abaft of the foremast, John McFall, the Bosun, was dancing a hornpipe to a well-played violin. Near the funnel, three cornet players were rendering national airs and at the mainmast, the 'execrable' flute duo was attracting its usual appreciative audience.

Dancing was popular with all classes, and the frequent imbalance of the sexes did not necessarily inhibit matters. Samuel Archer was amazed by the sight in the Second Cabin mess room. 'There being no ladies, the gentlemen danced together and looked very ludicrous, many of the men wearing great sea boots coming above the knees and with great beards and moustaches.' A little steward known as 'Ballarat Billy' acted as Master of Ceremonies and 'kept them all a-going'. In sunnier climes, dances were held on deck to a fiddle accompaniment and games such as quoits and Aunt Sally were played. There were frequent complaints that smokers indulged in the disgusting practice of spitting on the deck, which ruined it for games.

Homespun theatricals could reveal contemporary social attitudes. Thomas Conway, who sailed from Melbourne in 1860, inadvertently revealed the degradation wrought by the white man in a letter home.

> No little amusement was caused last night by two men dressing themselves like Australian Aboriginals or natives. A 'black fellow and his jin'. Poor jin sitting on the ground with a bottle in her hand and her husband or 'black fellow' as he is generally called with his spear and boomerang in hand dancing around her, and jin, whenever she could get a chance of getting a bottle to her mouth did so, and her husband when he saw her snatched it from her.

Bedlam

Charades were another form of entertainment. On her return voyage from India, the energies of the saloon passengers turned to this popular pastime. Dr Nicholson, Surgeon to the 9th Regiment of Foot, was indefatigable in his efforts, writing the script and building a stage on deck, complete with footlights, drop scene and 'everything *comme il faut*'.

An enthusiastic audience gathered on deck for the performance. The first scene showed a great row in a boarding house with all the lodgers roused from their beds in their nightshirts. The second scene showed a shepherd and a shepherdess, who were so full of each other that they neglected the sheep. The furious farmer entered, carrying a dead lamb and summarily dismissed them. The third scene revealed the word to those who had not worked it out. Samuel Archer played a physician visiting a ward at Bedlam. One lunatic 'looked so very horrible with his paint and chains that some of the children were quite frightened. It was very effective'.

After the interval, the second word was presented. The first scene showed a schoolroom where the master was enraged when all the boys went up at once to mend their pens. In the second scene, a midshipman dressed as a lady eloped through the pantry window with her lover. A disappointed suitor found the ladder and raised the alarm. The father, servants and suitor set off for Gretna Green and arrived just in time to prevent the marriage. The last scene was a tableau representing the return of Ulysses, with another midshipman playing Penelope. The evening concluded with champagne and hock 'flying about and every one was much pleased'.

Judge and Jury Societies

'Judge and Jury' societies performed mock trials on most voyages. During the day, a passenger appeared wearing a fantastical costume, ringing a bell and announcing that 'The Supreme Court of the *Great Britain*' would sit that evening. The occasions were full of ludicrous characters and situations. At an elaborately prepared 'Breach of Promise' action on the second Australian voyage, Joseph McBain, the Plaintiff, appeared on behalf of Fanny, his 'once fair' ward, a 'young lady' of 30 played by Henry Fayrer, an 'old voyager' aged 20. The three judges and six counsel wore white wigs and chokers made from Neptune's headdress and 'would not have disgraced ... the Old Bailey on a foggy day'. One judge, a gambler from the After Saloon, was drunk through the whole business.

Counsel for 'Miss Fayrer' opened the proceedings by stating that she had been shamefully treated by the 'base and cowardly' Philip Moore, which had caused her to be afflicted with serious illness and nervous excitement. The Defence Counsel replied that Mr Moore was 'sweet 19' and must have been *non compos mentis* to have squandered all his money and embittered his youth with 'one who was considered ... a "Flirt" (Here hysterical sobs were distinctly heard from Miss Fanny Fayrer) and not by any means a good looking Person (sobs), indeed rather the reverse (sobs).'

Some 'ludicrous' love letters were read before the first witness, the landlord of the Bedford Hotel in Brighton brought a hint of naughtiness to the proceedings. Star turn was 'Paddy Money', the ostler, who wore a rabbit skin waistcoat, white cord 'unmentionables' and top boots. None of his evidence was to the point, but his eloquence and rare Irish wit convulsed the court. After he stepped down, he got noisily drunk. After a few words from the 'Lord Chief Justice', the jury retired. Eight were for awarding a farthing's damages, but the foreman held out for an acquittal. Such was the success of this first mock trial that another was held a week later. Robert Saddington played the lady in a case of elopement involving assault and battery. The verdict was in favour of his 'husband' and there was a touching scene when the two men innocently rushed into each other's arms.

Sometimes the Mock Court dealt with real petty incidents. On an outward passage in 1860, it was alleged that one night, some passengers had become 'a little elevated in mind' and one locked another in a cabin for some time. When he was released they threw water at each other, disturbing the other passengers. The 'delinquent' was charged and brought before a 'Court of Justice'. After a hard-fought action, the all-lady jury found against the defendant who was fined a bottle of whisky, which was produced and drunk.

'The Most Vociferous Applause'

Occasionally, the standard of entertainment was raised by the presence of professional artistes, out to revive their careers in the colonies. One such was Mr Jacobs. 'He causes many hours amusement and provokes hearty laughter', wrote an admiring Thomas Dunn, 'by his tricks of legerdemain and comic songs improvised at the moment. He is a great acquisition to while away the tedious monotony of a long voyage.'

In 1862, 'the distinguished Tragedienne and Shakespearean Reader', Mary Aitken, a 41 year-old Glaswegian, who was travelling with a gentleman who went under the name of Professor J Marquis Chisholm, 'kindly consented' to give a performance. In a crowded After Saloon, Professor Chisholm opened the programme with his arrangement of popular airs on the harmonium, at 'which he justly stands at the head of his profession'. Miss Aitken then recited Sheriff Glasford Bell's *Mary, Queen of Scots.* 'This beautiful poem, so touching to the heart of every son and daughter of Auld Scotland, drew forth the most unqualified marks of applause and approbation.' What was 'unanimously conceded to be the gem of the evening' came when Miss Aitken recited Miss Landon's 'pathetic' poem, *The Ruined Cottage.*

> Many eyes, unaccustomed to tears, were literally flooded; and when the fair reader gave the sentence where the incarcerated father burst the bars and stood forth a free man, every one felt electrified and at the conclusion, one long breath, followed by the most vociferous applause, evinced that the audience fully appreciated that the fair artiste was justly entitled to the rank of the best reader now before the public.

Miss Aitken concluded with Sir Walter Scott's 'admired ballad', *Young Lochinvar.* No-one doubted that the couple would achieve 'an immortal fame ... in the Southern Hemisphere'.

Another professional who gave great satisfaction was a theatrical manager, Mr G V Brooke, who returned to England in 1865 in the company of a young actress called Lavinia Jones. He rigged up a theatre in the saloon and they gave Shakespearean performances for the passengers. Only later did it emerge that he was accused of absconding with the enormous sum of £30,000. The police had actually searched the ship for him before the *Great Britain*'s departure, but he had been hidden in a cupboard by one of the officers. Later the charges were dropped and the couple resolved to return to Melbourne aboard the ss *London,* but sadly they were drowned when the ship went down in the Bay of Biscay.

'Our Noble Defenders'

On many voyages a cadet force was formed which drilled up and down the deck. It was known as 'The Black Ball Company of Volunteers' in honour of the owners. The Bosun would present them with their colours, but standing at ease was difficult owing to the movement of the ship.

On a voyage in 1864, the corps of volunteers was led by the professional magician, 'Colonel' Jacobs, who marched his men round the deck with the German band playing a quick march. As they passed the forecastle, the crew ambushed them. Their 'guns' were pocket-knives 'loaded with lucifer match heads' and their 'cannons', the brass nozzles on the hosepipes. 'Twice', wrote Thomas Dunn,

> did our noble defenders stand the withering fire without replying. Third time of coming that way ... fire was again opened on them. They immediately stormed the outworks and attempted to take the battery which was gallantly defended by the sailors ... with basket sticks and an old pocket handkerchief on a pole as their flag. A hand to hand melee took place. The advantage was decidedly on the side of the sailors who had already secured one gun from the assailants.

The battle was waging 'hot and strong' when the Chief Mate appeared and put an end to it. Thomas Dunn was annoyed that the good-hearted brawl had been curtailed. 'Terrible as was the onslaught and fierce and desperate the defence, it resulted in the following casualties: killed 0, wounded 0, prisoners 0, 1 gun left in the hands of a sailor.'

'A Floating Bank'

Chess, whist, draughts and backgammon formed the main indoor amusements. One morning John Chatterton overheard an old man boast that he would never be able to play chess or draughts again as nobody could beat him. He challenged him immediately. They adjourned to the Fore Saloon. John soon lost the first game, so they played another.

> The old gentleman, thinking to have an easy victory, played too carelessly and the result was that he was compelled to resign. We played another for the rubber and I lost. This was as I expected, for he was much the better player, but he won't be able to boast any more that he has never been beaten.

'The gambling, song singing and all other sorts of games and vices', wrote William Bray, 'are carried on to such an extent that those on board who have previously travelled across the Atlantic and to other parts of the Globe, say that they have never witnessed anything in all their past experience to equal it.'

A daily book was run on the ship's progress. The bar stocked 500 packs of cards which sold for 2/- each. Even Captain Gray was not averse to a rubber of whist at 3d a point, although he vetoed attempts to introduce a roulette wheel in the saloon. The ship was awash with cash, which encouraged the gambling urge. 'At that time', recalled the old sailor, 'a passenger ship going to and from the colonies was a floating bank. Money was flowing about the same as pebble stones.'

Steerage passengers left less record of themselves than those in superior accommodation, but they generally laid on a minstrel show. In 1865, the ship's newspaper was 'much gratified' at 'seeing our Captain down in the steerage actively and forcibly reprimanding several of the passengers who were gambling with cards'. The report was headed 'A STEP IN THE RIGHT DIRECTION'.

The card schools went on into the night. Robert Saddington was irked when the men in the next cabin lit a candle and started to play a game. The Purser came round and ordered it put out, but they relit it when he had gone. At midnight he returned and made them go to bed, but, in the early hours, they roused and finished the hand before they polished off the stake, which was a bottle of brandy.

As a good nonconformist, Robert resisted the gambling urge. 'I have been pressed to join a card game composed of a few friends ... where for the prevention of "Excess Gambling", the counters or fish will be valued at 1d or 2d per dozen. I gave a denial and have not touched a card. I hope I may be kept in this determination as I have already seen the evil effects of indecision in this matter. Several of the Lower Cabin have lost every penny.'

Stakes could be as high as a sovereign a game. One night a man named Schoemann, who was considered 'uncommon keen' lost the princely sum of £50.

> The natural consequence of this is that robbery is on the increase – this afternoon Mr Smith found a tin belonging to him broken open. He does not know if anything is missing, but has offered £5

reward to discover the offender. The Officers of the ship have suspicions of several, who, I need hardly say, are narrowly watched.

The Long Arm of the Law

Some were made thieves by their dissolute habits, while to others, larceny was a way of life. Once a cadet named Swan mislaid his pocketbook which contained quite a lot of money. At bedtime he missed it, and a fellow cadet told him that a little boy had been seen with a similar pocketbook. They discovered that his name was Ramsey and his mother an Irishwoman called Griffiths. They went to see her immediately, but 'she began abusing them in the vilest manner, swearing her son knew nothing of it'. When Captain Gray heard about it, he decided to question the boy who confessed that he had found the pocketbook and taken it to his mother, who mixed the sovereigns with her own and threw it away. When she was searched, 150 sovereigns were found.

Thefts were more prevalent on the return voyage when those who had done well were returning home. Passengers in Steerage, where space was confined and luggage largely unguarded, were particularly vulnerable – and often they were carrying large sums of money. In 1865, a man had gold nuggets and sovereigns stolen. Fortunately, they were recovered and the thief consigned to prison. However, not all the claims of larceny were what they seemed. On a voyage in 1863, a passenger with a reputation as an imbiber claimed that one of his cabin mates had stolen 11 guineas from him. The resultant investigation ended badly for the accused when the Captain mistook him for a man he had seen drunk in bed one evening. When he discovered his mistake, he apologised profusely and let the matter drop. The passengers took the part of the accused and presented him with an address expressing their confidence in his integrity. It was considered that the man who reported the loss had done so in the hope that a subscription might be raised for him. 'He is a drunken fellow', was the general view. 'The other is a perfect gentleman.'

A small number of people took passage to evade the law. Duncan Patterson was a young man employed by the Commissioner for Roads and Bridges in Melbourne to collect the takings from toll-houses and pay it into the bank. One day, he collected £186:4:6d from the keeper of the St Kilda Gate. He returned a forged receipt to the office and embarked immediately for England under the name of Clarke on the *Great Britain*. He was accompanied by a woman purporting to be his wife. The fraud was discovered immediately, and although the telegraph link was by no means complete, a message was conveyed to Liverpool requesting that Patterson be arrested on arrival. Sergeant John Ryall of the Melbourne force embarked by the next packet to bring him back to be charged with forgeries and embezzlements to the tune of £400. Probably because they were unaware of his assumed name, Patterson evaded the police at Liverpool, but Ryall succeeded in tracing him and had him arrested before obtaining a warrant for his return to Victoria.

At around this time, on 12 June 1862, Robert Steward, aged 37, the bailiff to Mr Charles Caldecott of Holbrook Grange near Rugby, left his wife and six children and absconded with £400 he had progressively embezzled from his master. After four days of hearing nothing. his anxious and trusting employer informed the police of his disappearance. Extensive enquiries traced him to Liverpool where he had taken a first-class passage on 15 June on the *Great Britain* with one of the ladies' maids in the Caldecott household. He had registered as Robert Martin and his 'wife' as Jane Martin. As soon as Steward's whereabouts were discovered, Sergeant John Palmer of the Warwickshire Constabulary was dispatched by fast mail boat. The *Great Britain* made the passage in 60 days. Only once had she done it faster, but for Steward it was not quick enough. Palmer reached Melbourne twelve hours before him and he was arrested. At least he had enjoyed the trip of a lifetime. Of the £400 he had embezzled, he had only £121 left on his person.

Curiously enough, Steward had become a great friend on the ship of Duncan Patterson, who was being escorted home by Sergeant Ryall. The policeman had taken the painless decision to book into First Class, on the grounds that his prisoner would have had to share accommodation elsewhere on the ship, and gave him his freedom during the passage. In Melbourne Gaol, Steward applied to be lodged in the same cell as his new friend, but the request was refused.

'Jane Martin' was not charged with any offence and decided to remain in Australia, possibly because she had no means of returning. The saintly Mr Caldecott instructed Palmer to provide her with funds if she were in need and the detective generously ensured that Steward was provided with better fare than the prison food. The two felons appeared at the City Court on the same day – August 18th. Steward was remanded back to Warwick. Next day Palmer escorted him aboard the *Wellesley*, bound for London.

Steward was a credible character. At Warwick Assizes, the Captain, officers and passengers of the *Wellesley* presented a testimonial on his behalf. Even the prosecutor pleaded for a mitigated sentence, citing his aged parents and wife and children and the plea was supported by Mr Caldecott. Nevertheless, the Judge stated that the public required protection from a man, 'who with a liberal salary, and in a position of great trust, plundered his employer of a large sum of money' and sentenced him to six years penal servitude. The prisoner remained impassive, but his wife set up several piercing screams and had to be removed from the court. The fact that Steward's apprehension had cost the Warwickshire ratepayers £250 cannot have gone unnoticed by the judge.

FOURTEEN

'To God be All the Praise'

Despite the dubious diversions that prevailed, Victorian piety was the strongest influence on the *Great Britain*. 'There was a ball on deck this evening', wrote the somewhat unctuous Anglican clergyman, the Reverend James Maughan, 'for which great preparations in the way of fancy programmes were made.'

> Balls are not in accordance with my taste. My own recreations, when able to enjoy them, are worth a million balls. The nervous and physical energy wasted in dancing would conquer an empire for Christ.

John Campbell, the Chief Steward, expressed similar reservations. 'Oh that Christmas Days were more wisely spent. More love for Jesus and our fellow men; less love for self and selfish gratification.'

Generally there were clergy of the various denominations on board to officiate at services. In 1873, a group of five nuns from the Presentation Order went from Limerick to help with Catholic education among the burgeoning population of Melbourne. They were led by Mother Mary Paul Mulquin, who noted that although there were several Anglican ministers on board and 'preaching men and women in the 2nd and 3rd class cabins', there was 'a defect of clergy of our own dear church'. The absence of a priest was felt all the more keenly since there were 250 Irish emigrants in Steerage. 'Consequently given to quarrelling amongst themselves', she added cryptically, 'holding out for their religion, however little the practice may correspond with the profession. They regale us with national songs and frequently come to ask us for Agnus Deis, scapulars, beads and other articles of devotion.'

The class and ethnic base of the denominations was further revealed in the regular announcement that there would be 'A Roman service in the Steerage and the service of the English Church in the Fore Saloon.' The Reverend James Maughan noted that we 'have had prayers read each Sunday by Mr Wilson, a Church of England clergyman, and services in the steerage, led by Mr Cooper, a Wesleyan local preacher, and also by a Christian disciple'.

The shipboard Sunday was an austere festival – perhaps Captain Gray's Presbyterian heritage was a factor in that. 'Everything so still', wrote Mother Mary, 'as Protestants keep the Sabbath so strictly, do no writing and sing nothing but hymns – all in their best.'

'All saloon passengers are English and Protestants', she observed. The first appearance of the nuns in the dining saloon was a process of mutual discovery. 'Imagine our sensations at the sight of so many strange faces, all turned on us, the greatest novelty ever seen there for some time. The mortification of that Friday dinner I can never forget.' Yet things turned out well. 'When first we arrived everyone was afraid to approach thinking, as they tell us now, we would freeze them with long austere faces – soon the ice melted and they consider us quite social to use Mr Engall's expression – "The brightest lights on the *Great Britain.*" '

The Protestants of the saloon possessed a view of the religious life that must have been gleaned from Gothick novels.

> The greatest surprise is caused by our being enclosed nuns – this cannot be understood at all – so people pity us very much – for being caged birds – beautiful imprisonment! Little they know of the sweetness of its chains.

After breakfast on Sundays, the bells tolled and a drummer beat *reveille.* The sailors looked very smart in their white trousers and blue jackets bearing the ship's name. Midshipmen in their 'best toggery' and officers in full uniform assembled on the quarterdeck and marched to church. Their attendance could be brief, as all hands could be called to man the sails if the wind changed. Services could be very dull. On her first Sunday aboard, Mary Crompton attended Matins in the saloon, 'conducted by a dreadful old stick of a clergyman. I shall not like to stay away, but really he will be a dreadful affliction.' On Captain Gray's suggestion, she formed a choir to enliven things.

On the third Australian voyage, life in Steerage was enlivened by 30 'Ranters' who were mocked by some of the other passengers. 'When one of them begins to pray', observed David Patterson, 'the rest of them groans and moans and cries amen.' One evening he was amazed to see them praying at the other end of the long table from a card school.

The Irish nuns missed saying their daily office. 'It is on board a steamer like this that one feels the want of sweet duties of piety. With them every labour is light, but without them, at least partially, one cannot settle the mind down to any business.' On their first Sunday aboard, the nuns felt 'sad indeed at our desolate Sabbath', but they did their best to fulfil their obligations. At dawn, they said prayers in the Ladies Cabin and then recited their morning hours on deck, but with 'no meditation at all', it was 'too confused to fix one's thoughts'. As they were reading out loud from Butler's *Lives of the Saints,* they could hear the service in the saloon, 'but we did not do ourselves the honour of profiting by the opportunity', wrote Mother Mary ironically. At 5 o'clock they recited the office for the dead and the dolour's from the rosary.

The nuns were anxious to pray with the poor Irish and were allowed to do so in the evening. The dark passage down to steerage was 'really terrifying, and the spot itself confined and narrow', although Mother Mary did note it was very clean. The 'Holy Ladies' were alarmed by the prevalent fierce sectarianism. An evangelical service had been held there earlier and may have been somewhat inflammatory. Some of the 'patriotic' Irish were for 'throwing down the preacher, so it is a wonder some trouble did not result from it ...'

> When some of the Protestant population of 3rd class and steerage passed some cutting remarks on our dress Paddy at once took up our cause and threatened to strangle the offenders.

The nuns handled the explosive situation with great tact. They promised them articles of devotion 'and hope to make them more civilised before we part from them'.

Such religious partisanship was endemic. Mother Mary found 'all on board ... particularly courteous and anxious to become acquainted with our order, even Lord George Hervy, the Protestant clergyman and his brothers in arms – seek to ingratiate themselves in our good grace – doubtless hoping', she added with characteristic irony, 'to convince us of our errors'. She recognised the virtues of many of the Protestants, but regretted their churchmanship. 'It is a pity that people who are so good are not of the true faith.' The nuns, believing that every human soul was worth saving, shared the proselytising spirit and saw the good in all. Miss Hackforth, the flirtatious governess, sat on their table, 'a sweet creature, whose brother and sister are Catholics, so it would be easy to sway her'.

The conversion programme even extended to Captain Chapman, the new commander.

> The captain is a very obliging person, a Protestant, but his family are Catholics. He shows us particular attention, perhaps we might work the mission on him before we land.

In this project, the nuns enjoyed the support of his daughters, who had left the ship with the Liverpool pilot. 'They are most anxious to have their father a Catholic, begging us that we would use our influence to convert him.'

Whatever their religious allegiance, most Victorians shared a belief in a Divine Providence which watched over those with destinies to fulfil. 'An unseen hand led us', wrote the ship's newspaper in 1862, 'and a sleepless eye kept watch over us, and we were brought in health and safety to the land of our adoption.'

'You will, I know, fully understand me', wrote Robert Saddington to his parents, 'when I say that, during my first absence from the parental roof, I have been subject to many trials and temptations of the strength of which I previously had no adequate conception.

> And feeling as I do that it is owing to the watchfulness of an overruling providence that I have been preserved from many of those snares (which, alas, prove fatal to so many young and inexperienced men) connected with Life on board ship – I would say 'To God be all the praise'.

The marvels of nature encountered on the voyage were seen as manifestations of God's Majesty. 'What words ought more appropriately to express our feelings than those of the 107th Psalm', wrote one passenger. 'They that go down to the sea in ships and do business in great waters thus see the works of the Lord and his wonders in the deep.' 'In their grandeur and beauty, in their silence and strength', wrote the Reverend Dr Cairns after he beheld the icebergs, 'they are impressive witnesses of Him who for his own pleasure did create them'. Mother Mary was absorbed by the sight of the birds flying over the mountainous waves and 'resting on the top quite peacefully. 'How beautifully does not God provide for these children of the ocean, away from all the habitations of men.'

This belief led to a stoical attitude towards death and misfortune. 'In the midst of life we are in death' was an everyday statement to the Victorians. Misfortune was a reminder of the judgement to come and the sacrificial nature of their religion, rather than as a cause to shake a fist at the heavens. 'Sad accident this morning', John Campbell wrote in his journal. 'The Boatswain's son fell from the yard to the deck and is killed.'

> A few minutes before sporting with glee, George's voice is now hushed and still; the ribald jest and swearing talk is quiet for a time, a gloom is over the face of the most thoughtless ... Sad news for his mother, God help her to look up to Himself in her need. Has any presentment come to her of her trial, or dream of impending ill news? ... surely there is something in that voice that has spoken today or why the gloom on the faces that used to be the other way? ... Is it sympathy for those left, or is it ... (haste from it, or stifle it as we may), a voice reminding us of our own death?

To Mother Mary's nuns, the anguish of seasickness represented a small opportunity to share her Saviour's sufferings.

> We were so ill – however we offered it to God, knowing so well how little the inconveniences are in comparison to the sufferings of our Blessed Lord.

Yet, the anguish was not without purpose.

> A few short years of suffering it may be, and we shall again be united to our darling sisters – a thousand times more dear now than when amongst them.

Yet, even in an age of deep religious feeling, some escaped the ecclesiastical net. Mother Mary noted that the stewards never attended any religious service 'being too busy in Business. They make the beds, sweep the cabins, etc – It is in truth sad to see so many souls wholly blinded to the sweet life of faith. The stewardess is Presbyterian, but she never has the leisure, she says, to say even morning or night prayers.'

On a return voyage in 1869, the earnest Evangelical, the Revd James Maughan tried to render spiritual consolation to Thomas Court, a Canadian who was dying of consumption. He was shocked to discover that he had never attended a place of worship.

> But he had some religious friends and good thoughts; and beautiful passages of scripture sometimes crossed his mind ... I spoke kindly but faithfully to him both as to his present and future condition. I tried to lead him by simple faith to Calvary, and sang to him 'The Blood of Jesus cleanses me'. I then said I would pray with him. He looked at me in apparent astonishment. I said 'You don't object to my praying with you, do you?' He shook his head and whispered 'No'.

The ship was lurching considerably, so Maughan grasped the side of the bed with one hand and the door handle with the other to support himself.

> I pleaded his cause at the Mercy Seat with as much simplicity and earnestness as I could command. But I have reason to fear that I displeased him by telling the Lord that he came before him a poor sinner – publican-like – having nothing and needing everything.

Not surprisingly, Court declined the clergyman's offer to visit him again by telling him that he felt too weak to talk, but that he would be obliged if he would send for the steward and get one of the passengers to bring him a bedpan. He died two or three days later. Maughan could not help 'asking for what end did such men live. Theirs is vegetation, not life'.

Some facets of religion verged on superstition. When one of a party of Welshmen had his watch stolen from his berth, a reward was offered for its return. This produced no response, so they placed a key on an open Bible. As they read a chapter out loud, the owner of the watch pondered who the thief might be. When he thought of one of the cooks, the key suddenly moved. To them this was proof that he had the watch and he was reported as the thief. The Purser and Chief Steward were given the 'disagreeable duty' of searching a man's box that they thought had nothing to do with it. Naturally, the cook was 'much put out'. John Campbell felt that some supporting evidence should have been produced before the fruitless search was made, but orders had to be obeyed.

> I thought we had got past the time of such nonsensical convictions, making the man a thief and no circumstantial evidence but a Welsh superstition.

His conclusion was a religious and radical critique of the spirit of the age, with its assumption that man could be educated out of his folly.

> Education is to clear us from all this bosh. Will it? Yes, if He in whom we live, move and have our being is our teacher and acknowledged guide. More love and forbearance we need our teaching to be. Less pleasing of the social position and hunting after its verdict on our conduct in life. More of a seeking to honour those who are trying to be Kings of Men and Queens of Women, be their social standing what it may.

In the Midst of Life

In his passion for fitness, Captain Gray enjoyed the support of the ship's doctor, who reported on the community's health in weekly bulletins and made gradual rounds of all the cabins. 'How are we all?' he would ask cheerily. 'As dirty as usual', was Robert Saddington's reply. The doctor prescribed drugs freely. When the Reverend James Maughan suffered a spasmodic attack at dinner, he was given sulphuric ether. 'On the whole I think it has made me worse', he commented modestly. A few days later he suffered a second attack. Inhaling vapour from boiling extract of *bella donna* gave him partial relief, but it was not until he was able to vomit freely that the spasm relaxed.

The close quarters at which the voyagers were packed meant that illness could spread rapidly. 'Mr Way', wrote the James Maughan of a fellow cleric, 'seems to have caught the prevailing bronchitic influenza which is quite endemic in the ship.' In 1869, a number of children in the saloon caught scarlet fever and were put in isolation. All recovered except one who died of a combination of the disease and of water on the brain. 'Poor Mrs Ward looks very mournful', wrote Rosamund D'Ouseley of the bereaved mother, 'and only comes up on deck in the evening to walk with the Colonel, who is coming out to Melbourne as master of the mint.'

Smallpox scares were frequent, but after the disastrous second voyage when the entire ship was put in quarantine, it became the practice to isolate sufferers and to undertake a programme of selective vaccination. 'We have got one passenger, a lady in the saloon ill of smallpox', wrote Thomas Dunn.

> The Captain has got most of the crew vaccinated by the doctor and many of the young children and there is some talk of doing the same to the passengers. They built a house right aft for the patient abaft the wheel and have made it nice and cool by putting up canvas around it to keep the sun off and as the wind has been all most ahead any infection has had a good opportunity of blowing away ...

'I did not care to be vaccinated', he concluded, but there was no help for it, as anyone not submitting then would be put in quarantine and kept in it for days when we got to Melbourne.'

There were births on many trips, 'During the night', wrote Mary Crompton, 'one of the Steerage passengers, a Mrs Moses, had a baby, but it was born dead: the poor woman has been ill ever since we sailed. She has one little girl, though she is only twenty.' 'Last night', she wrote two days later, 'a child was born in Steerage and a poor old man died. He was upward of 80 and had none of his relatives with him; he was buried early this morning.' At least one of the shipboard arrivals went through life bearing the name of the illustrious commander. 'But one birth,' recorded a passenger in 1870, 'a little boy, the son of poor parents, who was duly baptised "John Gray Britain" '.

Some went to Australia in despair. Pulmonary tuberculosis was a scourge of the age and sufferers sought warmer climes. 'Mr McVey', wrote Mary Mulquin, 'is a most gentlemanly person, quite young, all his sisters died of consumption and he too has the seeds of the disease so he is ordered to Australia for the winter or rather summer and returns in ours.' Often the hopes of the sufferers were doomed to be dashed. When The Revd James Maughan recorded that the dying Thomas Court had left Montreal believing 'that a voyage to Australia and back would cure his consumption. Terrible delusion. Such a voyage has often corrected consumption its incipient stages, but never cured a real abscess of the lungs'. Mr Court had been comparatively well when he left home, but he had embarked on a 'wet ship' that landed him in Melbourne in a much worse condition than when he set off.

> He was now struggling to get home again and, though at the very door of death, feeble as a little child, with his hand tremulous, his voice hushed to a whisper, the hectic flush on his cheek and the death glaze in his eye, he was quite sure, if he could only get rid of the dreadful diarrhoea, which was wasting him, he would be all right again when he got to England. Poor fellow, he was at that moment within a few hours of his great Eternity.

Maggie Brown was moved by the plight of a young lass of 17 or 18 who had 'been in consumption for some time ... As her father is in Melbourne, she was recommended to try this voyage as a last hope of restoring her health, but she has been getting weaker every day and though this was the case, we hoped that she would be spared to land and die beside her father, but this was not to be the case for yesterday about 9 o'clock, she passed away and at 3 o'clock her body was, in a very solemn manner, committed to the deep. We all thought she might be taken ashore but on account of the adverse winds and because there are one or two cases of smallpox on board, the Captain thought it better not to do so.' 'There was no one particularly interested in her', she added, 'but her nurse, an Irish girl, and she was in a dreadful state.'

The lack of concern about the death reflects its everyday immediacy. Few voyages passed without a funeral. William Bray attended the obsequies of a Cornishman called Dinstone who died after a stroke. As soon as Captain Gray heard about it, he changed from his white uniform into black and went on deck with the officers and passengers. The body was sewn in canvas, with iron bars attached to make it sink. It was carried on deck by six men and placed on a hatchway at the ship's side. The clergyman read the burial service 'amid much silence and solemnity'. When he came to the words 'We therefore commit his body to the deep', the end of the board was lifted up and 'splash went the body into the waters, there to remain until the sea yielded up her dead. The scene was truly impressive. Not more than an hour had elapsed after his death ere the waters rolled as usual over his grave.'

PART FIVE: DECLINE AND FALL

FIFTEEN

'What a Sad Tale for Home'

Despite his fondness for the company of young and attractive women, Captain Gray was a good family man. At each homecoming, his wife, five daughters and only son were at the landing stage to greet him. But in 1866, his beloved son died and the Captain's friends considered that he never came to terms with the loss. His depression worsened in 1869, when this robust figure contracted severe congestion of the lungs. He never fully recovered and suffered further from neuralgia. Like many fitness fanatics, he was a hypochondriac and his condition was not improved by his habit of taking an array of patent medicines.

On 27 August 1873, the *Great Britain* completed the voyage to Melbourne in the record time of 54 days. Yet even the continuing prowess of his beloved ship gave Captain Gray but temporary relief. His condition worsened. He developed pains in his kidneys and severe constipation. His haggard appearance shocked all who knew him, but he retained his dogged independence. When the ship returned from Melbourne on Christmas Day, he was persuaded to go to a spa resort, noted for the curative properties of its waters. He returned a week later, saying it would kill him to drink such stuff and if he was going to die he would rather it was on board his ship. He returned on board and refused to leave before her next departure.

At Melbourne, Captain Gray told a friend who visited him on board that he thought he would never return and that he had been long enough at sea. During the bustle of departure, he rested on a couch in his cabin, which was unprecedented. During the voyage, he remarked frequently that he was not getting any better. Yet his power of command and humanity were still manifest. One of the passengers was deranged and the Captain ordered him to be locked up and watched night and day lest he do himself harm.

On 25 November, the Captain complained about the pain in his bowels and a stewardess advised him to apply a bran poultice. He lay in bed all day. The Chief Officer suggested that his servant stay in his cabin that night, but Captain Gray, who was sitting at his desk writing a letter, dismissed him. When the retiring bell rang that evening, a steward called John Prout screwed down the large stern ports in the Lower Saloon. When Captain Gray's servant took in his tea next morning, he was not in his cabin. He went back a little later and, finding him still missing, raised the alarm. A search of the ship revealed that one of the stern ports was open. The lanyard had been released and the crossbar removed. The lamp that hung by it was extinguished and it appeared that Captain Gray had carefully put it out before sliding through the gap into the sea. The letter that he had been writing could not be found.

'That he should take his life is the last of our thoughts', wrote John Campbell, 'though he was unwell ...'.

> My mind can hardly realise that him who has been to me (withal his faults) a good Master for over twelve years, is gone ... Listless and heartless we are, and those of us who have sailed with the late Captain Gray [taken] aback ... I can hardly think it true and go looking for him here and there ... The least noise or shout of the men seems to grate on the feelings. A smile or a cheerful word seems cruel. The ship is the same, and the dark blue sea, and yet we cannot look on them with the same feelings. I can't realise that I won't see him more, and ask his servant what he is going to take; how he is this morning.

He found it ironic that the man who would do himself harm was still alive and the Captain, who had sought to save him, was dead. Nor would it have been any use if any of the crew had seen him going down to the Lower Saloon. 'We would have thought he was going to the water closet.'

The First Officer, Peter Robinson, assumed command and convened an inquest with the purser and the surgeon. The verdict was recorded in the ship's log. 'Captain Gray not to be found supposed to have committed suicide by going through one of the stern ports.'

'What a sad tale for home', Campbell had written and this was borne out when the ship reached Liverpool on Christmas Day. Mrs Gray and one of her daughters were waiting to meet him on Princes Landing Stage. The news of Captain Gray's death arrived in Melbourne by telegram on 3 January. It spread rapidly through the city. 'In places of public resort', reported the *Melbourne Daily Telegraph,* 'all other topics were forgotten, and it seemed as though everybody had lost a personal friend, the lamented gentleman being known either personally or by reputation to every man in the city.' Captain Gray's friend recalled their conversation. He had thought at the time that he was announcing his intention to retire, but now he thought that the remarks were indicative of his troubled state of mind.

Brisbane

It was now 30 years since the ship had been launched. 'Our good old ship is getting behind the times', John Campbell had written in 1871. 'Folks think her too old now.' Increased concern about safety at sea led to the establishment of a Royal Commission on Unseaworthy Ships, which ordered the examination of the older ships in the Merchant Marine. The *Great Britain* did not escape scrutiny. 'Having carefully examined this vessel', William H Bisset, a marine surveyor, reported, 'I beg to state that I consider her to be in first rate condition; her plating is perfectly sound and she is in every way seaworthy.'

Charles Chapman, the former First Officer, returned to command the ship on her next voyage to Australia, which began on 27 October 1873. She was sailing into new waters, conveying emigrants to Brisbane for the Government of Queensland. These were the poor Irish to whom Mother Mary and her nuns were shipboard pastors. At Melbourne, the ship did not occupy her usual mooring off Sandridge Pier, but brought up at her old outer anchorage, presumably to prevent the immigrants from jumping ship.

On New Year's Day, the *Great Britain* became the first steamship to arrive at Brisbane 'in the ordinary course of maritime trade'. As with everywhere she first dropped anchor, her arrival was 'a red letter day' and a large party of dignitaries came aboard to extend 'the heartiest of greetings' to the shipboard company. Among the visitors was the correspondent of the *Brisbane Courier*, who found the contrast between the Saloon and the Intermediate and Steerage accommodation to be 'striking – indeed, almost painful'.

> Here had been the abode for two months of 230 persons destined to increase our population. Although little fault could be found with the various berths ... still its *tout ensemble* presented a very gloomy appearance, the whole department being so dark and dreary-looking that a visitor would imagine to prove anything but a pleasant recollection to a steerage passenger in after years. The married men's division was an improvement on the single men's division, but neither it nor the accommodation for ladies are what they ought to be.

While the visitors were looking round the ship, the immigrants were presenting themselves, one by one, to Mr Gray, the Immigration Agent, to state whether they had any complaints about the voyage.

Eight of them accused William Smythe, the ship's doctor, of neglect of his duties. He had entertained the nuns on the run to Melbourne with anecdotes of his travels. It would appear that his talents as a raconteur were superior to his medical care for the poor.

The reporter found the new arrivals even less impressive than the accommodation they had occupied.

> It may as well be stated at once that the *Great Britain*'s immigrants are not the most desirable class to introduce into Queensland, and before the steamer leaves this port it is hoped that the Government will make the proper inquiries into ... the advantage of introducing such persons as the large majority of the *Great Britain* immigrants seem to be.

The reporter was unflagging in his disapprobation.

> No impartial visitor could fail to be struck ... with the unsatisfactory reflection that there is apparently not on board that close discipline which almost universally characterises British vessels. The *Great Britain* almost throughout was, we regret to state, far from being in a credible condition.

This was to be the ship's only visit to Brisbane. The reporter's scathing comments may have deterred the colonial government from employing her again. The validity of his criticisms is difficult to assess, as he only saw her at the close of a very long voyage and his view was not shared by an acute observer like Mother Mary, who remarked on the high standards of cleanliness throughout the ship.

The Procession of the Dead Horse

The discipline that Captain Gray had imposed on the crew was relaxed after the appointment of Captain Chapman. The bacchanalian excesses of the Crossing the Line ceremony were not restored, but the crew initiated its own festival, 'The Procession of the Dead Horse'. The ceremony originated in the custom of paying the crew a month's wages in advance when they signed up for a voyage. For most, the money went to support their families in their absence. Thus the month after sailing was a 'dead month' and the procession celebrated the renewal of the weekly wage.

At 3 o'clock, 'all on deck mounted on every conceivable elevation to witness the fun'. The sailors paraded around the deck three times, singing choruses such as *So We Say – So We Hope* and *Poor Old Man.* Two sailors dressed as a doctor and his assistant, who wore wigs and long white beards and carried a basket of medicine bottles, led the procession, enquiring of the spectators if they needed their services. 'No one accepted the offer'. Behind came other sailors dressed 'as niggers with musical instruments', then an 'interesting female (of the male sex) with Grecian bend, chignon and parasol, laughing at her dignity and strutting along most comically – then came the hero of the day' – the horse. It had a barrel for its body, a canvas head and a mane and tail made of rope yarn. Its rider 'presented a laughable spectacle – with painted cheeks and whip spurring on his beast'. The rear guard consisted of 'police and other officers, keeping the peace'.

The procession stopped at the main mast. One of the 'niggers' put up the horse for auction, declaring that he could cover 50 miles in half an hour, although he confessed he had never seen him do it. Meanwhile, two other sailors were busy rigging a tackle in the yards. This was made fast to the horse, the rider got on and both were hoisted up to the main yard. The rider pulled a slipknot and the poor horse went down into the sea amidst the loud cheers. Little Dickie Bright, aged 3, was disappointed that the rider did not drop into the sea as well. Mother Mary's nuns enjoyed the whole business hugely. 'The poor fellows', she wrote, 'are in great form on these occasions and do their parts astonishingly well.' A collection was held for the sailors, and that evening, they raised more funds by holding a concert in their quarters.

Georgiana

Peter Robinson commanded the *Great Britain* on her two voyages in 1875. On 7 August, she left Liverpool on her last Australian voyage to embark passengers from London but the reason for this is unclear. Perhaps another large party of immigrants was to be conveyed. It is not even certain that this was intended to be the last trip – John Campbell, now promoted to Chief Purser, makes no mention of it in his diary.

The ship anchored at Gravesend on 10 August and waited for the tide to take her up to the Pool of London. It took her three hours to get upstream, but, on arrival, she had to return to Gravesend. 'Not water enough', recorded John Campbell laconically. 'Proceeded to London Dock this morning', he wrote four days later. 'Got in all right.'

Amongst the passengers embarking at London was the Hon. Anna-Maria Georgiana ('Minnie') Bright, the last in the line of formidable women who voyaged on the *Great Britain*. She was the daughter of Viscount Canterbury, the Governor of Victoria from 1866 to 1873. She had married Charles ('Charlie') Bright, who represented the family's shipping interests in Australia, in 1868. Now the couple were returning home to Melbourne, with their four children, Alfred, aged 6; 'little Charlie', 5; Dickie, 3; and Georgy, aged 18 months. They were travelling with their 22 year-old nephew, Robert ('Robin') Bright and a considerable entourage, consisting of Miss Broxholme ('Brox'), the Australian governess, a formidable figure of whom she was not a little scared; King, her lady's maid; Druscilla, the nanny, 'a first rate girl'; 'Old Margaret', a family retainer and the steward from the family home in Norwood who they were taking back to work for them in Australia. As her contribution to the general good during what she must have assumed would be an uneventful voyage, Minnie agreed to play the 'wretched little harmonium' at Sunday services and train the choir.

Brox had seemed affable and component enough when she was appointed, but she was trouble from the start of the voyage. Minnie was to suspect that she had been shipped to England for her health and that she was the 'catspaw' for her return to Australia. One evening, Alfred threw a book at Brox. She had told him that he dared not do it again, and if he did she would box his ears. He did and she did and Minnie put him to bed, 'as I was so terrified myself that I daren't go on deck'.

> I sadly fear that Brox lost her temper and did not conduct herself in a way becoming her years. However no doubt poor Broxie is in a poor way today for she sat in a draught yesterday and has got a swelled face. Then, when she was in bed, in the middle of the night she heard something nibbling and put out her hand and found she had got hold of a rat!! – and finished the night walking about in the saloon. I am responsible for all these miseries and do them on purpose.

On the following night, Minnie was awoken by loud screams. King was at the door of her cabin, vowing she had a rat in her berth. She told her that it was only the family kitten.

> Having said so, I was obliged to show I believed what I said by putting my hand in the berth (pitch dark it was) and most thankful I was to find that I had got hold of the poor little kitten instead of a great rat. What a bite I should have got!

'I have had a headwind with Broxholme – old cat!' she wrote the following day. 'I think she is possessed! Of all the mistakes I ever made, I do believe Brox is the greatest. She is a perfect changeling and has been ever since she came on board.' As if this was not sufficient trouble, King retired to bed with a sleeping draught from the doctor ('which I should think would make her sicker tomorrow') and

Druscilla had come out in boils. Robin Bright was very ill with what was diagnosed as liver trouble, brought on by the heat. Georgiana started to cook his meals.

Nevertheless, she retained her capacity to look on the bright side. The children were well 'and so long as that is the case, the rest don't matter'. 'I breathe again', she wrote a week later, 'for Brox and I are two.' The governess had made unkind remarks about the children, so she had plucked up courage and dismissed her. She took over their lessons herself. 'It seems such a sad pity for them to lose all that has been taught them with so much trouble and expense.' The relief at getting rid of Brox compensated for the fact that King was now confined to bed, which meant that she had to do her own hair, which did 'not look very grand, but it keeps up and is fairly tidy'.

Her spirit seemed unquenchable, despite getting a cold in her eyes ('probably I shall hear tomorrow that Charlie has been beating me'). 'There was a great practice of the choir today', she wrote to her parents, 'and what with giving the boys their lessons and paying visits to several people who are sick and mixing and cooking meals for Robin, I have been so busy that I had no time to go on deck until this evening. It is a first rate thing having a lot to ado as it makes the days pass so much more quickly.' Her energies could contain the troubles, but not overcome them. 'A great breaking out in Georgy's mouth has utterly spoiled her beauty', she wrote. King had 'such a terrible fainting fit that the doctor thought she would never come round,' but she did, 'by dint of champagne brandy'.

A few days later King had lost 'all heart and hope and even *wish* of getting better – and stays like a great log in her berth'. Things stayed much the same until the Captain decided to visit King and tell her that she was to be transferred to the ship's hospital. 'Extraordinary to relate, she got up today, went on deck and has never been sick once.'

'Then I am nearly frantic about Robin – my chief thought is now that we may get him to Melbourne. The doctor thinks we shall, but he has such bad symptoms that I am miserable about him.' Next day, the doctor told her that he thought Robin had typhoid. She engaged a 'charming old women' to nurse him. The deck above his cabin was cordoned off and there was no singing at the church service. Charlie, her husband, was 'in a terrible way', thinking that she might catch it too. 'I have given up going into the cabin to please him, but I can't desert the poor sick boy and must go to the adjoining cabin and to the door to see that he gets all his comforts ... It would be wicked to do otherwise'. 'I don't believe it is catching at all', she added in a correct medical assessment.

Robin appeared to revive, but 'took a dreadful change' on 30 October, but brandy revived him and he took 'an immense amount of nourishment both yesterday and today ...'

> His life *now* hangs on a mere thread. He is better one day and may be much worse the next. Dear Boy, if he is taken he is perfectly prepared to go ... It is very distressing and sometimes a selfish horror comes over me – that I may catch it or give it to Charlie or the children – but it is so clearly my duty to go to the Boy. There is no one else to speak a word of comfort or love to him. I could not leave him to die alone.

Two nights later, Robin became insensible and the doctors said that he was passing away when he suddenly opened his eyes. He was given some wine and then he said: 'I have been in a trance.'

> We asked him if he saw Heaven and he said, 'not quite' – if he saw the Saviour? He said 'I was just on the point of it.' Soon after ... he said, 'When they are all gone I want my Aunt.' I came to him and he said 'I had just got a glimpse of Jesus and they came and said "revive" and a cloud came.' Afterwards in speaking of what he saw he said 'I saw Jesus on a throne, but the light was so great it knocked me down.' I heard him saying to himself with his hands clasped 'O my God, I thank Thee for making my soul so happy.' And in speaking of what he saw, he said 'It was splendid. How I did envy them up there.'

King had returned to her bed. Her temporary recovery when threatened with the hospital finally led Minnie to question the genuineness of her illness.

> She has not stirred from her bed for two days and has not been in my cabin for I think nearly a month. She can eat plenty of mutton chops and drink brandy and water which now I have stopped giving. Human patience has an end and mine has come to an end with King. She says she is going to repay all my kindness when she gets to Melbourne – but it is *now* that I want it – and after being worn and weary all day it adds to ones fatigue having to do every little thing for oneself.

She had given up hope that Robin would live. It was his 23rd birthday on 2 November and he died next evening. Minnie thought of the distress of his parents, but knew that they would feel 'consolation and intense comfort in the knowledge of the perfectly happy condition of mind he was in – never being harassed by (I believe) a single doubt or single fear. His faith and certainty of going to Jesus never forsook him.' After Robin's burial at sea the next morning,

Georgiana and Charlie had the sad task of packing up 'all his little odds and ends and treasures and gifts'. It was decided not to reveal the cause of his death. 'If people knew it was typhoid fever there would be 20 people ill of it tomorrow.'

Under these circumstances it is not surprising that she finally lost patience with King, telling her that when they got to Melbourne, she would be obliged to leave her on board until she could send her to the hospital.

> Extraordinary to say, up she got and walked to my cabin. This was my trump card. I have had it in my hand for a long time and not liked to play it but really thought it was no use bottling it any longer ...

King made a rapid and complete recovery and two days later was running Georgy's bath. 'I think I must give the Hospital a donation', wrote Minnie with her usual dry wit. The thought of getting rid of the hypochondriac maid never seems to have occurred to this generous spirit. She could only conceive of the mildest possible censure. 'I shall never take King on any little expedition I may make – so (as usual) good comes out of evil.'

Inevitably, the traumas of the voyage were beginning to get to her. 'My sea legs are utterly gone and I tumble about everywhere and nearly break myself into bits. I suppose my nerves are gone for I am perpetually tumbling across my cabin and bruising myself everywhere.' Even then she could think of others, sending spare food to the passengers in steerage. Her courage and generosity amply demonstrate that, for some at least, privilege involved duties as well as rights.

'A Ship of more than ordinary Interest'

On 1 February 1876, the *Great Britain* completed her 32nd and final passage from Melbourne in 66 days. Her passenger usefulness over, she was laid up in the West Float at Birkenhead. After a long period of idleness, she was auctioned in the saleroom of Messrs Kellock & Sons in 1881. The auctioneers had decided that was 'admirably adapted' for the cattle trade across the Atlantic.

> Her high 'tween decks and side ports affording grand ventilation; she can carry livestock on three decks. For a sailing ship her beautiful lines particularly adapt her and with her machinery taken out she is calculated to carry 4,000 tons deadweight.

The *Liverpool Post* reported that the sale of this ship 'of more than ordinary interest ... attracted a very large attendance of gentlemen who are closely identified with the shipping interest of the port'. Despite this, she failed to reach her reserve price. The bidding reached £6500 and there being no further advance, the lot was withdrawn.

In the following year, the ship was saved from the breaker's yard when she was acquired by Antony Gibbs, Son & Co of London, a firm related to Gibbs, Bright & Co. The company followed the auctioneer's suggestion and converted her as a sailing cargo ship to carry coal from Cardiff to San Francisco, returning with wheat. The recent completion of the transcontinental railroad had opened up California, but the cost of transporting bulk products was prohibitive. As a result the great square riggers enjoyed a sudden boom, shipping cargoes to the eastern seaboard and to Europe. Between 1881 and 1885, 761 British and 418 American ships, as well as ones from most other maritime nations, passed through the Golden Gate. Only the strongest ships and the most experienced crews were fitted for the 14,000-mile voyage, as grain and coal were treacherous cargoes, liable to shift. The trip out around Cape Horn, when ships battled against the strength of the prevailing winds, was especially hazardous. The *Great Britain*'s accommodation and engines were removed at H&C Grayson's shipyard. The mainmast was moved forward to regain the balance after her funnel was removed. Three large cargo hatches were installed and pitched pine cladding bolted round the hull, probably to protect it when lighters came alongside.

Captain Stap

The *Great Britain* embarked for San Francisco on 2 November 1882, carrying the massive cargo of 3292 tons of coal. She was under the command of Captain Henry Stap, an experienced merchantman. He was desperate for a commission and took this one at very short notice, but he was to wish that he had joined the ship a week earlier and picked his crew, rather than have it hired by others. An attempt to hire some competent sailors failed, when the authorities in the Liverpool Sailors' Home would not cash their vouchers. 'They don't like a man to leave the home while he has money', wrote Captain Stap cryptically. He was even more scathing about their replacements.

> A more useless lot I never was with. Half a dozen of them no sailors at all, substitutes shipped on board at the last moment with only what they stood upright in and are no earthly use.

The First Mate was a good man, but the Second 'too quiet' and the Boatswain 'not much account'. In all there were only three good sailors on board.

The drinking water for the voyage was very bad. Captain Stap took up the issue with the owners and was told that it was cement in the tank that made it taste so awful, but he came to the conclusion that the tank was leaking and that salt water was getting in.

The voyage was beset with difficulty even before the *Great Britain* had left the Irish Sea. Her tug stayed with her in adverse winds, but this made her more difficult to control and the Captain ordered her to be cast off. 'The caper the ship cut that night is indescribable.' Next morning the crew came aft and told Captain Stap that the ship was not safe and asked him to put back to Liverpool. Realising that he would lose them all if they returned, he told them that he would endeavour to reach Queenstown, 'thinking if I once got that far I might go on'.

'After rocking about the Channel for two days', the ship was 40 miles north of the Scillies. Captain Stap was clearly hoping that, if conditions improved, the crew would be happy to push on, but the men refused to pull another rope if he did not make for Queenstown. 'I told them now this wind had set in it would take days to reach there, but still they refused, so I had no alternative but to keep the ship to the wind.' As a result of the turn, the *Great Britain* had to tack against the wind in mountainous seas. The ship rolled and laboured so much that Captain Stap expected the mainmast to go at any minute. Much of the rigging went and the sails split. It was the original canvas and he came to the conclusion that it was rotten. Attempts to repair it were abandoned when a sailor fell overboard and was drowned.

'What with one half of the crew sick (loafing) and the rest next to useless I had a most anxious time of it, I can assure you', wrote Captain Stap to his brother, 'and wished that I had never seen the GREAT BRITAIN.'

After rudimentary repairs at Queenstown they set out again and made good progress, but the storms had made the water much worse and the men complained bitterly. Captain Stap gave them oatmeal to drink with it to mask the acrid taste. 'I have not drunk a cup of tea or coffee since I left', he wrote, 'being much worse when boiled.' There was no condenser on board and nothing in which to catch rainwater. They tried to condense 'by putting the steam pipe onto an empty beef cask' and managed to make about 4 gallons, but it tasted of the cask and was almost as bad as the other.

He privately concurred with the crew's view that the ship was unsafe.

> I think Mr Bright has been imposed upon in the fitting out of this ship for her sails though numerous are of no account and the

running gear bad, both sails and gear look good, but they are constantly giving way.

The coal was loaded too low. There was only 300 tons in the 'tween decks where there should be 1000 tons. 'It is that makes her roll so heavily and be so laboursome and she is too deep for her build.' It was said that Mr Bright had laid out £30,000 for the ship's conversion. 'Someone must have had good pickings for I don't see myself where that money could be expended on her.' The ship was 'well found' in stores and provisions, 'but everything else has been slopped, things just put in their place, and I believe old running gear in place of new. 'They certainly could not have had any practical man to superintend the fitting out.'

He thought of putting into Mindelo for water, but decided to hold out for Montevideo. The water that they were condensing was carefully allocated and got them through. He almost wished that he had not taken the command. Had he been sure of another opportunity in a month or two he would have waited, 'for to leave my children so suddenly makes me very sad at times to think about it'. Montevideo was reached on 30 January. Nineteen of the crew deserted next morning, but in view of Captain Stap's comments, it is unlikely he missed them. While in port he got 500 tons of coal shifted from the lower hold to the 'tween decks, which made the ship much more stable when she sailed around 30 days later.

The voyage to California proved less eventful and the ship moored at Mission Street Wharf in San Francisco on 2 June 1883, after a voyage of 182 days from Britain. Her arrival evoked considerable interest. At 2736 tons gross, twice the size of the average full-rigger, she was an impressive sight. 'She carries us back to "Auld Lang Syne" ', enthused the *Daily Alta*, 'and shows conclusively that they put good work and materials into vessels in earlier times. Captain Stap is one of the best shipmasters in the service and I hope his stay among us will be a pleasant one.'

On the return voyage, the *Great Britain* carried a large cargo of wheat worth $125,683 on a long passage which took 153 days. The second trip went more smoothly. Departing on 11 May 1884, she carried 2870 tons of coal on a voyage lasting 160 days, returning in 150 days on 12 February 1885.

The third voyage to California began on 6 February 1886. In the South Atlantic the ship ran into heavy weather. On 26 March, a small fire was swiftly put out. A spell of plain sailing followed, but on 16 April, off Cape Horn, a south-westerly gale blew up. The sea broke over the deckhouse, causing it to leak badly, and the old hull was straining in the mountainous seas. Next night the winds grew to hurricane strength. At 8am, the crew came aft in a body and asked the Captain to put back. Perhaps mindful of the heavy losses the owners would incur, he refused. By 21 April, the gale had abated, but the cargo had shifted, causing a list to port. Two days later it was discovered that most of the coal on the 'tween decks was saturated, considerably increasing its weight. These hazards were overcome by mighty efforts, but another gale blew up which continued for a week, increasing to hurricane strength on 10 May, carrying away the fore and aft top gallant masts. Three days later, the crew came aft again and this time, Captain Stap agreed to put back to Port Stanley, considering it impossible to reach Valparaiso.

The ship's troubles were not over, however. On 24 May, she arrived off Cape Pembroke on East Falkland. While running to the lee of Williams inlet, she ran aground, but freed herself after half an hour. She anchored in 60 fathoms of water at Port William in the Stanley outer harbour, but ran aground again while swinging at anchor. The steamer *Rance* pulled her clear and towed her into Port Stanley on 28 May.

EPILOGUE

'Forever as a Monument'

The cost of repairs was prohibitive in such a remote place as the Falkland Islands, so the *Great Britain* was sold for £2000 to the Falkland Islands Company as a storeship on 8 November 1886. Her vast stocks of coal tendered visiting steamers for a year. She was stripped down to the lower masts. Her wheel was installed in the sailing ship, *Pengwern,* in 1899. The ship's bell, her Captain's sword, a hatband and a paysheet were removed to the local museum. Most of the other items were destroyed in a fire, but the bell survived and found its way to a local farm.

The Battle of the Falkland Islands, 1914

Despite this diminution of her former glory, the ship still had a moment on the stage of history. On 1 November 1914, the German Pacific Squadron defeated a scratch British naval squadron at the Battle of Coronel off the coast of Chile. The German commander Admiral Graf von Spee decided to run for home, but hearing that the Falklands were only lightly defended, he resolved to destroy the port facilities and wireless station on the way. Unknown to him, however, when Winston Churchill, the First Lord of the Admiralty, had heard of the disaster at Coronel, he had dispatched two battlecruisers, HMS *Invincible* and HMS *Inflexible,* to the South Atlantic under the command of Vice-Admiral Sir Richard Sturdee. On 7 December, they arrived at Port Stanley.

Next day, when Von Spee's squadron arrived off the Falklands at 7.35am, both sides were oblivious to the other's presence. The German fleet was spotted by a lookout on Sapper Hill, who telephoned the news to Port Stanley. Admiral Sturdee was not intending to put to sea till that evening and his ships were in various stages of preparation for what he assumed would be a long chase. His flagship HMS *Invincible,* was coaling alongside the *Great Britain* and would take two hours to complete the process. When he received the news of the German arrival, he was still at his morning ablutions. He gave an order which passed into national mythology. 'Then send the men to breakfast.' The order carried less *sang froid* than it would appear. Only the ship's stokers and engineers had an urgent job to do. To order the rest of the crew to action stations would lead to them sitting about amidst increasing tension, waiting for the battle to start.

As the German ships, SMS *Gneisenau* and SMS *Nürnburg,* approached Port Stanley, their lookouts noted the tall masts of the wireless station they had come to destroy. Anticipation turned to perplexity when a column of smoke rose from the middle of the harbour beyond the low promontory. It was assumed that the British were firing the coal stocks on the *Great Britain,* but alarm followed as the tripod masts of the battlecruisers were discerned. The bad news was conveyed to Admiral Spee, lurking over the horizon.

Had Admiral Spee decided to attack the British ships at their anchorages, he could have wrought great havoc, but he had no means of knowing their unpreparedness. Instead he decided to run for it, although he was hampered by the slowest ship in his squadron, SMS *Leipzig.* Once Admiral Sturdee's squadron got under way at 9.40am, the Germans, outrun and outgunned, stood little chance. After a chase lasting most of the daylight hours, four German ships were sunk. Only the light cruiser, SMS *Dresden,* escaped.

A Hulk

After this dramatic episode, the *Great Britain* continued to fuel passing ships, but, in 1933, it was decided that she was no longer serviceable. She was replaced by the *Fennia,* a Finnish naval training ship. The circumstances of her arrival curiously paralleled the *Great Britain*'s. She had been bought by the Falkland Islands Company after being dismasted in fierce storms off Cape Horn and towed into Port Stanley.

The *Great Britain* lay redundant at her moorings for three years. In 1936, the Company offered her to the Government. The Governor, Sir Heneker Heaton, proposed an appeal to return her to Britain, but a survey showed that it would cost well over £10,000 to preserve her and the project was abandoned. The Royal Navy, out of respect for the nonagenarian ship, declined an offer to use her as a target. There seemed only one option. Much of the internal decking was torn up and used to build a bridge over the Fitzroy River and a jetty in Port Stanley. On 12 April 1937, steered by her own rudder and tiller, she was towed out by two tugs and beached in Sparrow Cove in the outer harbour. Holes were knocked in her sides so that she could not float away. A local newssheet, *The Penguin,* expressed the hope that she might become 'an attractive spectacle' for tourists in her new setting of calm water surrounded by quiet hills.

The *Great Britain* became the haunt of seabirds and was left to decay. The mussels that clustered thick on the boards below her waterline became a local delicacy. Yet her significance was not entirely forgotten. In 1943, in the midst of another war, the islanders celebrated her centenary. In 1952, Karl Lellman, the Town Clerk of Port Stanley, visited her while he was gathering seagulls' eggs. He swarmed up the starboard mooring chain and found that the greenheart sheathing was still sound. He removed two dowels and discovered that the heads of the galvanised boxes were 'as good as new'. The frame of the 1882 deckhouse remained, but between decks the iron plating was very rusted and holed, although it seemed better lower down. 'She is still an impressive sight', he wrote, 'and at close quarters her curves are amazing. I don't know that there can be a straight line in her.'

Recovery

In 1958, Karl Kortum, Director of the San Francisco Maritime Museum, wrote to the National Maritime Museum at Greenwich, urging the *Great Britain*'s return to England. In 1965, he visited the Falklands with a wealthy potential backer, William Swigert, to examine the possibility of bringing the ship to San Francisco. On 8 November 1967, a British naval architect, Ewan Corlett, wrote to *The Times*, urging that 'the forefather of all modern ships' should be recovered, or, at least, fully documented. In 1968, two meetings were held in England to decide whether an attempt at salvage was practicable. Swigert generously declared that the British had a prior claim on the ship. The 'SS Great Britain Project' was formed, with the initial objective of bringing her back to the Great Western Dock. That autumn, Corlett went out to the Falklands. With valuable help from the crew of the survey ship HMS *Endurance*, he surveyed the *Great Britain* and decided that she was in 'surprisingly sound overall structural condition', despite a 13-inch crack which had opened on the starboard side as a result of 30 years of tidal action.

Funds trickled in. In 1969, the main financial problem was solved when Jack Hayward, the noted philanthropist, promised backing up to £150,000, but in November, the designated towing firm withdrew because they considered that the ship was too dilapidated to be made seaworthy. In fact a technology existed to overcome this problem. Risdom Beazley Ulrich Harms, an Anglo-German salvage company had developed a method in Hamburg just two years before of rescuing salvaged vessels with a submersible pontoon. A charter was agreed, subject to an assessment on the spot by the firm's Salvage Officer, Leslie O'Neill. He rated the chances of getting the *Great Britain* back to Bristol at 80 per cent – exactly Ewan Corlett's assessment.

The drama of these developments was dampened by the fact that it was felt that no public announcement could be made until it was felt that opinion on the Falklands was reconciled to the attempt. Few local people thought it possible, which made it difficult for Sir Cosmo Hazard, the Governor, to recommend the release of what was an Official Crown Wreck. It was decided to take a chance. Fortuitously, the pontoon, *Mulus III* and its tug, *Varius II*, were in West Africa, a third of the way to the Falklands. While they were on the way south, in February 1970, the Governor cabled his recommendation of release. In Montevideo planks were bought to make walkways on the rotten deck of the *Great Britain* and steel tubes to use as sheerlegs to hoist out her three massive masts, which could damage the hull if they broke on the long voyage home.

At Montevideo, a BBC film crew joined the German crew of fifteen. Invaluable help was given by the detachment of Royal Marines based in the Falklands. Another 15 tons of stores, including welding and pumping equipment, were shipped directly from England. The party dropped anchor in Sparrow Cove on 25 March 1970. They were daunted by what they saw. Although it was the end of summer, the weather was cold and there were frequent gales.

The pontoon was lashed end-on to the port of the ship and the sheerlegs erected. The masts were removed and three divers patched the holes below the waterline. The mainmast and main yard were shipped back to Bristol where they lie on the quayside at the Great Western Dock. The other masts remained in the Falklands. After the 1982 Falklands War the mizzen mast was erected at Goose Green as a monument to the men of the 2nd Battalion of the Parachute Regiment who died in battle there. Thirty-foot steel strip plates were bolted across the crack on the starboard side at each of the three upper deck levels. The crack itself was stuffed with a dozen old mattresses. Bad weather and a miscalculation about the depth of the water delayed the process of getting the *Great Britain* onto the submerged pontoon for several days, but on 13 April the pontoon was pumped out and the ship lifted clear of the water. As its full weight was taken by the pontoon, the crack closed and a slight twist to port in the stern straightened itself, just as Ewan Corlett had calculated. The straps were cut, straightened and welded back into place and concrete poured in as a seal.

Two days later, the flotilla entered Port Stanley. Ten days were spent fixing the ship more firmly on the pontoon for the 7000-mile tow. Montevideo was reached on 2 May amidst scenes of great public enthusiasm. After further checks, they set off again on 6 May, arriving off the Welsh coast on the evening of 22 June. Here Captain

Herzog handed her over to Bristol tugs. Next morning every ship's hooter in Avonmouth greeted the arrival of the *Great Britain.*

The ship was taken off the pontoon in Avonmouth Graving Dock and made watertight for her journey to Bristol on her own keel. On 5 July, 100,000 people lined the banks to see her towed up the Avon. For two weeks she lay afloat in Bristol City Docks, waiting for a spring tide high enough to get her through the shallow entrance to the Great Western Dock. By a happy coincidence, this came on 19 July, the anniversary of her laying-down and her launch. Prince Philip, great-great-grandson of that Prince Albert who had cracked a champagne bottle over her bows, was on board for her return.

Restoration

The preservation and restoration of the ship's hull required detailed examination of the structure before drawings and specifications could be prepared. The heavy wooden cladding of 1882 and its 10,000 bolts were removed, blanking tapes taken off the portholes and the original hawse-pipes uncovered. Rust and scale were removed from the ironwork with high-pressure hoses, followed by flame-drying and painting. Considerations of economy and durability dictated the use of modern materials, including fibreglass lamination to repair the plates. A number of original artefacts were found on board, including one of the Trotman-designed anchors, which was discovered in the hold.

The crucial question was whether the ship could remain in the Great Western Dock, which would reduce the scale of restoration necessary, since she would not have to float again. The dock, which belongs to the City of Bristol, was leased to the timber merchants, Charles Hill and Sons, whose commitment to the project has been vital. In 1975, the dock was leased to the Project for a peppercorn rent. The *Great Britain* has a permanent home.

Despite generous help in cash, time and kind, limited resources have meant that progress with the restoration was slow. Maritime heritage projects involve a high level of conservation as well as restoration, but the ship has become a noted landmark and attraction. Now over 150 years old, the *Great Britain* constitutes a unique exhibit: a ship of huge historic significance on display in the very dock where she was built. Over 4 million people have visited her since her dramatic return. In the words of Ewan Corlett: 'the iron ship has come and has gone. It is to be hoped that this ship created at the beginning of the iron shipbuilding era will remain forever as a monument to it.'

Sources

Manuscripts in the Archives of the SS **Great Britain** *Trust*

Journals of Samuel Archer, MRCS, Captain William Bennison, Thomas Henry Brain, William Bray, Haywood Bright, Louise Buchan, Edward Byrd, John Campbell, Thomas Cowley, James Duck, Thomas Dunn, Rosamund D'Ouseley, Dr E M Grace, Margaret Graham, William Henry Griffiths, J A Gurner, William Harrold, Gus Hatton, Augusta Jacobs, Revd James Maughan, Mother Mary Paul Mulquin, Thomas M Park, Davis Patterson, Arthur Anthony Robinson, Robert Saddington, Robert Tindall, Edward Towle

Anonymous Journals of a Lady in 1863, a Steward in 1863, a passenger in 1865, an Irish passenger's log of 1875

Letters of Thomas Brewer, RN, the Hon Anna-Maria Georgiana Bright, Heywood Bright, Tyndall Bright, Margaret Brown, Mrs F I Dubely, Sir Charles Fremantle, Captain John Gray, William Hadfield, Elizabeth Joseph, John Lewis, Alexander MacLennan, Stephen Perry, Captain Henry Stap.

Ship's Logs of the SS *Great Britain, 1843-1876.*

Newspapers and Periodicals

The Files of *The Australian Women's Weekly*
The Files of *The Brisbane Courier*
The Files of *The Cape Monitor*
The Files of *The Daily Telegraph*
The Files of *The Hampshire Telegraph and Sussex Chronicle*
The Files of *The Illustrated London News*
The Files of *The Illustrated Melbourne Post*
The Files of *Jack's Cutting Book*
The Files of *The Melbourne Argus*
The Files of *The Melbourne Daily Telegraph*
The Files of *Sea Breezes*
The Files of *The Times*
The Files of *The Town and Country Journal*
The Files of *The Warwick Advertiser*

Ship's Journals

The Great Britain Times, 1852, The Great Britain Gazette, 1861, Our Voyage, 1862.
The Cabinet, Repository of Facts, Figures and Fancies relating to the Voyage of the 'Great Britain' SS, from Liverpool to Melbourne, with The Eleven of All England and Other Distinguished Passengers. Published by J. Reid, 56, Elizabeth Street, 1862. [A photographic facsimile produced by the SS Great Britain Project.]
'The Great Britain Times', A Weekly Newspaper published on board the Screw Steamship 'Great Britain' during the Passage from Melbourne to Liverpool, 1866. [A photographic facsimile produced by the SS Great Britain Project.]
The Great Britain Chronicle, 1868.

Articles

M K Stammers, 'Letters from the Great Britain, 1852' (the letters of John McFall), *The Mariner's Mirror* 62/3 (1976).

Reports and Official Documents

Proceedings of the Royal Commission on Unseaworthy Ships, 1873. Board of Trade.
Thomas Guppy, *Proceedings of the Institution of Engineers, 1845.*
War Office, *Disembarkation Returns for the ss Great Britain, 1855-1856.*

Books

Adrian Ball, *Is Yours an SS Great Britain Family?* (Emsworth, Hants 1988).
Adrian Ball and Diana Wright, *SS Great Britain* (Newton Abbot 1981).
Ewan Corlett, *The Iron Ship, the Story of Brunel's SS Great Britain* (London 1990).
J W Fortescue, *History of the 17th Lancers (Duke of Cambridge's Own)* (London 1895).
E H Nolan, *Illustrated History of the War against Russia* (London 1857).
L T C Rolt, *Isambard Kingdom Brunel* (London 1985).

Pamphlets

Anonymous, *Men who have earned Success, Messrs Spiers and Pond,* pub Empire Hotels, undated.
Grahame Farr, *The Steamship Great Britain,* pub Bristol Branch of the Historical Association, 1965.

Index

Abbreviations
AB = Able Seaman; HMS = Her Majesty's Ship; HRH = His Royal Highness; MP = Member of Parliament; Revd = Reverend; RN = Royal Navy; Sgt = Sergeant; SS = Steam Ship

Index